HOW TO WRITE FOR
Animation

HOW TO WRITE FOR

Animation

Jeffrey Scott

THE OVERLOOK PRESS
New York, NY

First published in paperback in the United States in 2003 by
The Overlook Press, Peter Mayer Publishers, Inc.
New York, NY

NEW YORK:
141 Wooster Street
New York, NY 10012
www.overlookpress.com
For bulk and special sales, please contact sales@overlookny.com,
or write us at the above address.

Library of Congress Cataloging-in-Publication Data

Scott, Jeffrey.
How to write for animation / Jeffrey Scott.
p. cm.
1. Animated films—Authorship. I. Title
PN1996 .S36 2002   808.2'3—dc21   2001055435

Book design and type formatting by Bernard Schleifer
Manufactured in the United States of America
ISBN 978-1-58567-428-2
7 9 8 6

Contents

To Walt Disney, who wallpapered my mind with beautiful animated pictures, and who transformed a middle-American Main Street into the closest thing to Utopia on our less-than-perfect planet.

Acknowledgments

A PRODUCER ONCE TOLD ME he never acknowledges his writers' work with praise because he felt they'd ask for more money. But when I get acknowledged for my writing it energizes me to work even harder, even better. It makes me feel like someone cares. That's why I'm a big believer in acknowledgments, especially for those who have helped me along the way.

It's an old show biz tradition to list the cast in order of appearance, so...

First I want to thank my father, Norman Maurer. It helps to grow up in a creative environment, and my father was an artist at everything he did. And thank you to my mother, Joan, who gave me the freedom to light firecrackers along with the brains to throw them as far as I could.

I want to thank my grandfather, Moe Howard of the Three Stooges, who not only gave me insight into comedy, but also gave me his genes. I should probably also thank my great uncles, Curly and Shemp, because without them there wouldn't have been three Stooges, Moe wouldn't have moved to Hollywood, my Mom wouldn't have met my Dad at the USO, and God knows where I'd be now.

Next I want to thank Walt Disney for making all those wonderful cartoons which formed the foundation of my animated imagination.

I want to thank Sunny for returning my love-at-first-sight in the fifth grade, putting up with the Tasmanian Devil in me, and giving birth to my two adorable children, Caroline and Moe.

I want to thank Orville Hampton, my father's assistant story editor at Hanna-Barbera, for quitting back in 1976, allowing my father to hire me in his place. Getting paid to learn those first six months at H-B was a priceless experience.

Thanks to Bill Hanna and Joe Barbera for giving birth to the animated television industry, and for letting me write so many scripts.

Many thanks to Peter Roth who, while Director of Children's Programs at ABC back in 1978, gave me such an acknowledgment for my writing that it virtually launched my career.

Thanks to Joe Ruby and Ken Spears for being super friends while I was story editing *Superfriends*.

Thanks to Stan "Spider-Man" Lee for introducing me to the marvelous world of Marvel Productions, and to Lee "Business-Man" Gunther for making me an offer I couldn't refuse.

Thank you, Judy Price, for giving me the chance to write over a hundred scripts for ABC and a hundred more for CBS.

Thanks to Jean Chalopin and Andy Heyward for asking me to develop and write DIC's first network series, *The Littles*, but especially to Andy for asking me to do so many series after that.

A special thanks to Jim Henson who was a dream to work with, and who kept his promise to work with me after I left the *Muppet Babies*. I miss you, Jim.

My sincerest thanks to those who gave me so much creative freedom and paid me to fill up blank pages with my ideas, including Margaret Loesch, Fred Wolf, and Will Vinton.

Five percent of all my thanks go to my entertainment attorney and friend, Gregg Homer.

Thanks to my literary agent, Shawna McCarthy, and my animation agent, Barbara Alexander.

Thanks to Gary Richardson for letting me use the *Teenage Mutant Ninja Turtles* in this book, to Patric Verrone for sharing his insight into prime-time animation writing and to Jack Mendelsohn for the inspiration that led to this book.

Thank you to my editors at Overlook, Tracy Carns and David Mulrooney.

And finally, if I've forgotten anyone, this THANKS is for you.

Foreword

ONCE IN A WHILE YOU MEET a person who is so hard-working and dedicated to his craft that his work stands above the rest. Less often you meet such a person who is also willing to take the time to cut a trail so that others can follow in the footsteps of his success. Such a man is Jeffrey Scott.

Fortunately for me, Jeffrey learned the ropes of animation writing at Hanna-Barbera—and learned them *fast!* Within six months he was made full story editor on *Superfriends*, which became one of the most successful action series we had ever produced. So successful was Jeffrey's first story-editing assignment that ABC ordered an additional thirty-two half-hours of the series, a record at that time. Remarkably, Jeffrey didn't just edit these scripts, he wrote them all! Over the next three seasons he wrote nearly a hundred more! And that was just *Superfriends*. He continued his high-quality, high-production output on *Captain Caveman*, *Trollkins*, *Pac-Man*, and *Wake, Rattle & Roll*, writing over 200 scripts for H-B, more than any other writer in the history of the studio.

Anyone who loves movies and television knows the importance of a good script. Though today this is equally true in animation, it wasn't always the case. I should know, because H-B was responsible for developing the current script writing process for TV cartoons.

When Bill Hanna and I were doing *Tom & Jerry* for MGM, like Disney and other studios, we never had scripts. Instead, we'd come up with a notion, then brainstorm gags with our artists, stringing them together to make a cartoon. At that time, animation relied much more on action and far less on dialogue. But animated action was getting more and more expensive, and by 1958, MGM stopped production of *Tom & Jerry*. So Bill and I decided to try our luck in television.

Unfortunately, we quickly discovered that there was even less money for TV animation than theatrical. So we had to find a way to drastically cut our budgets. This forced us to come up with what we called "limited animation," a concept that turned the classical structure on its head, creating cartoons with more dialogue and less action. Though we used fewer and simpler drawings, by timing the action correctly we were able to create cartoons that were just as funny as those produced in full animation.

Luckily for Bill and me, we had more than good animation timing—our timing was perfect to get into TV. Movie audiences were no longer enraptured by the beauty of full animation. Pretty pictures alone weren't enough to keep them interested. In television animation, the most important elements were clever gags, funny dialogue, and good stories.

That's when we realized we needed scripts. *Lots of them!*

And that's why today's animation market is story driven. Whether full-length animated feature, prime-time animated sitcom, or Saturday morning cartoon, it all begins with the script. A producer can no longer rely solely on artists. He has to have someone who understands story structure, character development, and dialogue. In other words, he has to have a *cartoon writer*.

And if you want to become one, you have to read this book!

With *How to Write for Animation*, Jeffrey has cut a clear path that will take aspiring animation writers from their first confrontation with the dreaded "blank page," past the dangers of falling anvils, all the way through to a confident understanding of how to write for animation. Jeffrey has done a masterful job of condensing twenty-five years of experience into an easy-to-read, step-by-step journey through the cartoon writing process.

If you're new to cartoon writing, this book will give you the tools you need to come up with clever ideas, flesh them out into well-structured stories, develop interesting characters, and transform it all into professional quality scripts. In it you'll find valuable secrets that will help you create your own series and show you how to sell it. But this book isn't just for the novice. If you're already an animation writer there are plenty of helpful tips and tricks gleaned from knowledge that can only be acquired after writing a staggering six hundred scripts for virtually every kind of animation.

I can tell you from personal experience that to really succeed in this business you need to create your own style and fight for your ideas. But first you need to learn the fundamentals of your craft and learn them well. And that's exactly what this book will teach you.

So if you want to become an animation writer, just turn the page and get ready to *Yabba Dabba Do It!*

Joseph Barbera

Joseph Barbera
Co-Chairman, Founder
Hanna-Barbera Cartoons, Inc.

Author's Introduction

CAN YOU PICTURE YOURSELF CHASING after a beeping bird, your legs a blur, absent-mindedly running right off the end of a cliff? Can you see yourself stopping over thin air, looking down at the canyon bottom a mile below and starting to sweat? Can you envision looking into camera with a loud "gulp!" then dropping like a rock, your neck stretching like a rubber band as your head tries to catch up with your body? Can you feel yourself exploding with a muffled thud and distant puff of smoke?

If you answered yes to these questions, your friends probably think you should have your head examined. But don't! You're not loony—you're Looney Tunes!—and, like millions of others around the world, suffer from a passion for animation. If you think it's fun to watch cartoons, imagine how much fun it could be to write them! Now imagine the joy of making a living doing this. That's exactly what I've done for the past twenty-five years, and it's a blast! So if you can picture yourself chasing fowl off a cliff you're not insane. You're in luck! You might just have what it takes to be a toon writer.

Of course, if you're like most toonheads, your parents probably told you to stop wasting your time watching "those stupid cartoons!" and insisted you go back to your homework. They may have encouraged you to become a doctor or a lawyer despite your artistic tendencies. You may even have tried to resist and sneaked comic books into your calculus texts and doodled on your history exams (like I did).

If you're feeling guilty about dropping out, or having trouble deciding what career to pursue, perhaps this will help: When lawyers gather round the judge's bench they talk about contingent liability, estoppel by contract and demurrer to interrogatories. When doctors gather round a patient they talk about the pathology of mycobacteria, the treatment of echinococosis, and the procedure for panhysterosalpingo-oophorectomies. On the other "four-fingered" hand, when toon writers gather round the conference table they talk about how deep of a hole a grand piano makes when flattening someone onto the pavement, the proper tone of a frying pan smacking a guy in the face (personally, I prefer boi-oi-oi-oi-oiiinnnggg!), and how to properly pull a cat inside-out by reaching into its mouth and yanking it's tail!

If you want to be a doctor or a lawyer, I'm afraid you've got the wrong book! But if you prefer smashing pianos, flattening faces, and squealing cats, this book is definitely for you.

Okay, let's assume you're interested in writing for animation. How is this book going to help you? If you've read any books on live-action screenwriting you've probably learned a few things that can be of use in animation writing. But there are many factors in animation writing that are very different from live action. And applying the wrong live-action technique to animation can produce disastrous results.

Do you know the most significant difference between writing for animation and live-action? You'd better if you want to succeed in animation writing. The answer is that in animation writing there is a greater emphasis on the visual. And that means it's written very differently. You'll find out how in this book. You'll also learn the difference between live-action and animation form and content. For example, in a typical prime-time drama or sitcom the writing is restricted by the budget to a minimum of locations and narrowly defined characters and format, but in animation it costs the same to have a character jump out of bed or jump off the Titanic. Thus, the animation writer is freer to create worlds and characters from the depths of his or her imagination. This is why sitcoms all look the same but cartoons all look different. It's also why animation is generally more visually stimulating than live action.

If you were ever thinking about getting into animation writing, now is the time. Toon Town is a Boom Town! The reason animation is expanding so rapidly today is because for the first time we have a generation in which everyone under the age of fifty grew up on cartoons. The Baby Boomers might also be called the Toon Boomers because they're the ones who watched toons as kids and are now watching prime-time animation. And the executives who are now running the networks, and buying the animation, have been watching toons since their moms first plopped them before the set to get a few moments of peace.

The animation market has virtually exploded over the past ten years. When I started in the business, back in the mid-70's, there was only ABC, CBS, and NBC doing television animation, and Disney in features. That was it. Now there's ABC, CBS, Fox, UPN, WB, HBO, HBO Family, Fox Kids, ABC Family, Nickelodeon, Cartoon Network, PBS, and Noggin in television. In feature animation there's Disney, Fox, Warner Bros., Paramount, Nickelodeon, MGM, Sony, and Universal. And that's just the U.S. market. There are many foreign networks and studios, too. Add to this the huge success of animated features and prime-time animated series like *The Simpsons* and you can see why everyone wants to get into animation.

What this means is that animation is going to keep evolving and expanding until it is as accepted an art form for telling stories as live-action. *CG* (computer graphics) will be a major catalyst in this change. Writers and directors will make films or television productions in animation as they would live action, and the audience will be completely receptive to their art.

As the medium of animation expands, so to do the techniques necessary to write it. Preschool, Saturday morning, prime time, Internet, film. All of these genres are written, and all will be discussed in this book.

Because so many major studios (and even famous TV and film producers) are getting into animation, there is more opportunity for animation writers than ever before. As a result of this expansion, there is greater opportunity for animation writers to get into writing live-action TV and film. Once you write a successful animated movie or episodes for an animated series, studio execs or producers will ask you to write more important projects. Why? Because they know you, and know that you can deliver. Case in point: After developing the *Muppet Babies* series and writing the show for three years, Jim Henson asked me to write a live-action feature for him. This is how careers expand.

How high can a toon writer go? Chuck Lorre, the creator/executive producer of ABC's hit series, *Dharma & Greg*, started his writing career as a cartoon writer. His last deal with Warner Brothers was reported to be $30,000,000!

One of the more lucrative aspects of animation is licensing—the selling of rights to a name or character for use on products or in other media, such as toys, books, clothing, music, videos, etc. Over the past twenty years the major studios have focused on the importance of licensing the characters created in their films. An early example of a huge success in this area was *Ghostbusters*. Columbia Pictures not only made a sequel, they made two animated series and sold gobs of toys. Disney's *The Lion King* not only broke box office and video records, it sold over a billion dollars in toys and merchandise. The real gold mine of Hollywood is not the box office but the after-market licensing of the property. This is why there is so much interest in animation today. The success of an animated feature often means an animated series won't be far behind. A successful animated series also guarantees a licensing jackpot. *The Rugrats Movie* proved that the expansion can also go the other way, with an animated series being turned into a feature-film blockbuster. All of this translates to big profits.

And all of it starts with the writer!

So if you've ever dreamed of creating the next mega-hit animated film or series, or if you just want to experience the joy of getting paid to write, then your best chance of doing it is to learn how to write animation. *Yup! Thar's gold in them thar animated hills!* The way to mine it ain't with a pick and shovel, but with a computer keyboard.

As a professional cartoon writer, I will stick primarily to animation. I will lay out everything I believe you need to know. If you want to learn the art of cartoon writing, or already write cartoons but want to improve your skills, you'll find what you need here. And if you're a live-action TV or film writer, this book will teach you what you need to know to leap the chasm from live to animation without landing at the bottom with a dull thud and puff of smoke.

There are several reasons I wrote this book. First, I believe that anyone who knows a craft has a responsibility to see that its technology is written down and available to others. Second, I'd like to help develop better cartoon writers. There has been much complaining over the years about the sorry state of children's television. This book is my chance to do something about it at the very root—the stories. My final reason for writing this book is a selfish one. After years of writing, I wanted to finally be an author and have a book to put on my shelf. I wanted to hold it and caress it. I wanted to be able to autograph it and give it to my friends.

So here it is.

If you get only one good piece of usable information out of this book it'll be worth the price of admission. If you improve your writing skills you will have gotten quite a bargain. If you use this book to launch a successful career in toon writing then you will not only have accomplished your goal, but mine as well.

Good luck!

JEFFREY SCOTT
Toon Town, USA

How To Read This Book

THIS BOOK IS WRITTEN so that anyone can understand it, whether you're a professional writer or someone who's never written anything more creative than "the quick brown fox jumps over the lazy dog." Because scriptwriting has its own terminology, if you're not familiar with scripts you will come across words in this book with new meanings. All animation and writing terms are defined within the text or in the glossary. Words in the glossary have been italicized where they first appear in the text. The most important information has been **bolded**.

Don't expect to read this book straight through and understand and apply everything. There is just too much information in it to absorb all at once. Learning takes place in small steps, gaining little bits of understanding which gradually expand into larger areas of certainty. And certainty is only gained from *doing*. This is not a novel. It is a series of steps which, if understood and applied, should give you the ability to be a cartoon writer.

Remember one thing: the only truly effective way to learn to write is *to write*. You will not be a cartoon writer when you have finished reading this book. You will simply have been familiarized with the tools. You will be a cartoon writer once you have applied these tools again and again and can produce the product of a cartoon writer, which is a well-written script or a well-developed series *concept*.

If you are already a cartoon writer then you'll probably do fine just reading straight through the book, noting whatever points may help improve your skills. If you are a writer from a different field, such as live-action television or film, and want to supplement your income by writing cartoons between "real" script assignments, I suggest you start from the beginning and proceed slowly. Some of your habits may need to be shaken loose.

The very best way to learn any subject is to balance theory with practice. Thus, it is best to read about a new idea, then immediately put it to use. Learn about methods of creating ideas, then go out and think up a few (or a few hundred). Study story development, then write three or four short stories. Learn the form and content of a script, then write one.

Being a professional means learning your craft, then practicing, practicing, practicing, until you can produce a high quality product. So even though cartoon writer is probably one of the silliest professions in the world, you do need to get a little bit serious if you want to learn to be one.

Now, take that anvil off your head, tie a giant ACME rocket to your backside and get ready to light the fuse. You're about to learn how to write cartoons!

Ssssss...FWOOOOOMM!!

PART I
GETTING READY TO WRITE

"Writers are the most important people in Hollywood . . . and they must never find out."
—Irving Thalberg

Chapter 1

Understanding the World of Animation

BEFORE I DISCUSS HOW to write cartoons I want to give a brief overview on the medium of animation. This will provide a general understanding of what's happening in the world of animation. After all, the cartoon writer is the first link in the production chain, and the better you understand what's going to happen to your script after you write it, the better able you will be to help make the best cartoon. A failure to understand the basics of animation production and the various types of animation will put you in the center of a mystery. You won't know what's happening around you, and won't be able to communicate with the production people.

One of the most important concepts to understand about the production side of animation is budget. As a writer, you are responsible for writing a script that can be produced, both technically and financially. If you write too many scene changes in your script, which necessitate too many *background* drawings, you can go over budget. Similarly, if you put too many characters into your story, requiring too many actors, you can also go over budget. A good cartoon script that can't be produced is not really a good cartoon script. The ultimate goal of all screen writers is to get their work produced. It's fine to sell something and make a little money, but seeing your work on the tube or the big screen is not only emotionally rewarding, it's a much better calling card to use to get more work.

A Brief Overview of Animation Production—
From Script to Finished Cartoon

There are a few steps that come before the script, but we'll go over these later in more detail. Suffice it to say, the animation production process, whether for television cartoons or full-length animated feature films, begins with a script.

A script describes the entire story, including a *description* of all of the environments in which the scenes take place, all the *action* that happens in those environments, and all the *dialogue* spoken by the characters. In television animation, unlike live action, the cartoon script lays out every detail of the story. Almost nothing is left to the imagination of others. That's not to say that others along the production chain cannot or should not creatively contribute to the story, dialogue, or gags. They can and should, for this often makes for a better cartoon. But a television animation script should be a complete blueprint of the final production. In feature animation, months are spent perfecting gags with sketches and *pencil tests*. But in television, what's in the script is what will be animated.

Once the script reaches *final draft*, work begins on the *storyboard*. A storyboard is a visual interpretation of the script, made up of small, thumbnail drawings. The storyboard shows every scene in the script, and indicates action and camera moves by means of various symbols and sequences of pictures. A storyboard artist doesn't just literally translate the script to pictures, his job is to act somewhat like a director and editor, setting up the scenes properly, adding dramatic camera moves and *transitions* where necessary to improve the telling of the story. A good storyboard is so complete that the script is no longer necessary except, perhaps, for dialogue *recording*.

On the facing page is an example of a scene from a *Teenage Mutant Ninja Turtles* storyboard.

Once the storyboard is put into production, the design stage of artwork is begun, consisting of background designs (sketches of interior and exterior environments that will be used in the cartoon), character *models* (sketches of the characters and their wardrobe), as well as designs for any vehicles, *props*, or anything else that might appear in the cartoon.

Another production step that can begin during the storyboard process is the *casting* of voice talent. If the script is an episode of an ongoing series, the main characters will have already been cast, but any new characters created in the script would now be interviewed and hired.

Once the storyboard is completed and approved, the dialogue is recorded. This is done before any animation is created because in cartoons the animation is drawn to match the *dialogue track*.

Next comes *layout*, which is the process by which the lead animators lay out the basic movements of the scenes, including how characters will move between the backgrounds and foregrounds and in relation to other characters. In most cases, after the layouts are done, and the key background art is designed, the material is sent overseas, along with the storyboard and dialogue track, where the remainder of the animation is produced. When completed, it is shipped back to the studio, where it is reviewed and any errors are noted so that *retakes* can be made and the errors corrected.

The *2-D* animation process consists basically of drawing the individual animation frames on paper, then either *inking* them on acetate *cels*, *Xeroxing* them onto cels, or *scanning* the drawn images into a computer which then turns the pencil lines into black "inked" lines. These cels, whether real or just computer *frames*, have to be colored in. In the case of real cels, they are *painted* with acrylic paint on the backside, one at a time. In the case of computer frames, one simply has to point the cursor, click the mouse and . . . *voila!* The area is instantly colored in.

In *3-D* animation, the characters and vehicles, once designed on paper, are then "built" in the computer in the form of three-dimensional *wire frame* models. These computer models are made to move in accordance with the storyboard. 3-D animated models are *texture-mapped* with whatever surface is desired. If, for example, the character is a robot, it's surface might be mapped with a reflective metallic covering. By programming the computer so that the light comes from a specific direction, the skin of the robot automatically reflects light, falls into shadow, etc.

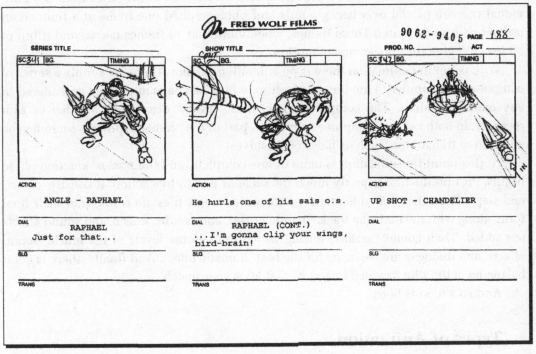

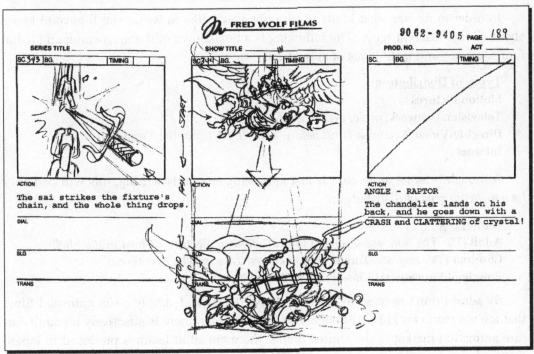

Next, the animation must be photographed. In the case of cel animation, the individual cels are placed over backgrounds and photographed one frame at a time on an *animation camera stand*. These frames, when viewed at 24 frames per second (film) or 30 fps (TV) give the appearance of motion.

With computer animation there is no animation camera. There are simply a series of computer files, similar to the frames of a film, which can be manipulated and altered in any manner desired. The computer sends these frames directly to a video or film recorder. In both cel and computer animation, part of the "camera" process includes the addition of transitions (such as fades or dissolves).

At this point the animation is more of less complete, and the *post-production* phase begins. Post production is pretty much the same as it is in live action. It consists of several steps. First, the film, video tape, or computer movie files are edited into their final form, along with the dialogue track. Opening titles, end *credits*, music, and sound effects are added. Then comes the *mix*, during which the volume levels of the music, sound effects, and dialogue are balanced for the best dramatic effect. And finally, there is color balancing of the film or video image, so that all scenes match.

And so a toon is born.

Types of Animation

In order to decide what kinds of cartoons you'd like to write, you'll have to know about all the different types. The following is a breakdown of the most common media, forms, genres, and techniques of animation.

Types of Distribution:
Motion Pictures
Television (network, cable, syndicated)
Direct-to-Video (Features: *Land Before Time II, III*; Episodic: *Vegetales*)
Internet

Although Internet animation is just appearing as of this writing, this will certainly be a growing area of distribution.

Audiences:
Adult (TV: *The Simpsons, King of the Hill, Spawn*; Features: *Ghost in the Shell*)
Children (TV: *Rugrats, Tiny Toons*; Features: *Tarzan, The Iron Giant*)
Preschool/Educational (*Blue's Clues, Dragon Tales*)

By adult I don't necessarily mean R- or NC-17 rated; I simply mean animated films that are not made for kids. Although, as of this writing, there is effectively no adult feature animation market in the United States, there are adult features produced in Japan. Just as Japanese animation such as *Pokémon* is becoming popular for kids, Japanese *anime* is likely to become popular in America, and the adult market will expand.

Types of Animated Media:
2-D (*The Flintstones, Little Mermaid*)
3-D (*Beast Wars, Shrek*)

Clay/Foam (*Wallace & Grommet, The PJ's*)
Paper Cutout (*South Park*)

Actually, *South Park*, though originally done with paper, is currently produced by computer animation made to look like paper.

<u>**Genres of Animation**</u>:
Action-Adventure (*Batman*)
Action-Comedy (*Teenage Mutant Ninja Turtles*)
Anime (*Dragonball Z*)
Comedy (*Hey Arnold!, Doug*)
Dramatic (*Prince of Egypt*)
Educational (*Dora the Explorer, The Magic School Bus*)
Musical (*Little Mermaid, Beauty and the Beast*)
Preschool (*Blue's Clues, Dragon Tales*)
Sci-Fi (*Starchaser: The Legend of Orin*)
Sitcom (*PJ's, King of the Hill*)
Squash and Stretch (*Catdog, Ren & Stimpy*)

There are other categories, but these are the most common and should give you more than enough options to choose one that best suits your creative bent.

There are two distinct areas of television animation, so different that they are practically two different industries. These are prime-time animation and the rest of TV animation. Prime-time animation, at present, consists mainly of animated sitcoms like *The Simpsons* and *King of the Hill*. Non-prime-time animation consists of everything else, including Saturday morning, daytime, preschool, and network specials. The big difference between these two areas is that prime-time animation is written by live-action sitcom writers, as opposed to what most in the industry would call "cartoon writers." The inner workings of these two divisions of the animated television industry are completely different.

Non-Prime-Time Animation

For the most part, non-prime-time animation is written by writers, whether staff or *freelance*, who work independently of one another rather than as a group. The vast majority work on a freelance basis. Most non-prime-time toon writers submit story ideas (called *premises*) for free. If the idea is approved, the writer is contracted to do an *outline* and *script*, with varying numbers of rewrites. A known writer may be guaranteed payment for both the outline and script, whereas a less qualified writer might be cut off at any stage without further compensation.

Half-hour animated script fees currently range from around $6,500 on the high end to $3,000 on the low. A staff writer might get anywhere from $1,500 to $2,500 per week, and the average *story editor* fee for a U.S. network series is probably around $7,500 per episode.

It's quite common for non-prime-time writers to get their assignments, disappear for a week or more, then e-mail their scripts to the story editor. The story editor is responsible for reading the script and giving the writer notes so that he can do the rewrite. After that, the story editor usually revises the rewritten scripts and does any further changes the producer or network may request. There are some shows that have staff writers who meet and discuss storylines. But they, too, usually go off and write their scripts, deliver them to the editors, and do their rewrites as above.

That's the life of a non-prime-time cartoon writer. Life in the fast lane of prime-time animation is remarkably different.

Prime-Time Animation

Many children's cartoon writers aspire to writing prime-time animation. But even a great deal of experience in non-prime-time toon writing may leave you clueless when it comes to writing prime-time animation.

To get a glimpse of the way a hit prime-time animated series is written I consulted Patric M. Verrone, the Supervising Producer of Matt Groening's *Futurama*. According to Patric, Sam Simon, one of the executive producers of *The Simpsons*, worked out the following system, which is now used by virtually all prime-time animated series. Here's how it works:

Animated prime-time series typically have a staff of between seven and twenty-two writers, depending on the show. Newer shows have fewer; older (spelled s-u-c-c-e-s-s-f-u-l) shows have more. The networks buy somewhere between thirteen and twenty-two half-hours for a single season.

The stories are all *broken* (meaning the story ideas are conceived and approved) *in house* by the staff. The story ideas are then assigned to the staff writers. So if there are seven staff and thirteen episodes in total, each writer would get about two scripts. The writers then go off in groups of four or five and *beat out* their stories (work out the *beats*) along with the *lead writer* (the guy whose name will wind up on the script).

Each half-hour script will have roughly thirty scenes and is generally made up of three acts. After a story is beat out, the staff all get together and do a *joke pass*—adding, deleting, and improving the gags, and adding any new beats that may be needed. They generally develop three to four times the amount of jokes that will be used in the final script.

At this point, the lead writer has a week to write an outline. The executive producer reads the outline and gives notes to the lead writer, who then has two weeks to do a first draft script.

Once the first draft is finished the *table process* begins. The "table" is simply the big conference table at which the staff can work en masse, and the "process" is a series of steps whereby the staff continues to develop the script.

The first step of the table process is for the staff to rewrite the script according to the executive producer's notes. This step takes from five to eight days, during which the staff use a large computer monitor to view the script and go over it line by line. The executive producer attends the *table polish,* which is the final stage of this step.

Next comes the *table read.* At this stage the actors participate, coming to the table and reading their lines in real time (meaning the actual time it will take during the episode). The writers note which jokes don't work and any other problems as the story plays out.

After the table read comes the *read rewrite.* Here the staff does another rewrite, based on the table read notes, which usually takes about another day and a half.

At this point they *record*. Recording, in animation terms, means recording the actors' dialogue. Sometimes a read is done just before the record, and the script might even be fine tuned *while recording*!

About a month later a storyboard and an edited dialogue track are returned. During dialogue recording, actors may have to say their lines several times before getting it right. The director will note which *take* is the best and these takes are edited together, with pauses between them. The lead writer and executive producer go over the board and make changes, as needed, to ensure it conforms with existing gags and to fix any gags that don't work.

About one and a half to two months later the *animatic* is finished. An animatic is a series of still drawings and pencil tests, edited together with the dialogue track to form a rough draft of the cartoon.

Next comes a process called the *animatic rewrite*. This is a one to two day rewrite, during which the writers view the animatic and punch up gags.

Three to four months after the animatic rewrite, the finished animation comes back from overseas. Typically, a show has around $5,000 budgeted for elective retakes in each episode.

And that's the prime-time animation writing process. It generally takes about nine to ten months to complete a season of twenty-two half hours. Typically, prime-time toon writers work from 10 AM to 7 PM, five days a week. However, it's not uncommon to work till midnight.

The good news is that virtually all animated prime-time series are now covered by the WGA. Unless you're an animation professional you may be surprised to know that up until recently, no animation writing was covered by the Writer's Guild of America. Even today, only a small percentage of animated series are covered by WGA contracts. Most prime-time series are covered, but almost no non-prime-time. Thus, other than prime-time animation writers, almost no cartoon writers receive residuals. While all live-action television writers receive periodic residual payments as the studios continue to air and generate profits from their work, over 90 percent of cartoon writers get paid only a small, flat fee. Believe it or not, most of them have no union representation whatsoever. The small percentage who do, have historically been covered by The Screen Cartoonist Union Local 839 of the International Alliance of Theatrical and Stage Employees (IATSE)—the same union that represents inkers, painters, and animators. To change this, the Animation Writers Caucus (AWC) of the Writers Guild of America, an ad hoc group of WGA members who also happen to write animation, organized for the purpose of gaining better contracts and fairer representation for animation writers. To learn more about the AWC you can contact the WGA. The bad news is that, per WGA regulations, only one script in every thirteen goes to a freelance writer. And script submissions for most, if not all, prime-time animated series must be made by agents. So don't go mailing your scripts to prime-time story editors expecting them to be read.

It is a general rule that prime-time animated series editors want to read live-action sitcoms or prime-time animation scripts as examples of a writer's work. They're not interested in non-prime-time toon writers, no matter how successful, unless they've written a good sitcom *spec*.

Staff salaries for prime-time animated series that have signed with the WGA are governed by the WGA Minimum Basic Agreement. Currently this is $2,500-$3,200 per week for a staff writer, and between $4,500-$6,000 per week for a story editor. Most staff writer deals are for one to two years, with an option for more if the series is picked up (the same as sitcoms). The minimum staff deal is thirteen weeks. But that's just the salary. All scripts are extra. Presently, the WGA half-hour prime-time script minimum is $18,659. WGA minimums go up every year according to guild agreements, so check with the WGA if you want the most current figures.

Wait! There's more! All prime-time animation covered by the WGA pays residuals at the same rate as WGA prime-time live-action rates. This means that on a hit show the money can roll in for years.

So, although it's much harder to break into prime-time than non-prime-time animation writing, there are several good reasons to shoot for the prime-time stars, including higher script fees, residuals, and the chance to make the "jump to light-speed" and get into live-action television.

Choosing Which Type of Animation to Write

I've been blessed with a varied and exciting career. I've written animated features, television, and videos, in genres as diverse as sci-fi, action-comedy, comedy, fantasy, children's, and preschool. Frankly, I love them all, because I love to create fun and different stories.

If you want to start off with something easy don't start with comedy. It's more difficult than dramatic scripts because you not only have to write a good story, it has to be funny. Comedy can be difficult, unless you're a self-propelled-automatic-comedy-making-machine like Robin Williams. If you want to get your feet wet with comedy you might try an action-comedy. These are action stories with fun characters, like *Teenage Mutant Ninja Turtles*.

Because they aren't as detailed in story plotting and structure, short scripts are easier to write than long scripts. Seven-minute squash-and-stretch cartoons, such as *Tiny Toon Adventures*, have a hair-thin plot with lots of physical schtick. If you like to just come up with wild and crazy visual gags then this is the form for you.

Speaking of short scripts, I wrote some scripts for Warner Bros. Online's Entertaindom website. The series, *Li'l Green Men*, was made up of two-minute episodes that are about three-and-a-half pages long. You can't get much shorter than that. A simple setup—gag-gag-gag—and you're out.

There's also animated feature films. Who wouldn't like to write the next *Lion King* or *Toy Story*? But despite the allure of feature animation writing, it's a simple mathematical fact that there are a hundred times as many available opportunities in TV than in animated features. So do yourself—and your career—a favor, and start out with television. You'll get paid while you improve your skills, and thus have a better chance of selling that feature you have your heart set on.

Above all, follow your passion. If happiness is what you experience as you succeed in life, then succeeding at something you're passionate about *has* to result in the most happiness of all. Who knows? Maybe the next $500 million grossing animated feature will have your name on it. Anything's possible in Hollywood.

Chapter 2
Tools of the Trade

If you want to be an organ grinder you have to have an organ and a monkey. If you want to be a cartoon writer you need a few things, too. Fortunately, you don't need much. And what you do need doesn't bite or crap on your shoulder!

In this chapter I'm going to briefly discuss the basic tools of the toon writer (which are the same for any script writer). They are:

paper and pencil
computer
word processing software
reference works
internet access

The reason I include paper and pencil in this computer age of ours is because I've discovered something very interesting when I write. Every now and then it helps to switch from computer to paper and back to computer. If you find that typing or staring at a monitor is getting monotonous or uncomfortable, or if you feel creatively blocked, try pulling out a legal pad and pencil, or your favorite fountain pen, and doing it the old-fashioned way for a while. When I'm working out the beats for a story I generally write longhand for around fifteen to thirty minutes, until I get jammed and need my computer to spread my ideas out and more easily manipulate them. Then I'll work on my computer for hours until I need a change of pace again.

So don't discount ol' "No. 2". It can be quite useful.

I'll never forget when I started out as a story editor at Hanna-Barbera and they delivered my first brand new IBM Correcting Selectric typewriter. Wow! That was state-of-the-art. I could correct my typos without getting White Out all over my fingers. But compared to the ease of working on today's computers, typing on a Selectric is like chipping your scripts onto stone tablets (which can get very messy if you have to edit your commandments). So do yourself a favor and *don't* try to write a script on a legal pad or a typewriter. It is so much easier to manipulate your ideas on a computer that you will be giving yourself an unnecessary creative barrier. Trust me, cutting and pasting paragraphs, moving blocks of dialogue around, and editing scenes is infinitely easier on a computer. I should know. When I started writing with my Selectric I had to literally cut with a pair of scissors and paste with scotch tape to move things around.

The nice thing about computers for writers is that the cheapest of today's new computers, with the slowest chips, is lightning fast when it comes to word processing. For $500 you can get more power than you'll ever need. And there's nothing special to know about buying a computer for writing. If writing is your profession, or you hope it will be, you deserve the best tools. Period!

I'm a fast writer. In fact, my speed is limited by only one thing: how fast I type. And I type up to 100 words per minute! So do yourself a big favor, and if you don't already know how, learn to touch type.

If you're a hunt-and-pecker, and type like a child playing Chopsticks on the piano, you're going to find that you actually type slower when you begin to learn touch typing. When I got my Selectric I had to make a decision. Should I learn to type correctly and slow down? Or should I keep on hunting and pecking? I took the plunge. You should, too. If you stick with it you'll get faster and faster. I taught myself to type. But you don't need to. There are several good computer typing programs on the market. Find the best one for you and practice. If you're going to be a professional writer your ten most important tools will be your fingers!

I haven't tried voice recognition software and I'm not inclined to. Call me old-fashioned, but an 800MHz Pentium III computer with 256 MB RAM is enough for me. I don't need to have my voice digitzed, analzyed, and transmogrified into type. That's a little too mechanical for my creative taste. Makes me want to pick up my pad and pencil just thinking about it. But if it works for you, do it!

Speaking of software, one of the most important tools a writer will choose is word processing software. While just about any decent PC will do, many word processors are not ideal for script writing. I've used Microsoft Word for nearly fifteen years. I've always found it to be the best word processor for writing anything, including cartoons. But there's another reason for the toon writer to use it, and that's because it's the most common word processor used by the studios. This is important, because you can waste time if you have to convert your scripts to some other software so a studio can read and/or revise it. And converting sometimes screws up the margins and page breaks. This can make scripts come out longer or shorter than they should be, and can give you grief when trying to get on the same page as someone else.

I use Microsoft Word for all my TV and film writing, including premises, outlines, TV scripts, and screenplays. With MS Word's styles—automatic format settings—you can automatically set all your script margins, indent *character names*, and word-wrap the dialogue. You can also set up a template that will allow you to start a brand new document that is automatically formatted for script writing. If you need a Word for Windows script template, go to my website at www.jeffreyscott.tv and click on the FAQs page where it will explain how to download one of my scripts and turn it into a template.

In addition to conventional word processors, like Word, there are also some word processing programs that are specifically designed for scripts. At the request of Fred Wolf Films, I wrote the animated *Zorro* series using Movie Magic Screenwriter, which automatically generates *scene numbers*, recalls character names, adds *revision marks*, creates *A-pages*, and lots more. It's not a must for writing *sample* or spec scripts, but if you wind up doing any production work it can be very helpful and time saving.

There are several basic reference books that every writer should have on his or her desk. These include a good dictionary, a thesaurus, a slang dictionary, a multi-language dictionary, a rhyming dictionary, an atlas, an encyclopedia, and a book of names. Of course, if you have a computer you actually don't have to have any reference books because you can find them all online. But getting data from the Internet takes time no matter how fast your connection is. So, for basic reference, I use *Microsoft Bookshelf* CD-ROM. I keep it in my drive at all times. It is, as its name implies, a reference book-shelf, containing a dictionary, encyclopedia, thesaurus, atlas, book of quotations, historical chronology, and almanac. For quick, one-stop reference at the touch of a key, it's indispensable. In conjunction with Microsoft Word you can literally click on a word in your script and instantly get its definition, even an audio pronunciation! I use *Bookshelf* to check historical or technical facts, search locations on the atlas, and find synonyms.

For the six people out there who are still not on the Internet, this paragraph's for you. There isn't enough room in this entire book to tell you how helpful the Net can be to a writer. It's like being connected to every research library in the world, plus a few hundred million independent researchers (known as people). If you're not already a "surfer" you really *must* put your feet in the water. If having billions of facts at your fingertips sounds intimidating, just try some of the basic search engines like Google, Yahoo, HotBot, GoTo, Alta Vista, and Research-It. All you have to do is type in a question and very often the search engine takes you right to the answer. I once needed some research for a *Zorro* script and just typed in "1820 Southern California Spanish history." I got pages and pages of information on the subject, and it took all of thirty seconds (with a very slow modem). There's no longer any excuse not to do story research.

One of the coolest things on the Net for writers are all the dictionaries. There are hundreds of them, on every subject you can imagine. Not to mention every language, with translations to English. I found a rhyming dictionary where all you had to do was type in your word and it instantly gave you a list of every rhyme in the dictionary. One of the best dictionary sites I've found is www.onelook.com.

Another reason you must eventually get on the Net if you want to be a working writer is because of e-mail. I've written scores of scripts for shows without even setting foot in the studio. I just attach my script to an e-mail, send it in, get notes, revise it, then e-mail it back.

So if you're one of those six people who isn't online, don't procrastinate any longer. Get on and start practicing so you'll be grooved in by the time you really need it.

PART II
ANIMATION WRITING

Chapter 3
Basic Overview

NOW THAT WE'VE HANDLED the preliminaries let's get down to animation writing. As noted earlier, there are far more animated television episodes produced each year than animated features, so you're much better off starting out with TV. For that reason, a majority of this book will focus on TV toon writing.

With respect to TV, the most common script form is a half-hour episode, though 11-minute scripts are quite common as well. As there is more to the structure of a half-hour story than an 11-minute one, we'll focus our attention on a half-hour episode. If you can write a half-hour you can write an 11-minute script.

So let's assume that the product we're going for is a half-hour animated series script. With that as our goal, let's look down the road and see what we'll have to do to get there.

There are three basic steps to the toon writing process:

premise
outline
script

The Premise

A premise is a simple telling of the story, generally from one-half to three pages long. It lays out the beginning, middle, and end of the story, and not much else. A premise is what the writer gives to the story editor or producer as the initial attempt to get a script assignment. The writer receives no fee for the premise unless the producer wants to buy the idea and have someone else write it, in which case they'll pay a small amount, generally no more than a few hundred dollars. But the goal is not to sell the premise. The goal is to get a script assignment, at which point you are paid to write the outline and then the script. New writers may be cut off at the outline stage if the outline is not up to par, in which case their outline will be given to another to rewrite and go to script. (But if I do a good enough job with this book that shouldn't happen to you.)

For the writer, a premise has two purposes: first is to *communicate* the story; second is to *sell* the story—so you don't want to skimp on the quality of a premise.

It is a common understanding in writing that it is harder to write short than it is to write long. Thus, the expression "less is more" is quite true for the writer. It is hard to keep a premise down to one or two pages in length, but it's important to do so for several reasons. Most important is the fact that story editors and producers are busy people. They have tons of premises, outlines, and scripts to read. So the shorter the premise is, the more willing they are to read it. **Make your premise as short as possible, but long enough to tell the story.**

Perhaps the most important thing about writing a premise (and outlines, too) is that every word should count. Don't be redundant or say the same thing twice (that was just a test to see if you were paying attention). Don't use lots of unnecessary adjectives or flowery prose to try to sweeten your story. Just tell it effectively, dramatically, humorously—whatever it takes to get it across. No more, no less.

The most important thing to remember when you're trying to sell a premise is that it must work well in the context of the series. It must therefore fit the characters and the format.

If you want to win in this business—or any business, for that matter—the best way to do so is to have your work stand out. For your story idea to stand out it needs to be different. Most premises received by story editors are stories they've seen before. I've written so many stories that it's not uncommon for me to get story ideas submitted which I've already written myself.

I made a decision when I first started writing that I would always try to make my ideas unique in some way. I owe a lot of my success to the fact that I was able to come up with new ideas instead of regurgitating material already seen in other cartoons.

But what makes something different? The answer is not necessarily in the basic idea itself, but in the way it's executed. You can take a familiar story and change its setting or its date or its characters, and make it fresh. For example, take *Run Silent, Run Deep*, the classic World War II film in which a sub captain (Clark Gable) is obsessed with the sinking of a Japanese destroyer that sunk his previous vessel. Make it two starships, and it's a fresh idea.

Old idea + new time, place, or characters = fresh idea.

I borrowed an "old" idea known as *Raiders of the Lost Ark* and changed the setting (to a basement) and the characters (to Kermit, Piggy, and Gonzo) and got a fresh idea that turned into the "Raiders of the Lost Basement" episode of *Jim Henson's Muppet Babies*.

Another way to create a good premise idea is to have the story grow out of a character. A terrific example of this was the 1999 movie, *Muppets in Space*. The character Gonzo has never known what the hell he is (other than a weirdo). From this character need—to know about himself—came a story about Gonzo learning that he's really an alien.

Although a clever writer can write a story about anything, some things are definitely more interesting than others. As a basic rule, adults are more interested in people (they've seen enough action so that it's harder to keep their attention with it), while kids are more interested in action (they're learning how the world works and meet all the weird characters they need in school). This is, of course, a generality, and the rule is often broken. Witness all the mega-action movies that make hundreds of millions at the box office and the character films that die a swift death.

One way to get good story ideas is to look at what currently interests people (or kids). See hit movies, read the hottest magazines, go to toy stores, malls, the beach, or wherever, and you'll get great input. I've even gotten story ideas from the Yellow Pages!

Of course, one of the most important working rules of all is **keep it simple**. Don't get too complicated with your ideas or your writing. Simpler is always better, especially in animation.

A TV writer needs to train himself to come up with lots of ideas. If you're *pitching* premises you'll need them, because most premises are not accepted, including mine. The solution to a rejected premise is another premise. How many ideas can you come up with? Two? Six? A dozen? The answer is: As many as you think you can.

When I was story-editing the *Superfriends* series for Hanna-Barbera, ABC ordered eight half-hours consisting of three seven-minute stories each. So they needed a total of twenty-four ideas. I came up with fifty-two one paragraph ideas in one afternoon and got thirty-five of them approved. Of course, it helped that I had already run the show for three years, so the network had no doubt that I could deliver the scripts. Nonetheless, it proves that it can be done.

By the way, whenever you happen to get a good idea for a story, write it down and put it in your idea file. You never know when something that popped into your head in the shower will turn out to be just the idea you need for a script.

Another important rule in coming up with premise ideas is to **stay real to the reader (or viewer)**. Don't go too far out into space or you'll alienate your audience. This brings up another important point. **Your initial audience is not the viewer of the cartoon but the story editor or producer who is going to buy your idea.** He or she is the one you want to sell. Which brings up yet another important point. **Always try to find out what the buyer wants.** If you limit your ideas to those that *you* think are terrific you might miss the mark. You'll have a much better chance of selling something if you know what's wanted (and not wanted) first. It's not always easy to find out what people want in this industry. But try to find out whatever you can before you start dreaming up ideas.

Next Comes the Outline

After you have sold a premise—or after you have conceived your basic idea if you are writing a sample or spec script—it's time to *flesh out* your story into an outline.

An outline is a complete story, in written prose form, laying out every scene that will be in the final script.

In writing parlance, scenes are often called beats.

A half-hour outline has anywhere from fifteen to twenty-five beats, and should be from ten to twenty pages in length. Beats can be anywhere from five seconds long to three or four minutes.

Although dialogue is not necessary in most outlines, if you come up with any good lines while writing your story it's perfectly acceptable to include them.

Then Comes the Script

After you've completed your outline it's time to write the script. A script is a story written in a special form, laying out every scene in the story by means of:

description of the physical environment and any action;
dialogue;
transitions, *camera angles*, **and** *camera moves* **where necessary.**

Animation scripts come in various lengths. Though the underlying form of the writing (i.e. action and dialogue) is the same for all, the structure differs for each length.

The seven-minute cartoon is the length of the classic Warner Bros. and Disney cartoon shorts, such as *Tweety & Sylvester* and *Donald Duck*. Most seven-minute cartoons are squash-and-stretch comedy. There's not much time for story or character, but plenty of time for the frantic, nonstop gags that this length has become famous for.

The eleven-minute cartoon is a quarter hour, thus there are two of them in a half hour of programming. Many cartoons fall into this format, shows such as *Rugrats* and *Dragon Tales*, for example. With eleven minutes you have time to develop a *story arc*, get into some minor character changes, and perhaps develop a short *B-story*. Most eleven-minute shows have no act breaks, as the break comes between the two eleven-minute shows that make up the half-hour program. To read a sample of an eleven-minute script, go to my website and download one. You can also download samples of seven-minute scripts and other twenty-two-minute scripts.

The twenty-two-minute cartoon is called a half hour. *Jim Henson's Muppet Babies* and *Batman* are examples of half-hour cartoons. Plenty of time for A-, B-, and C-stories, and a good amount of character interaction. Half hour scripts consist of two or three acts, and sometimes have a thirty- to sixty-second *teaser* at the top of the show. They run anywhere from thirty to forty-five pages.

You might want to think about choosing the story length that best utilizes your particular likes or skills as a writer. If you're great at gags but your story structure leaves something to be desired you might want to focus on seven- or eleven-minute cartoons. If you're good with story structure you might want to focus on half-hours. If you feel you have a specific lack in some area you may want to consider getting a writing partner. For example, if you're great at dialogue, but can't write a story to save your life, teaming up with your opposite might help you both write well-balanced scripts.

Now that you understand the basic elements, we're going to take a much closer look at the process of cartoon writing.

Chapter 4
How to Write a Premise

ARTOON WRITING IS THE SAME as any applied technology—the more you do it the more proficient you become. Once you've written a hundred scripts you'll become very skilled at toon writing. But what if you haven't even written *one*? In that case it's all a big mystery. Take heart! Mysteries are only mysteries until one has acquired the information. Once you study the basic concepts of cartoon writing, and drill them by developing some stories and writing some scripts, you will begin to grow familiar with the process just as I did.

If Confucius was a toon writer he would have said, "A career of a thousand scripts begins with one story."

As noted earlier, animated television series have several formats. It wouldn't be practical to go over every step of every form and genre, so instead I'm going to focus on the broadest genre, half-hour action-comedy.

Rather than plod through the dry details of story structure, I'm going to make this a little more action-packed (and hopefully fun) by going step by step through the process of how I create a half-hour episode. I'm also going to ask you to contribute to the process.

I was fortunate enough to get permission from Mirage Licensing to use an actual episode I wrote for the mega-hit CBS series, *Teenage Mutant Ninja Turtles*. This will allow me to show you the development of a story from the premise stage, through the outline stage, to the final script, based on a series that many of you will be familiar with. The episode we'll be working with was produced, so some of you may have even seen it.

For those of you who missed the comic books, the zillion toys, the nearly two hundred cartoon episodes, and the live-action feature films, the Ninja Turtles are a group of four mutated teenage turtles named Leonardo, Donatello, Raphael, and Michaelangelo. (In case you noticed the misspelling, don't blame me. It was the creators of the Ninja Turtles who inadvertently spelled Michelangelo with an extra *a*.)

Turtles at birth, they were contaminated by toxic waste and became humanoid turtle dudes who battle various evil bad guys seeking to dominate the world.

During the final season of *Ninja Turtles*, which I story-edited and wrote for Fred Wolf Films, the recurring villain of each episode was an evil alien from Dimension X named Dregg. Dregg's goal was to take over the Earth by means of a "vortex warp" device which allowed him to transport warships and alien accomplices to our world.

With that as my series format, I was asked to come up with eight stories. One of them—and my favorite of the bunch—was "The Mobster from Dimension X." That's the one I'll be using as an example.

Over the course of my career I've come up with a story development method that works quite well. And it's really simple. We're now going to begin to put together a half-hour animated TV episode, beginning with the premise.

In coming up with a story premise for a series you want something that:

1. **Is as unique and creative as you can make it;**
2. **Fits well within the format and characters of the series;**
3. **Has some familiar elements that the audience can relate to and that you, the writer, can have fun with in terms of action and/or comedy.**

In fulfilling these three points for my "Mobster From Dimension X" premise I chose to have Dregg attempt to gain possession of a sophisticated computer chip, which would enable him to control every piece of computerized equipment on Earth with thought alone. This satisfied number 2, fitting in well with the Dregg-tries-to-conquer-the-Earth format for the season. But Dregg, like Darth Vader, is not the kind of guy who hangs around with his buddies during an entire story, so I needed another sub-villain to focus on while Dregg plotted from afar. Thus, I decided that Dregg would get help in acquiring the computer chip by using his vortex transporter to import an alien monster made of oozing green slime. To satisfy number 1 and make the story as unique as possible, I decided my slimy alien monster would be a "mobster" in fedora and pinstriped suit, just like Earth mobsters of the 1930s. This also satisfied number 3 by allowing me to have some fun with familiar gangster elements. For example, I added a pun and called him the Globfather.

With the above plot points in place I next needed to lay out my story. To do this I generally begin with the *A-story*—the main action plot—and first work out the basic beginning, middle, and end.

As his vortex transporter was destroyed in the previous episode, I knew I was going to have to have Dregg rebuild it. His reason for doing so was to import the alien mobster to help him get the chip. This gave me my A-story:

> *Dregg rebuilds his vortex transporter in order to import an alien mobster whom he needs to help him get the thought-controlling computer chip.*

Next we need a character-related complication for our heroes. This will be our *B-story*. **A B-story is a sub-story that is usually character driven and complicates or places a barrier in the way of the A-story.** To figure out a B-story let's examine our A-story a little closer.

So far we have (1) Dregg rebuilds the vortex transporter, and (2) He imports the alien mobster to help him get the computer chip with which to control the world's electronic equipment. You'd be surprised how much story material you can establish by simply looking at what would happen next. For example, you might ask the question, "Where would the alien mobster logically get a sophisticated computer chip?" The simple answer is a chip designer.

Remember, we're looking for a B-story to complicate the A-story. This means that our B-story must somehow prevent the villain from getting the chip. So you might ask, "Who or what would prevent the villain from getting the chip?" You could answer this question a thousand ways. A good way to start is to look within the environment of the story. In this case, the environment would probably be a computer chip lab.

Since it's generally *people* who complicate stories, not things, we should look for who would prevent the villain from getting the chip. It can't be the Turtles, because that would still be part of the A-story. It could be a lab technician, a janitor, a guard, a pizza delivery guy, the chip designer's wife, or his son, among others. I chose the son because kids are going to be more real to our audience, and they're going to provide more suspense when in trouble.

Thus, a simple but effective B-story would be to have the chip designer's innocent son somehow get the chip, forcing the Turtles to rescue the boy before our alien mobster can get him.

Now the son could just get the chip. But that's kind of dull. In order to add even more fun to the B-story I chose to have the son playing with his remote control car at the lab, thus being somewhat of an annoyance. Our B-story is now as follows:

> When the alien mobster comes to the lab to steal the chip, Dad hides it in his son's RC car. Son, not knowing Dad did so, grabs his car and runs for his life. Thus, the Turtles are forced to find the son and the chip before the villain can get them.

There was one more thing I needed to add to the premise based on the format of the series. I had to include TV reporter April O'Neil, the Turtles' friend and a recurring character in the series. As the Turtles will be chasing the kid in much of the story, April will help the Turtles find the kid. As a reporter, April would use the Internet, so it makes sense that she could get her local Internet buddies to help her search.

So, the villain is after a computer chip, brings in an alien mobster to help him get it, and the chip falls into the hands of the designer's son, whom the Turtles rescue with the help of April O'Neil. We've got our basic beginning, middle, and end. Now it's time to flesh out these elements and turn them into a premise.

As your first writing exercise, I'm going to ask you to write a draft of the premise yourself, before you read any further. When you've done that, go ahead and read mine. You'll be surprised how much you can learn by comparing the two.

On the following page is the *Teenage Mutant Ninja Turtles* premise: "Mobster From Dimension X."

TEENAGE MUTANT NINJA TURTLES

"Mobster From Dimension X"

by

Jeffrey Scott

Dregg, the self-appointed Supreme Warlord of the Galaxy and nemesis of the Turtles, rebuilds his Vortex Transporter and uses it to procure an infamous alien mobster from Dimension X, known across the galaxy as *The Globfather.* A Tommy gun-toting, slimy green amoeba in a pinstripe suit and fedora, The Globfather can infect humans with a touch of his oozing finger, turning them into spineless blobs.

At Dregg's command, The Globfather uses this power to organize Earth gangsters into a ruthless mob to do the evil warlord's bidding. And in this case, Dregg bids them to get "THE CHIP" — a state-of-the-art computer processor that allows brain waves to control computers. If Dregg can get his evil hands on it he can telepathically control every computer in the world and take over the Earth!

But before The Globfather and his gangsters can get it, the chip's inventor hides the tiny processor in his son's toy RC car. Bad idea! Now the Globfather and his gang are after the inventor's son!

With the help of reporter April O'Neil, who attempts to locate the kid via the Internet, the Turtles must find the young boy, and the chip, before the Globfather and his gangsters get their hands on it!

Other than some exciting prose, I didn't add much to my initial ideas to get the final premise. There's a bit more description of the Globfather, and I added some threat with his infectious touch. Note that I laid out the basic beginning and middle, but left the end a mystery. Needless to say, the Turtles are going to defeat the villains, so the end is really obvious. The premise is short, fast-paced, and sounds pretty exciting so far.

At one page, double spaced, this premise is on the short side. That's fine for an established writer like me, but if you're a new writer, a producer or story editor will probably want to see more of the details. Producers and editors will tell you what they want to see in the premise and will give you samples to read.

If your premise was a bit meatier than mine, that's good. If not, you might want to do another drill and see if you can flesh it out a bit.

The above premise was approved by Fred Wolf and I was asked to go ahead and write the outline. But before a cartoon writer begins the outline there is an intermediate step—the most important step in the toon writing process...

Chapter 5
Developing Your Story Beats

I T MAY SEEM LIKE A DAUNTING TASK to turn a thin premise into a tightly paced, precisely structured outline, with fully developed A- and B-stories, exciting action, and whimsical comic relief. And it would be daunting if you tried to start writing your outline from the beginning of the story straight through to the end. In fact, that's just how to give yourself a good case of writer's block, or what I call blank page syndrome. Fortunately, that's not how stories are written. Writing this way would be like trying to build a house without any blueprints. You'd start, of course, with the foundation. But you wouldn't know how to structure it because you wouldn't know what rooms are going where.

Writing a story is similar to building a house. When you build a house you know you're going to have bedrooms, bathrooms, a kitchen, garage, and a family room. These are the basic elements of any house. A story has its basic elements as well. These are the scenes, or as writers often call them, story beats.

Just as you decide on the rooms you want before you build your house, you work out story beats before you start writing an outline. A story beat is simply a *short* description of what a scene will include. For example, in the opening scene of *Star Wars*, a description of the beat might be as simple as "Vader captures the princess while C-3PO and R2-D2 escape." This gives the writer enough information to have a conceptual understanding of the scene, which is all he needs to know in order to begin stringing scenes together to form a coherent whole.

So the next thing we want to do in developing our "Mobster" story is find all of the beats. When we're done with that we'll put them together and write our outline. It is at the beat stage where your story really begins to take form. If you get your beats right, the rest is easy. The beats are where you find your structure, the backbone of the story.

Typically, in a half-our episode, you need from fifteen to twenty-five beats, depending on how long you make each one.

Be careful not to give yourself too many beats, as you may not have time to fully develop them. If this happens, your story will feel shallow and rushed. Also, **give yourself more time for comedy beats than action beats.** You need time to milk a comedy scene for all the fun it's got.

Now, how do we come up with all these story beats? To the novice writer this may sound like an overwhelming question. You look at that ream of paper or blank monitor, and the thought of filling pages with meaningful words sends you spinning. There's an infinity of ideas out there. Where do you start? What do you do?

Relax! The answer is simple. All you have to do to start the process is ask yourself one question: **"What are the scenes that *must* be there?"**

If we look over our premise we will see that we already have several scenes that *must* be there: We *must* have a scene in which we introduce the Globfather and his goal of getting the "chip." We *must* have a scene in which the Globfather and his men attempt to steal the chip. We *must* have a scene in which April O'Neil uses her computer to search for the missing kid, and we *must* have one or more scenes in which the Turtles search for the kid and chip. All of these beats are right there in the premise, so we don't have to start from scratch.

One thing I find that makes it easier to start figuring out my story beats is bringing my premise up on my computer screen and dividing it into separate numbered lines, each of which will become a story beat. The next thing I do is cut out all the unnecessary description, leaving only the basic concepts of the beats. Remember, the beats are not for anyone but you, so they don't have to be well written, they only have to communicate to *you* what the beat is about. Keep them as short as you can—on one line if possible. After numbering the individual beats, you will have a list that looks something like this:

1. **Dregg rebuilds his transporter and brings the Globfather to Earth.**
2. **The Globfather organizes gangsters to get "the chip."**
3. **The professor hides it in his son's RC car before the Globfather can get it.**
4. **April O'Neil helps the Turtles locate the kid via the Internet.**
5. **The Turtles try to find the kid and chip before Dregg and the Globfather.**

You can immediately see how much easier it is to work with something this simple. You only have to glance at a numbered line to understand the beat. It also allows you to see much more clearly where scenes are missing and which scenes might be out of order.

Now let's find some more beats by continuing to ask which are the scenes that *must* be there in order to connect up what we've got and get from the beginning of our story to the end.

Considering that this is a Ninja Turtles episode, and that most episodes begin with their stars, we *must* have a scene in which we introduce the Turtles.

In order for the Turtles to chase after the kid, he *must* run away. Also, since we can't possibly have any fun or suspense if the Turtles are never with the kid, it's necessary to have a scene in which the Turtles find him.

What about Dregg? In all good action stories the villain almost succeeds. Therefore, we *must* have a scene in which Dregg gets hold of the chip and starts to use it, and so we don't waste the opportunity of a great scene between the Turtles and the villain, we'll need a scene in which Dregg uses the chip to mentally control things in an effort to destroy the Turtles.

Now, if the kid has the chip, at some point the villains have to get it. So we *must* have a scene in which the villain gets the chip from the kid. And of course there *must* be a final action scene in which the Turtles defeat the villains.

All of these scenes are, for the most part, essential story points that I didn't have to put much creative thought into because they are logically necessary to the plot. We've already got a dozen beats, so for an average outline of twenty beats we're over halfway to the finish line.

Life is a cause and effect process. When one thing happens it necessitates something else happening. Then the effect becomes a further cause, necessitating another action, and so on. You don't have to be totally locked into this. Your characters have free will (actually it's yours as the writer) and will do things based upon their established personalities. But for the most part, in order to maintain a coherent story flow, you will find that much of a story can be plotted by this simple cause-and-effect process.

It should also be noted that every series has different characters, settings, and complications, and many or all of these elements must be serviced in a given story. This will dictate additional scenes, not from the plot but from the series format. The above scene with April O'Neil is an example of this.

An important thing to remember about story plotting is that **every scene should advance the story**. If a scene does not advance the story it will feel gratuitous, as if it's just tacked on. It will likely be less interesting and will often slow the *pacing*. You can see how this principle was applied to the scene with April O'Neil. Rather than just having her show up out of nowhere, her character was used to advance the story by helping the Turtles find the professor's son.

It's important to realize that writing stories is actually very simple, and most of the story beats are right below the surface. Of course, this could be likened to Michelangelo (the artist, not Ninja Turtle) looking at a block of marble and saying that David is right below the surface. But with some practice you'll begin to see most of the beats that are essential to your story.

One of the things that makes this story development method so easy is that **when coming up with scenes you don't have to worry about the order in which you think of them.** While answering the question of which scene must come next, just write down all of your beats in the order they come to you. Keep them as short as possible so that you can view them at a glance. When you're done listing the beats, number each one. I use the auto-numbering feature in my word processor to do this, so that the numbers are always in their proper sequence. Then all you have to do is cut and paste the beat you think should come first to the top of the list. Find the beat you think should come next and paste it into the second line. Continue this until you've got them in the order you think is right. You may not be done with your beats at this point, but by having them in order you'll be able to tell which new beats you need, or which of the ones you came up with you don't really need.

But how does one know the right order? This brings us to the subject of logic.

Logic

As a producer/story editor I have come to realize that many writers overlook, or simply don't understand, the most basic principle in story plotting—logic.

In order to write a good story it must be logical. Logic can be defined as "a sequence or association of facts which create an effective condition, correctly determine an outcome, or resolve a problem." Thus, good stories have sequences of scenes that create a desired effect and/or effectively resolve a problem.

Let's look at the "sequence of facts" component of the definition. You plot a story out in a sequence of events or facts. This sequence must be logical, meaning that it must follow a reasonable or workable course of cause and effect.

An illogical sequence of events would be: A boy's beloved puppy dies, then he immediately goes to a party and has a great time. The sadness of the death of a cherished puppy and the joy of a party do not logically track (unless the boy is crazy and killed the puppy, but I'll talk more about that in a moment).

A more logical sequence of events would be: The boy's puppy dies, and when he goes to a party he cannot get into the spirit of it. To follow this sequence out logically, the boy might then meet a nice girl at the party, which brings him slightly out of his funk. She takes him home and shows him *her* dog's new batch of pups, which makes him feel better still. One of the puppies is attracted to the boy. She gives it to him, turns on some music, and now he's feeling like dancing again.

This is now a logical sequence. This is how life works. And that's really what logic is—how the universe, and the people in it, *properly* work.

When writing a good story you must make sure that every scene logically follows its predecessor. The only way you can leave a step out is if you make a time cut, or a dissolve, in which case your audience will assume things have happened in the interval. For example, if you see a character with a beard in one scene and clean shaven in the next, one could assume he shaved it off—*provided* it was logical. If he's in a car, racing down a highway with a beard, then in the next scene he pulls up in the same car clean shaven, this would be illogical. However, if he had a beard one day, and the next day had no beard while on his way to an important business meeting—this *would* be logical.

One simple way to help make your story logical is to ask the following questions: **What would happen next? What would (character) do/say next?** Then, with the knowledge of the series, characters, the events of the story so far, and life in general, answer the question as best you can.

If you've already written something, you can check its logic by asking: **Is this what would happen next? What the character would do/say next?** If it isn't, it's not logical. If it's not logical it's probably not going to make a good story.

Also, keep in mind that what a character would do next is very much based on their goal or intention as set out in the story. So in asking the above questions you have to use all the information previously revealed in the story, including action, dialogue, and any undisclosed facts that are a part of the format of the show.

You might ask, "Why do I have to be logical when people act illogically all the time?" This is true, yet there is underlying logic to their illogical behavior. It's called insanity (to a greater or lesser degree), and it consists of patterns of behavior that, though different than normal, have a consistency to them, and that follow the logical mechanics of the mind (or of a "broken" mind). In the example of the boy whose dog died, if he was evil it might be very logical for him to see his puppy die and then have a great time at a party. Thus, being logical is dependent on knowing all the data.

There are a few other important things to consider when you're trying to put scenes in their best order. I once read a quote of Einstein's in which he simply said, "Something's moving!" An eloquently understated yet universal truth.

This brings up another important writing fact: **Movement creates interest.**

You'll see at a glance that this is true in life. What does a wild animal do when it sees movement? It gets interested. What does a hunter do when he sees movement? He gets interested. It's a survival mechanism. Every living thing gets interested at the perception of movement, whether by sight, hearing, or touch. Movement in music or art can be equally interesting.

The opposite is also true: **No movement creates boredom**.

Ever been in a doctor's waiting lounge? More to the point, have you ever watched a movie where the story didn't move? I'll bet you were bored. In order to keep your audience's interest you have to maintain movement in the story. This doesn't just mean physical movement. We've all seen movies with megatons of action that still bored us. Even when objects are physically moving, the story or the characters will sometimes stagnate.

There is also the matter of predictability of movement. **Movement that can be predicted is less interesting than movement that cannot be predicted.** This is because it is our nature to try to predict it, either because it is necessary to survival (as in predicting where a rattlesnake is going to move next), or because it is fun (as in predicting where a tennis ball will land so you can have your racket there in time to make a perfect backhand).

So in order to keep a story interesting you need to keep it moving. And one of the simplest ways to keep a story moving is to cut back and forth from your A- to your B-story.

It's also best if you don't *end* your scenes. Let me explain...

Every story has a beginning, middle, and end. Every scene also has a beginning, middle, and end. In fact, everything in the universe has a beginning, middle, and end: a sentence, a game of bowling, a flower, a storm, a star, a panic attack, the blink of an eye.

The reason this is so important to writing is that an end is a *stop*. It says, "It's all over, baby." You don't want to create too strong of an end in any one scene prior to the end of your story.

Did you ever read a novel that you just couldn't put down? I'll bet the action in the chapters didn't fully end, or that the author set up actions, goals, or ideas in one chapter that forwarded your attention to the next.

If you end each scene at its conclusion you will have a very choppy script. It will thump along like an old jalopy, starting and stopping and starting and stopping. Thus, the worst stories will look like this:

Scene #1	beginning-middle-end
Scene #2	beginning-middle-end
Scene #3	beginning-middle-end (etc.)

A better way to write scenes is to begin one and get through a portion of it, then advance to the next scene before the first is completely done. You do this by leaving something yet to be done, or creating a mystery that leads you to the next scene, or by having a character get into a problem or confusion and ending the scene before he or she resolves it. You can then have them resolve that problem at the beginning of a later scene, and develop a new problem or idea or goal or action that won't be completed until later—and so on. So a better story might look like this:

Scene #1	beginning-middle
Scene #2	end-beginning-middle
Scene #3	end-beginning-middle (etc.)

Or this:

Scene #1	beginning-middle-end-beginning
Scene #2	middle-end-beginning
Scene #3	middle-end-beginning (etc.)

A word of warning! Don't take this advice so literally that you turn yourself into a writing robot, having to apply every rule to every line of every scene in every script. These are concepts to understand so you can apply them on your own terms. Use them when necessary, or use them to check your writing when you run into a problem area. Creating should be smooth and fun, not overly analytical and mechanical. If a rule doesn't improve your story, *fogeddabowdit*!

Putting The Beats In Order

In attempting to put the scenes into their best order, we need to apply logic, taking into consideration that we want to maintain a high level of story movement and that we don't necessarily want to end every scene completely.

First I'll simply put the beats down in the order I thought of them. I am including here the six additional "must" scenes we came up with earlier.

1. **Dregg rebuilds his transporter and brings the Globfather to Earth.**
2. **The Globfather organizes gangsters and goes off to get "the chip."**
3. **The professor hides it in his son's RC car before the Globfather can get it.**
4. **April O'Neil helps the Turtles locate the kid via the Internet.**
5. **The Turtles try to find the kid and chip before the Globfather can.**
6. **The Turtles are introduced.**
7. **The professor's son runs away.**
8. **The Turtles find the professor's son.**
9. **Dregg arrives and starts to use the chip.**

10. **Dregg uses the chip to try to destroy the Turtles.**
11. **The villain gets the chip from the kid.**
12. **The Turtles defeat the villains.**

Some of these are already in the right order because when I looked for what beats had to be there I was thinking through the logical time sequence in which stories unfold. But several of these beats are in the wrong place, and others could be moved or split into two or more scenes to make the story more interesting and better paced. Also, some scenes, though necessary for logical plotting, don't have to be shown. Instead, they can simply be implied or referred to in dialogue as having happened.

As a practical drill—and because you can't learn to write by just reading—why don't you see if you can put the above list in the order that you think would be best. If you're a conscientious aspiring toon writer you won't peek. If you're already reading on so that you can get to the list then you may not have what it takes to be a professional cartoon writer (though you might make a terrific studio executive).

Do the drill!

Here's how I would order them:

1. **The Turtles are introduced.**
2. **Dregg rebuilds his transporter and brings the Globfather to Earth.**
3. **The Globfather organizes gangsters and goes off to get "the chip."**
4. **The professor hides it in his son's RC car before the Globfather can get it.**
5. **The professor's son runs away.**
6. **The Turtles try to find the kid and chip before the Globfather can.**
7. **April O'Neil helps the Turtles locate the kid via the Internet.**
8. **The Turtles find the professor's son.**
9. **The villain gets the chip from the kid.**
10. **Dregg arrives and starts to use the chip.**
11. **Dregg uses the chip to try to destroy the Turtles.**
12. **The Turtles defeat the villains.**

These are not haphazardly ordered. They are placed in logical, cause-and-effect sequence.

Now let's do another drill. This one will be considerably harder. There are many missing beats in the above story. And some of the beats, as written, can be combined or deleted entirely.

Try to complete the beats and order them into the best story you can. Use the tools described above. Add any scenes you feel would fill in the gaps or improve the basic structure. Delete any you feel are not necessary.

Below you'll find the beats as I structured them for the actual episode. When you're done you can compare yours with mine and see how you did. Don't be surprised when you discover that my beats are very different than yours.

It's time to go to your computer and fill in the beats.

No peeking!

Okay, here's how—and why—I developed the story beats:

1. **When a group of gangsters try to steal the professor's chip they are thwarted by the Turtles.**

What I've done here is combined several of the "must" scenes into one. In one dramatic opening scene I've introduced the Turtles, set up the professor and his chip, and established the gangsters. I also started off with a bang by including Turtles fight action right at the top of the show. **It's generally a good idea to start off a story with a scene that hooks your audience, and action is one of the best ways to do this.** Just look at all those James Bond movies!

By revealing the gangsters first, without showing the Globfather coming to Earth and gathering his gang of gangsters, I've set up a mystery. Who are these gangsters and why are they after the chip? Mysteries are wonderful stuff. They stick the audience like moths to a light bulb.

You'll notice that I didn't play out beats #2 and #3. Instead, I decided to begin the story *after* these beats have taken place. One of the reasons I did this is because developing them linearly would be much less interesting. What I've done is sort of like starting to watch a baseball game in the bottom of the first inning, with the bases loaded and Mark McGuire at the plate. Contrast this to starting with the players warming up, everyone getting into the stadium, buying hot dogs, watching the teams come out onto the field, and the singing of the National Anthem, and you'll understand the logic. We've all seen this stuff before, so why not "cut to the chase," as they say.

There is a working rule of good writing that can be derived from this, and that is **"less is more."** In other words, **try to do it in one scene instead of three, and say it in one line instead of two.**

Looking back at scene #1, if we ask, "What would happen next?" the logical answer is: the Turtles would try to find the gangsters.

Once again, in developing a story you need to take into consideration the series format. In this case, a very important part of the show is the Turtle Lair, the underground home of the Turtles inside a big city storm drain. So rather than just have the Turtles race off after the baddies, it would be better, from a series standpoint, to have them return to their home base. This works especially well because Donatello has all sorts of computerized gizmos he can use to locate the gangsters. Thus, our next beat becomes:

2. **The Turtles return to their lair where they attempt to track the gangsters.**

Where should we go next? There are only two possibilities based on what's happened in the story so far: either a scene with the professor, or a scene with the gangsters. There's nothing more to be learned from the professor at this point. The real mystery lies with the gangsters and why they want the chip. The answer is to follow the gangsters and build the threat by introducing the villain (or, in this case, the sub-villain, with Dregg being the main villain). So the third beat becomes:

3. **The gangsters return to their hideout where they meet the deadly alien Globfather, who has been hired by a mysterious person to get the chip. They leave to try once again to get the chip.**

By revealing that the Globfather has been hired by someone else we keep the mystery of who the villian is. At the same time we heighten the threat to the Turtles by introducing the Globfather as a more dangerous adversary than the gangsters (whom the Turtles have already defeated). Now we can cut back to the Turtles.

> **4.   The Turtles track the gangsters to their hideout, find a clue, and continue to track them.**

Notice that I chose not to have the Turtles battle the villains in scene #4. There's an important reason for this. One of the most important storytelling rules I've ever come across is that **good stories have a balance between substance and meaning.** In terms of script writing this means **we need a balance of action and dialogue in a story.**

This is why we don't want to have too many Turtle action sequences, one after the other. It's too much substance without enough meaning, and will throw the story out of whack. So we must push the meaning of the story for awhile before going back to another confrontation.

This brings up another concept of good storytelling—*rhythm*. This is, perhaps, the most difficult thing to convey, as it is somewhat ethereal. Rhythm in storytelling is similar to rhythm in music. It's a recurring wave. The simplest form would be an action scene, then a talking scene, then an action scene, and another talking scene. But this kind of perfect rhythm can be too predictable and thus boring or hypnotic.

As with everything else, story rhythm can take on different forms, with varying modulations. It's important to understand that there *is* a rhythm to writing, as it may help you to spot the arythmia of a scene or story.

So far these are the beats we have:

> 1.   **When a group of gangsters try to steal the professor's chip they are thwarted by the Turtles.**
> 2.   **The Turtles return to their lair where they attempt to track the gangsters.**
> 3.   **The gangsters return to their hideout where they meet the deadly alien Globfather, who has been hired by a mysterious person to get the chip. They leave to try once again to get the chip.**
> 4.   **The Turtles arrive at the hideout, find a clue, and continue to track down the gangsters.**

In answering the "What would happen next?" question we have only to look at what's currently happening in the story. The Globfather is looking for the chip, and the Turtles are looking for the Globfather. Thus, everyone is essentially heading for the same place, which is the location of the chip. And that's where we need to go next. Thus:

> **5.   The professor and his son are established at the research lab.**

I chose a research lab simply because it's the most obvious place a professor would be developing a chip of this nature. The next piece of action is also very obvious. The Globfather must arrive. But how?

Here is where logic will begin to come in handy. Would it be logical for the door to burst open and the Globfather and his men to come in? No! Why not? Because research labs have guards and they're not that easy to break into. Also, the gangsters recently tried to steal the chip, so the security would logically have been beefed up. Thus, the most logical place for the Globfather and his gang to arrive on the scene is at some guarded perimeter. And so:

6. **At the lab's perimeter, the Globfather and his men cleverly get past the guards.**

Notice that I don't develop these scenes fully. I just jot down the basics of the beat. We'll develop them fully at the outline stage.

Now it's time for the baddies to enter the lab. This will be the scene in which the professor hides the chip in his son's RC car. There have also been four scenes since we've had any Turtle action, so it's time for a little ninja "substance" in this scene. Two other things must also happen. The son must run away with the chip (without knowing he's got it), and the Globfather and his men must get away.

Breaking a Scene Into Beats

You can see that there are a lot of things going on in this scene. When this happens it's sometimes a good idea to write out the beats *of the scene* just as you would write out beats for a story. So let's list the elements of this scene. As before, don't worry about the order at first. Just get them written down, then order them and fill in any missing beats later. Here's what has to happen:

- **Villians enter lab, after the chip.**
- **Professor hides chip in son's RC car.**
- **Turtles enter and battle gangsters.**
- **Professor's son runs away.**
- **Globfather and his men get away.**

There are a few other things missing from this scene. We know that the Globfather isn't going to get the chip yet, but he also isn't going to know that it's in the RC car. No one does except the professor. But if the Globfather doesn't know the chip is in the car, he must think it's somewhere else. Being a computer chip, it might logically be in a computer. So it would make sense that the Globfather would take the computer. It would also make sense for him to take the professor, just in case he needed any help getting the chip to work. Thus, in order to ensure the story continues to move, I decided to let the Globfather get away with the computer and professor as follows:

7. **Back in the lab, the Globfather and his men enter in search of the chip, but the professor hides it in his son's RC car. The Turtles arrive and try to stop the Globfather and his gang, who get away with the professor and his computer, while his son runs off in fear (with his RC car).**

The next beat on our list of twelve is #6: The Turtles try to find the kid and chip before the Globfather can. But the Turtles didn't see the professor hide the chip, nor did they see the kid run off. So they don't even know the kid has the chip and is in need of being found. Their obvious next action would be to simply chase the Globfather. But there are a few problems with this. First, we've already had them looking for the Globfather, so this would be somewhat redundant and boring at this point. The second problem is that we would be taking too long to get into our B-story involving the Turtles and the kid. So what we need in scene #7 is something that keeps the Turtles in the lab long enough to let the Globfather get away, after which the Turtles will be motivated to look for clues and discover what happened with the kid.

These are the kinds of puzzles that make writing really fun. I have a simple philosophy about solving such riddles, and that is: If you can pose the question you can find the answer. And the tougher the problem the better the solution.

Here's how I solved the problem: I mentioned earlier that this lab has tight security. Therefore, it makes perfect sense that there would be security cameras. All the Turtles have to do is play back the security tape to see if they can find any clues and— *voila!*—they see the professor hide the chip in his son's RC car, then spot the son take off with it. And now they know what they've got to do. And we know what our next beat is:

8.   **Still at the lab, the Turtles get out of the jeopardy the Globfather left them in. Looking for clues, they check the video security camera, which reveals that the professor hid the chip in the RC car, which his son has run off with. The Turtles take off to find the kid.**

The next beat on our list of twelve is #7: April O'Neil helps the Turtles locate the kid via the Internet. This one works fine here. The Turtles can call her from wherever they are via their communicators.

To develop the beat a bit I asked myself the question, "What would April do next?" Thus, I got the following beat:

9.   **Introduce April O'Neil, who is asked by the Turtles to help them find the kid. She calls a friend at police headquarters, who puts out an APB.**

The next beat on our list is #8: The Turtles find the professor's son. It's a little too soon for this to happen, so we have to find the interim beats first. But what do we do? We've got several pieces of action going on in several places. The story is developing and getting more complicated. How do we avoid getting lost? And how do we choose our next step? This brings up a very interesting and important part of good story writing.

Story Dynamics

Webster's New Collegiate Dictionary defines dynamics as "the pattern of change or growth of an object or phenomenon." For our purposes let's slightly modify this definition to mean all of the separate patterns of change that are taking place in our story. We'll call this *story dynamics*.

All of the patterns of change in our story, such as our heroes' goals, the villains' goals, our characters' emotions, character relationships, their individual or group states of action or jeopardy, make up the story's dynamics. All of these dynamics have logical cause-and-effect consequences. To handle one incorrectly, or omit one, is to leave a *hole* in your story. A hole, in writing parlance, means that there is something illogical in the story.

I cannot emphasize enough how important it is to **always keep track of all of the dynamics which are operating in your story!**

Depending upon the complexity of the story, following all of the story dynamics can be quite a job. But it must be done. One of the best reasons to keep a story simple, especially if you're an inexperienced writer, is so that there are less of these dynamics going on, which makes the story easier to control.

With this in mind, you might want to do another exercise and look over the previous story beats to see if you can list the dynamics that are operating. This list will tell you all of the things that you must deal with as the story progresses.

Here are what I found to be the existing story dynamics:

- **Dregg wants to take over the Earth (unexpressed in beats so far, but implied).**
- **The Globfather wants the chip.**
- **The Turtles want to find out who the Globfather is and what he's up to.**
- **They want to find the kid.**
- **They also want to get the Professor back.**
- **The Professor wants to prevent the Globfather from getting the chip.**
- **He also would be concerned about his son.**
- **His son wants to get to safety.**
- **And would also be concerned about his father.**
- **April wants to assist the Turtles.**

As a story progresses the dynamics will change. Some dynamics will end, while others will begin. All dynamics must be tracked, and must be resolved to their logical completion. This may sound very complicated, but in a good story it's just a smooth flow of interesting action and dialogue.

By listing the dynamics and following them you can more easily keep track of what's happening in your story, and keep them alive and moving. It is the cutting back and forth between these dynamics that will establish the movement and pacing of a story. It's much like juggling plates. As you spin one you find another slowing. You leave the one you're spinning and start spinning the slow one only to find another slowing down. You speed that one up, and so on.

At the end of your story you will find that all of your remaining dynamics converge and must be fully resolved in the final scenes. But we'll get to that later. Right now we need to put this principle into action and choose which story dynamic to deal with next. We can apply our rule of movement and our rule of not ending scenes and leave the Turtles and April before they resolve anything. There's nothing much to be gained at this point from going back to the kid. So let's return to the Globfather.

Before the Globfather can go after the kid he has to both discover that the Professor hasn't got the chip and find out where it is. This would be a good place to do that. The simplest thing for him to do is bring the computer back to his hideout. Then he'd probably just have his men tear it apart to find the chip. Not finding it, the Globfather would turn to the professor.

We can add a bit of menace to the scene by having the Globfather threaten harm to the professor if he doesn't give up the chip, forcing him to reveal that he put it in his son's backpack. But before the Globfather can search for the kid he's got to know what the kid looks like. This is easily solved by action that we set in motion earlier. Specifically, the APB that April's friend at Police Headquarters issued. The Globfather and his men need only be watching CNN (Cartoon News Network) to see a picture of the kid. Now they're all set for the chase to begin.

By the way, it would have been perfectly fine for one of the gangsters to find a picture of the boy in the professor's wallet, but spotting him on TV does a little more for us by establishing that the APB has gone out and that others are now looking for the boy as well. Thus, our next beat is:

> **10. Back at his hideout, the Globfather discovers the chip is missing and forces the professor to reveal that it's in his son's RC car. The baddies see the APB and head off in search of the kid.**

We've used neither our original beat #8, (The Turtles find the professor's son), nor beat #9 (The villain gets the chip from the kid). I chose to condense these two scenes into one and bring the Turtles and the bad guys together for another action scene, during which the Globfather gets the chip. However, in order to give him time to get away, it's necessary to separate the Turtles and gangsters. This problem is solved by using the kid. We'll simply have the Globfather put the kid in jeopardy, forcing the Turtles to save him and giving the Globfather and his men time to escape. And so our next scene becomes:

> **11. The Turtles and gangsters search for and find the kid. After a battle, the Turtles save the kid, but the Globfather gets away with the chip.**

The next three beats in our list of twelve all have to do with Dregg arriving and using the chip. But those are our ending beats, and we're not ready for them yet. We've still got several things to do first.

Because cutting back and forth between the A- and B-stories generates movement, pacing, and rhythm within a script, I chose to cut from the B-story back to the A-story as follows:

> **12. The Globfather informs Dregg that he has the chip, and Dregg reveals his plan to take over Earth and destroy the Turtles. He'll come as soon as he finishes rebuilding his vortex transporter.**

By revealing Dregg's goal we raise the threat to a higher level while building some additional suspense into the story.

We've just had an action scene and a threat-raising scene. Now would be a good time to take a breather from the action and suspense and further develop our B-story between the Turtles and the kid. Having saved the kid, the Turtles' basic motivation is to find the Globfather and get the chip back. This is routine Turtle stuff. Donatello would use some of the turtle gizmos to try to pick up the villains' trail.

For character conflict between the Turtles and the kid I chose a simple yet very familiar conflict that would be very real to adolescents: the don't-bother-me-kid-I-know-what-to-do adult (Donatello) versus the kid who really *does* have some helpful answers. This fits in perfectly with the story we've developed so far, as this is the son of a brilliant professor, so it makes perfect sense that he would be a brilliant kid. Here's how I chose to develop the next beat:

13. **In the Turtle van, the kid annoys Donatello by using his Turtle gizmos to lock onto the Globfather. Donatello dismisses the kid and boasts at having found the Globfather's trail himself.**

At this point the Turtles would take off after the Globfather. So we can leave this scene now.

In asking, "What would the Globfather do next?" we could either assume he's done his job (getting the chip) and would do nothing, or we could have him be more active. It's more dramatic to bring Dregg in at the end, so I chose to postpone his entrance and have the Globfather set the groundwork for Dregg's takeover. Dregg plans on using the chip to take control of Earth equipment, so one could ask where the best place would be for someone to try to tap into electronic equipment. Although any telephone jack would suffice, a more dramatic location to accomplish the same thing would be a central telephone switching center.

Checking over my story dynamics, I see that I have to do something with the Professor. Rather than leave him tied up at the Globfather's hideout, I chose to bring him along. This isn't just an arbitrary choice. We'll need him at the ending sequence in order to close out all of our story dynamics.

Finally, we don't want to merely have the Globfather take over the phone switching center. This would be dull and redundant action. As always, we want to raise the stakes as much as possible. To do this we simply have to demonstrate the capabilities of the chip. So here's how the scene would look:

14. **The Globfather and his men take over a telephone switching center where they force the professor to hook up his chip. The Globfather tests it by using his mind to control various pieces of equipment via telephone lines.**

Now, it's always a good idea to tie your story beats together whenever possible. The better they weave together the tighter and better constructed the story. So if the Globfather is going to test out the chip, rather than have him do so on a total stranger it would better serve our story to have him do so on a character we've already established. Who do you think would be the best person to test it on?

Well, you may have a better idea, but I chose April. We haven't seen her in a while, and don't want to just drop her. She's also alone, which is potentially more threatening. And we've already established that she's tied into the Internet—the perfect connection to the Globfather and his chip. Here's how I did it:

15. **April's computer goes haywire and she uses it to track down the source of the problem to the telephone switching center. When the Globfather discovers she's snooping on him he uses the phone lines to mentally control things in an attempt to destroy her.**

With April being attacked by the Globfather, the answer to "What would happen next?" becomes very simple. She'd contact the Turtles, telling them what she's found out about the Globfather. But when the Turtles find out where the Globfather is, what would they do? Donatello would use one of his gizmos to try to tap into the phone switching center to learn something about what the Globfather is up to. And what would the Globfather do if he got wind that the Turtles were snooping on him via the phone lines? Here's what I think would happen:

16. **April informs the Turtles that the Globfather is controlling the phone lines. Donatello tries to tap into the phone system, inadvertently allowing the Globfather to gain control of their Turtle van via the chip. The Globfather tries to destroy them, and the Turtles barely escape with their lives.**

In checking our story dynamics once again, we learn that the Globfather and his men are at the telephone switching center, April is in jeopardy, and so are the Turtles. Thus, we're at the highest point of threat in the story so far. How can we possibly raise the stakes and further the plot? Answer: By finally introducing the main villain of the piece—Dregg!

I chose to have Dregg commence his evil plan to use the chip to conquer Earth. But what will Dregg do? The question to ask is, "Which piece of electronic equipment at Dregg's disposal would be the most threatening to Earth?" The answer I chose for this is an orbiting satellite laser. Thus, my next beat:

17. **Back at the phone switching center, Dregg arrives and takes charge, gaining control of a military satellite weapon and threatening the world, demanding total capitulation.**

By asking the question, "What would the Turtles do next?" we get that they would work out a final plan of attack. The specifics of the plan can vary. There are hundreds of ways to skin an animated cat. Donatello is the brains of the bunch, so I chose to have him devise a gizmo with which to gain control of electronic devices through the phone lines, just like the villain. This will give us the opportunity for a dramatic finale, with the Turtles battling the villain, "brain against brain" and "device against device." The logical place for Donatello to build such a gizmo is the Turtle Lair. Thus...

18. **The Turtles return to their lair where Donatello builds a gizmo with which he hopes to mentally stop the villains from controlling things via the phone lines.**

With Dregg now threatening the world, and Donatello and the gang preparing to stop him, we are obviously ready to bring all of our story dynamics, and the story itself, to a close. Remember, in a beat outline we're not working out all of the details, just the basic beats. There are many things to be resolved, such as the relationship between the kid and Donatello, the reunion of the kid and his father, the demise of the Globfather, and of course, Dregg. We'll flesh these out in the outline. For our final beat it will suffice to simply state that everything will be resolved. And so we get:

19. **In a dramatic finale at the phone switching center, the Turtles battle the villains. Donatello, using his gizmo, enters into a battle of minds with Dregg, each of them trying to control things to destroy the other. The Turtles win and transport the villains back home. The professor is reunited with his son.**

That's the end of our beats. Let's see what they read like when we string them all together.

1. **When a group of gangsters try to steal the professor's chip they are thwarted by the Turtles.**
2. **The Turtles return to their lair where they attempt to track the gangsters.**
3. **The gangsters return to their hideout where they meet the deadly alien Globfather, who has been hired by a mysterious person to get the chip. They leave to try once again to get the chip.**
4. **The Turtles arrive at the hideout, find a clue, and continue to track down the gangsters.**
5. **The professor and his son are established at the research lab.**
6. **At the lab's perimeter, the Globfather and his men cleverly get past the guards.**
7. **Back in the lab, the Globfather and his men enter in search of the chip, but the professor hides it in his son's RC car. The Turtles arrive and try to stop the Globfather and his gang, who get away with the professor and his computer, while his son runs off in fear (with his RC car).**
8. **Still at the lab, the Turtles get out of the jeopardy that the Globfather left them in. Looking for clues, they check the video security camera, which reveals that the professor hid the chip in the RC car, which his son has run off with. The Turtles take off to find the kid.**
9. **Introduce April O'Neil, who is asked by the Turtles to help them find the kid. She calls a friend at police headquarters, who puts out an APB.**
10. **Back at his hideout, the Globfather discovers the chip is missing and forces the professor to reveal that it's in his son's RC car. The baddies see the APB and head off in search of the kid.**
11. **The Turtles and gangsters search for and find the kid. After a battle, the Turtles save the kid, but the Globfather gets away with the chip.**
12. **The Globfather informs Dregg that he has the chip, and Dregg reveals his plan to take over Earth and destroy the Turtles. He'll come as soon as he finishes rebuilding his vortex transporter.**

13. In the Turtle van, the kid annoys Donatello by using his Turtle gizmos to lock onto the Globfather. Donatello dismisses the kid and boasts at having found the Globfather's trail himself.

14. The Globfather and his men take over a telephone switching center where they force the professor to hook up his chip. The Globfather tests it by using his mind to control various pieces of equipment via telephone lines.

15. April's computer goes haywire and she uses it to track down the source of the problem to the telephone switching center. When the Globfather discovers she's snooping on him he uses the phone lines to mentally control things in an attempt to destroy her.

16. April informs the Turtles that the Globfather is controlling the phone lines. Donatello tries to tap into the phone system, inadvertently allowing the Globfather to gain control of their Turtle van via the chip. The Globfather tries to destroy them, and the Turtles barely escape with their lives.

17. Back at the phone switching center, Dregg arrives and takes charge, gaining control of a military satellite weapon and threatening the world, demanding total capitulation.

18. The Turtles return to their lair where Donatello builds a gizmo with which he hopes to mentally stop the villains from controlling things via the phone lines.

19. In a dramatic finale at the phone switching center, the Turtles battle the villains. Donatello, using his gizmo, enters into a battle of minds with Dregg, each of them trying to control things to destroy the other. The Turtles win and transport the villains back home. The professor is reunited with his son.

We now have a coherent and workable story. All of the beats are there. The "must" scenes have been properly ordered and connected to each other through intermediary scenes. There are no story holes (at least none that I found), and all of the dynamics that were started in the beginning of the story have been resolved.

As much as I'd like to be able to write stories in a consecutive stream of beats—one, two, three—it can't always be done. In laying out this story I went through a process of doing one or two scenes, then realizing that there was a logic problem and going back and revising an earlier scene, then progressing forward again until I hit another problem, and so on. It's a two-steps-forward-one-step-back process of taking the "must" scenes, finding those scenes that connect them up, then tinkering with them so that all of the holes are filled and the plot lays out logically.

A story can be written a million different ways, so maybe the way *you* laid it out is better. It's not important at this point to worry about whether or not a story is perfect. What's important is gaining an understanding of the basic structure of a story, and being able to lay it out, beat by beat, so that it is logical, dramatic, emotionally engaging, humorous where appropriate, and above all, entertaining.

Once you have the story beats laid out and you're pretty sure they track correctly, the next step is the outline.

Chapter 6
How to Write an Outline

WORKING OUT THE STORY BEATS is the most important part of writing a good script. If your beats are solid, the remainder of the work will be a lot easier. If they're really tight, fleshing out the outline should be fairly straightforward.

So how do you flesh out the beats? Well, if the beats are the bricks, then all you need to do is add the mortar. In other words, for the most part you'll just be making all of the pieces fit together better. Instead of short, staccato beats, you'll begin to turn them into a more stylish piece of writing that reads more smoothly. You might want to add some exciting adjectives, dramatic phrases, or a funny gag here and there. You'll definitely want to expand the beats so that the action is fully described. Rather than using simple statements like "the villain gets away," you'll want to explain how. You'll also need to flesh out the action so that the reader can *see* it. Although it's not necessary, you can even add some dialogue, but if you do, make sure it's good.

A good little maxim is: **When in doubt, leave it out!** Because your outline is your calling card to the script assignment, you want it to be written as well as possible. If they don't like your outline you may get cut off before writing the script.

In fleshing out your beats into a full outline you'll be doing the following things:

- **Filling in any gaps you left in the story.**
- **Correcting anything that doesn't work as you flesh it out.**
- **Adding details, like names of people and places.**
- **Expanding your sparse beats into more descriptive pictures.**
- **Further developing the characters and their interrelationships.**
- **Making it read easier and more smoothly.**

Fleshing out beats, to me, is one of the most fun parts of cartoon writing. You've already done the heavy brain work, now it's time to sit back and just do some creative writing.

An important thing to remember when writing is not to get stressed out, worrying whether it's good enough. Just do the best you can. You improve by practice. This means there is a definite "win" in everything you write, whether you sell it or not, because everything you write makes you a better writer.

There are many acceptable outline forms. One is just straight prose writing to tell the story from beginning to end, much as one would in a novel. Another is to number your scenes, just as you did your beats. A third is to start each scene with a *slug line*, thus setting up the location and time of the scene.

It's a good idea to number scenes for editing purposes. It's hard to find what you're looking for when someone says, "The fifth sentence in the third paragraph on page seven." It's easier to just call it "Scene 17." For this reason I always number the scenes in my outline. I also prefer to use slug lines because they instantly tell the reader exactly where they are.

It's time to get into the outline. In order to maintain the outline's integrity and let you enjoy reading it, there won't be comments interspersed throughout, as there were in the beat outline. Instead, comments will be in the form of footnotes. This way you can read the outline straight through, but be sure to read the footnotes as you go, because that's where the information is.

There's one more thing to remember. When you're developing a story from premise, to beat outline, to outline, and finally to script, there are many times, and many reasons, to change what you have written. You might change your mind and find an idea you like better. You might decide a scene is too long and choose to delete it. You might discover you need an additional scene to better connect two other scenes. You might find a story hole which needs fixing. Whatever it is, don't be afraid to change what you have written if you can make an improvement.

To be more real in this demonstration I am using the actual premise, outline and script I wrote for the Turtles episode. Thus, you will find that the outline doesn't perfectly match the premise. And the script doesn't exactly match the outline. I added, I changed, I deleted, but always with the intention of improving the final script.

Half-hour scripts, unless they're run on commercial-free TV, are broken into two or three acts. Most are two acts, but the Turtles was a three-act series. Generally, one should try to break up an outline into equal length acts, but they don't have to be exact. Don't worry if you have to make the acts uneven in length.

The criteria for choosing a spot for an act break is to find a place where you can leave the characters in jeopardy, cut in the middle of a piece of dramatic action, or somehow leave the audience in mystery. The main goal of an act out is to leave your viewer interested and curious about what is going to happen next. This is why you want to look for the most threatening or wild place to act out. If you can't find anything particularly exciting, just try to turn what you've got into something mysterious or interesting.

What follows is the *Teenage Mutant Ninja Turtles* outline, "Mobster From Dimension X," exactly as I turned it in to Fred Wolf and CBS:

TEENAGE MUTANT NINJA TURTLES

#9062-9606

"Mobster From Dimension X"

by

Jeffrey Scott

OUTLINE
March 26, 1996

Fred Wolf Films

TEENAGE MUTANT NINJA TURTLES
"Mobster From Dimension X"
ACT ONE

1.   **UNIVERSITY LECTURE HALL - DAY**

Dr. Alvin Huxley, a rather nebbish looking professor, is before a packed audience of academia, demonstrating his breakthrough: THE PROTEIN COMPUTER![1] Not only does it think as fast as the human mind, but it can be "linked" to the human brain as well! The Professor demonstrates by dramatically connecting his own brain to the protein computer and controlling the entire city (e.g. telephone switching, traffic signals, subways). The audience is awed![2]

Meanwhile, Donatello—interested in science as he is—is on the roof, watching the lecture through the skylight[3]. He's brought the other Turtles along, all of whom are bored stiff, except Donatello, who finds the lecture intellectually stimulating. Raphael, on the other hand, would rather watch paint dry. So he takes out a small can of paint and plays a practical joke on Donatello, painting a sign and putting it on the back of Donatello's shell. It reads: "I AM A TEENAGE MUTANT NINJA GEEK!"

But the boredom ends quickly when several earth gangsters burst into the lecture hall, taking out the security guards and attempting to grab the Professor! The Turtles go into action! They dramatically drop through the skylight and battle the gangsters, saving Professor Huxley and his protein computer, then chasing the gangsters off. And dissolve to...

2.   **THE TURTLES' LAIR**

Leonardo is concerned about their immediate problem: Why are those gangsters after the protein computer? And when will they strike again? Then the Turtles are alerted when Donatello's "Early Warning System" picks up telltale signs of "transporter" energy! They wonder if it could be Dregg, but figure that would be impossible. Dregg's down for the count. But who else could have a Vortex Transporter? There's only one way to find out. Donatello pinpoints the "beam down" location and the Turtles take off to find out who transported down and what they're up to. Wipe to:

---

1. In writing the outline, I decided it might be more interesting if, instead of a computer chip, I used something exotic such as a computer made of protein, like a brain.

2. By having the professor demonstrate the protein computer, I am setting up visually what it can do. This has a twofold purpose: first, to turn what would otherwise be dull dialogue into something visually interesting, and second, to set up the potential threat of what can be done with it should it fall into the wrong hands.

3. This is an example of using the character traits as defined by the series. Donatello is the brains of the bunch, so only he would be interested in such technology. It also gives a logical reason for the Turtles to be there.

3.   A SEEDY CRIMINAL HIDEOUT - NIGHT

The place is dark, and filled with the worst looking bunch of human criminal types imaginable. In the back of the joint, deep in the shadows at a table lit by an overhanging bulb, is a mysterious figure. The gangsters are in awe and fear of this being. Suddenly the gangsters who tried to steal the protein computer enter. They nervously approach the mysterious figure, explaining their failure. The mysterious figure becomes enraged. Then he steps out of the darkness into the light, revealing a large, slimy green amoeba in a pinstripe suit and fedora—an infamous alien mobster known across the galaxy as THE GLOBFATHER!

Unsympathetic to their excuses, the Globfather dramatically "slimes" the lead gangster. His green slime covers the gangster's body, eerily transforming him into a green, shapeless blob that oozes across the floor! The Globfather tells the others they had better not fail him again, or else they will suffer the same fate![4]

The Globfather explains that he's here on Earth to get the protein computer for someone who's willing to pay dearly for it[5]. Then the Globfather reveals a case full of hi-tech "alien" weaponry, handing it out to the gangsters, explaining that there's lots more where that came from, IF they get the protein computer[6].

After the Globfather and his gang get into several dark sedans[7] and take off into the night, the Turtle Van arrives. The Turtles check out the hideout, finding nothing...except for some "green sticky stuff." Leonardo wonders what it might be. Then Donatello uses a scanner to detect the infra-red trails of the cars that just drove off. And as they get in the van and speed away we wipe to...

4.   PROFESSOR HUXLEY'S UNIVERSITY LABORATORY - NIGHT

Professor Huxley is in his lab, working on his protein computer. His six-year-old son—RONNIE—is there, playing with his radio-controlled (RC) car. The Professor sees it's 6:30 PM and prepares to take his son home[8]. As he gets ready to leave we'll cut to...

5.   THE UNIVERSITY LAB GUARD STATION - CONTINUOUS

There is a chain-link fence around the lab, along with several military guards and a tank. Suddenly the Globfather's gang appears in a jeep, dressed as soldiers, along with a

---

4. By making the Globfather "ectoplasmically contageous" I am raising the threat level of the character and can use this device later in the story.

5. I chose not to mention who wanted the chip, thus creating a mystery.

6. The exchange of weapons for assistance sets up that the Globfather is powerful, and explains why the gangsters are motivated to help him.

7. I used dark sedans to maintain the familiar cliché of gangsters and big, dark cars.

8. The reason I put this scene here, before showing the Globfather arrive, is to establish the victims and thus set up the suspense of pending jeopardy

"General." They drive up to the gate and attempt to get in with a phony pass. When the guards are alerted to the ruse, more gangsters quietly come out of the shadows and subdue the guards like Marine commandos. As they all sneak up to the university lab we cut...

6.   **BACK INSIDE PROFESSOR HUXLEY'S LAB - CONTINUOUS**

As Professor Huxley is about to leave, the "soldiers" enter. They tell the Professor that due to the threat to national security, and to prevent the project from falling into the wrong hands, the "General" has ordered them to take the computer and the Professor to a safe place. But when Ronnie accidentally runs his RC car into the leg of the "General" and green stuff begins to ooze out, the jig is up. The Professor realizes these soldiers aren't on the level. But it's too late. The Globfather's gangsters blast away, taking out more guards[9], then tie up the other lab assistants. In the ruckus, Ronnie hides under a lab table.

Then the gangsters rip out the master computer, grab the Professor, and are about to leave when the Turtles arrive and dramatically battle them. During the fight, Professor Huxley surreptitiously places the small, "protein" central computer brain inside his son's RC car and stuffs it back into his son's pack.

Meanwhile, the Turtles battle the gangsters. But before they can stop them, the Globfather dramatically touches Raphael, who reacts with alarm as the green slime begins to ooze over him. The Globfather explains that once the green ooze covers Raphael he will turn into a glob just like the Globfather! And as Raphael is consumed by the green slime we fade out...

<u>END OF ACT ONE</u>

---

9. When I say "taking out" I mean to immobilize. Killing is not something that would get past *Broadcast Standards*.

<u>ACT TWO</u>

7. **UNIVERSITY LAB - CONTINUOUS**

We'll open with Raphael totally engulfed in the Globfather's green goo, about to dissolve into an amoeba himself. The Turtles try to help their buddy, but are afraid of being caught in the Globfather's sticky body.

During the commotion, the Globfather's gangsters hustle the Professor and his computer out of the lab. Seeing that his dad is in trouble, a frightened Ronnie grabs his backpack and runs away in fear.

Meanwhile, Leonardo dramatically uses his katana[10] blades to slice up the Globfather's slimy ooze, freeing Raphael in the nick of time. The Turtles figure they've handled the Globfather...until he suddenly reforms into one sticky mass (like the T-2000 from *Terminator 2*) and escapes by going down the drain. The Turtles blew it. The Globfather and his gangsters have gotten away with everything! And dissolve to...

8. **THE UNIVERSITY LAB - LATER THAT EVENING**

Donatello and the Turtles are investigating the lab for clues. Donatello examines the Globfather's green amoebic substance under a microscope to see if he can learn anything about who or what this guy is, but he's never seen anything like it before. Then Michaelangelo finds a TV security monitor and rewinds the tape. On it they see Professor Huxley place the protein computer brain in the RC car and into the backpack. Then they fast forward to see Ronnie grab the backpack and take off. He's got the goods! Which means he's in big trouble! They've got to find him before the Globfather and his gang do. Then cut to...

9. **INT. APRIL'S APARTMENT - NIGHT**

Raphael calls April and tells her what's up. He transmits a copy of the security tape via the Turtle Com, and asks her to get an "All Points Bulletin" out on the kid. April calls a friend of hers on the police force and gives him the picture and information re the kid and the stolen protein computer brain. Then wipe to:

10. **THE GLOBFATHER'S HIDEOUT - NIGHT**

The Globfather and his gang have the Professor tied to a chair. Several of the gangsters

10. A Japanese sword with a curved, single-edged blade two to three feet long.

get the master computer working and check it out. But something is wrong: The protein computer central brain is missing! The Globfather asks the Professor what he did with it, but he won't tell. So the Globfather places his hand on Professor Huxley's shoulder. The Professor watches as the slimy green ooze starts to cover his body, just like it did to Raphael. The Globfather assures the Professor that once he's been turned into an amoeba he'll tell all. The Professor watches in horror as the eerie green slime grows around him. And just when it's up to his neck he gives in, telling the Globfather that the protein computer is in his son's RC car, hidden in his backpack. The Globfather sucks his slimy green ooze off the Professor.

A moment later the Globfather and his gang catch a news broadcast on the missing Ronnie Huxley and see a picture of him (from the security tape). Now that they know what the kid looks like, the Globfather and his gangsters leave the Professor tied up and take off to get the boy.

11. **IN THE CITY - NIGHT**

We'll intercut the Turtles in their van, searching for the kid...and the Globfather and gangsters in their cars, also searching. Then intercut Ronnie as he sees both the Turtle Van and the villains' cars. Not knowing who's inside the van, he assumes that they're all bad guys and cleverly evades both the Turtles and the gangsters.

Finally, Ronnie is cornered by the gangsters. They grab him! But before they can take him away, the Turtles arrive and battle the Globfather and his hoods. The gangsters are losing badly until the Globfather shoots his "slime" causing Ronnie to slip down a roof, threatening to fall! The Turtles go for Ronnie, giving the Globfather and his gang a chance to snatch the protein computer out of the RC car and get away. After saving Ronnie, the Turtles hop into their van (with Ronnie) and take off. And dissolve to...

12. **THE GLOBFATHER'S HIDEOUT - NIGHT**

The Globfather and his gang are there with Professor Huxley. They have the protein computer, and it's time for the Globfather to contact the mysterious person he's working for. He turns on a strange looking inter-galactic monitor screen and makes a call. Then an alien face appears on screen—it's DREGG! He's pleased to see that the Globfather has gotten the protein computer, which is the key to his plan! With it he can hook his mind into the earth's computer networks and, using earth's own military defense systems, mentally take control of the entire planet. He won't have to lift a finger![11]

11. Notice that I waited until scene twelve to reveal Dregg's plan so that I could again raise the stakes of the story.

Dregg not only intends to return to earth and take it over, but more importantly, he intends to get rid of the Turtles for good![12] But his new Dreggnaut[13] is only half built. It will be days before it will be finished and he can reach earth. Fortunately, he's building a new Vortex Transporter aboard the ship. So he decides to put all of his micro-bots[14] to work on the transporter.

In the meantime, Dregg orders the Globfather and his gang to take control of the NATIONAL PHONE SWITCHING SYSTEM, a top-security installation which controls all public and governmental phone lines. They are to bring the Professor with them and hook up the protein computer to the main switching computer. He'll meet them there as soon as his Vortex Transporter is finished[15]. And as the Globfather and his gang head out...

13. IN THE TURTLE VAN - NIGHT

The Turtles are with Ronnie, who's quite a precocious kid! Without bothering to ask, he's already begun to fiddle with the van radar, looking for the Globfather. Donatello tells him "not to play with things he doesn't understand." Ronnie feels hurt, protesting that he does understand. But Donatello pays no attention to the kid and begins to fiddle with the radar himself, trying to track down the Globfather. Donatello intends to set the radar to detect the Globfather's amoebic structure. But it turns out the radar has already been programmed to do it. Donatello glances curiously at Ronnie, then figures it must have been an accident. Ronnie tries to say that he programmed the radar, but Donatello says "that's nice," just like a condescending adult. And as he starts to scan for the Globfather we wipe to...

14. NATIONAL PHONE SWITCHING SYSTEM - NIGHT

The place looks like an impregnable fortress with high concrete walls, guard towers, etc. The Globfather's gangsters cleverly cut the alarm system, then, in a perfectly choreographed break-in, cut the lights, take out the guards, blow out the huge steel door, and subdue the staff.

The Globfather and his gangsters enter the main switching area, where they find the most incredible computer ever seen. And it's theirs for the taking! Then the Globfather commands Professor Huxley to attach the protein computer to the master phone switching computer. We'll see inside the computer as the protein literally "infects" the circuit boards, growing new connections and taking over control of the computer like an ever-expanding brain!

---

12. This is his stated goal as part of the series format.
13. Dregg's huge spacecraft.
14. Also an established part of the series, micro-bots are microscopic robots that can build anything.

15. The reason I chose to construct the scene this way is so that I could make a more dramatic entrance for Dregg a little later.

Next the Globfather plugs his own brain into the protein and links his mind with the computer. He can now *telekinetically* control any computer equipment that is connected to the phone lines, anywhere in the world! He demonstrates, using only his thoughts to cause computers, vehicles, and machinery in various parts of the city to threaten people. And as he gets everything ready for Dregg's arrival we cut to...

15. INT. APRIL'S APARTMENT - NIGHT

April is working at her computer when it suddenly goes haywire. She gets it running again, then uses her Internet connection to track down the problem. To her amazement, she discovers that someone has just tapped into all of the world's phone lines! When the Globfather discovers that April is snooping on him, he cuts off her computer. April grabs her phone to call the authorities, but the Globfather is on the line. He laughs, insisting she can't get away, then shuts off her phones. So April rushes out, only to find the Globfather is in control of the elevator and won't open the door! Then he locks the fire exits, trapping her inside her apartment building. And as she grabs her Turtle Com, we cut...

16. BACK IN THE TURTLE VAN - NIGHT

...where April calls and tells the guys that some maniac has gotten control of the National Phone Switching System. When Donatello tries to link up with the phone company computer, Ronnie suggests that it might not be a good idea. Donatello tells him to be quiet. But when he hooks into the National Phone Switching System, the Globfather immediately senses Donatello's presence and gets control of the Turtle Van's computers. First he locks the doors! Then he gets control of the van's computer carburetion system and causes the gas to stream out and start the engine on fire. Then he causes the engine to race and takes control of the steering mechanism. And as the burning van heads for a cliff we fade out...

END OF ACT TWO

ACT THREE

17. IN THE TURTLE VAN - CONTINUOUS

The Turtles barely survive as they cleverly put out the fire and regain control of the van just in time. Donatello cuts all of the van computers off so that the Globfather can't control anything. It's obvious the Turtles can't just use the old "frontal assault" method on this guy. Then Ronnie tries to help with another idea, suggesting that if they can "tap into the main phone sys..." but Donatello cuts him off, coming up with a plan of his own. And as they head back to the lair we'll cut to...

18. NATIONAL PHONE SWITCHING SYSTEM - NIGHT

...where Dregg arrives in a dramatic transporter flash! Taking over from the Globfather, Dregg proceeds with his ultimate plan. With the help of the protein computer he uses his mind to infiltrate military computers, gains control of a satellite targeting system, and aims a dozen particle-beam satellites at as many cities. Then he gets control of the world's TV broadcast satellites and beams a message around the globe, demanding the governments of the world give him control of the planet or he'll begin firing the particle beams! And as the government leaders make plans to surrender we wipe to...

19. THE TURTLES' LAIR

...where Donatello is in his workshop, constructing a helmet which will allow him to tap into the main phone company computer, hopefully giving him mental access and allowing him to cut off the Globfather's control. Donatello tries the helmet on, but he can't quite control his thoughts, seriously fouling up. When the other Turtles try with similar comedic results, Splinter[16] lectures them on calming their minds and guiding their thoughts. But they still can't get it right.

Ronnie examines the helmet and thinks he knows how to get it working, suggesting that "perhaps the electro-brain-wave link can be stabilized if..." at which point Donatello grabs the helmet and says "Of course! If I can stabilize the electro-brain-wave link I should be able to focus my thoughts better. Glad I thought of it!" Donatello adjusts the helmet and gets it working.

---

16. For those of you who are not Turtles aficionados, Splinter is the large talking rat who is the Turtles' *sensei* (teacher and mentor). This scene with Splinter was cut from the final script.

Figuring that the Turtles don't need his help, a discouraged Ronnie leaves without the others noticing. When the Turtles are ready to go, they notice he's gone. But there's no time to look for the kid. So they grab the helmet and take off for the phone company. And wipe to...

20. NATIONAL PHONE SWITCHING SYSTEM - NIGHT[17]

...where the nations of the world (as seen on a large video monitor) are about to formally surrender control to Dregg. But before they can, the Turtles burst on the scene. As Leonardo, Michaelangelo, and Raphael battle the Globfather's gangsters, Donatello dons his helmet and heads for the master computer. He's got to plug it in before he can gain control! But the gangsters form a barrier, like a defensive football lineup—and a heavily armed lineup at that!

Before the Turtles can reach him, Dregg uses his telepathic mind control to activate the particle beams! And as a dozen of them begin to charge up, the battle continues. Donatello has only sixty seconds to get to the computer and stop Dregg before the particle beams will fire. But the gangsters have got him pinned down! Then Ronnie appears and cleverly uses his RC car to confuse the gangsters, giving Donatello the break he needs to get through to the computer. He plugs in his helmet and has a dramatic battle of the minds with Dregg!

Donatello telepathically commands the particle beams to shut down. Then Dregg concentrates, causing several computerized objects in the room—including a drink machine and photocopier—to attack the Turtles, causing Donatello to lose concentration and allowing Dregg to get the particle beams charging up again!

Donatello finally wires up the other Turtles to his helmet and, together, the four of them override Dregg, forcing the particle beam satellites to self-destruct before Dregg can fire them.

---

17. As you approach the end of a story you may notice that the scenes begin to get shorter, with less time and space between them, and the action becomes more continuous. This is what happens as the A- and B-stories converge and all of the story elements begin to come together. At this point we leave our relatively sparse beat outline and find ourselves in the uncharted territory of the story's ending. It's easy to write in a beat that the Turtles defeat the villain, but it's quite another thing to wrap up all of the story dynamics that are currently in progress and successfully bring the story to completion. There are, after all, various characters with various motives in various states of "incompletion." How do we tie all of these things together in an ending which resolves everything that has been established in the story? Just as with complex scenes, I find it very handy to jot down all of the dynamics that are currently in play. It makes it much easier to see, organize, and thus write the scene. All of these dynamics must be dealt with in the ending. You don't have to work out every detail in the beat outline, but it should be included in the regular outline. As you read outline beat twenty you'll see how I interwove and concluded all of these dynamics.

18. As an established writer I'm allowed to indicate that I'll write the gag later. I would not recommend a new writer do this.

Then the Turtles cleverly get control of a computerized vacuum cleaner and suck the Globfather into it. Finally, Leonardo links to the Dreggnaut's computer and telepathically activates the transporter. And an instant later Dregg and the Globfather are gone!

Professor Huxley gets a warm hug from his son. They're safe! And after a final gag[18] from the Turtles we fade out...

<u>THE END</u>

Now that you've read the outline, I suggest you reread the premise, beats, and outline again to see how they developed and expanded.

As a practical drill, you may want to take my beats and see if you can write an outline that follows these beats in a different way. You may even prefer to start from scratch and come up with your own premise, which you can then develop into beats and an outline.

Don't forget that the only way to become a good writer is to write.

Just as it is easier to write an outline if you have developed your beats well, it is much easier to write your script if your outline is well constructed and complete. Again, it's just like building a house. It goes much easier if you have good plans and a good foundation. If you don't, you'll be fixing problems all the way through.

So we've finished our outline and are ready for the next step. The thing we've been waiting to write from the very start—two bits worth of three-hole-punched paper covered with a few thousand words of dialogue and description that can turn a person who waits on tables into a player who gets waited on—*THE SCRIPT!*

Chapter 7
How to Write a Script

THE BEST WAY TO LEARN how to write animation scripts is a method I call The Three R's...

Read 'em! Review 'em! 'Rite 'em!

The first thing you need to do is read as many scripts as you can get your hands on. With a little e-searching, many animation scripts can be found on the Internet. For samples of some scripts I have written, check out my website, which is listed at the back of this book. Try to find the best scripts you can, ideally ones from successful series, and especially ones from the types of shows you want to write.

After you read an animation script, review it. Go over it with an analytical eye. Note what you like about it and what you don't. Try to understand what the writer was doing and why. Go through it and highlight the things you understood, agreed with, or liked best. I don't mean story ideas or funny lines of dialogue, but technical items, like how a scene was constructed, or that it was simple and short yet still conveyed the necessary information or humor. Pay special attention to the dialogue, description, structure, and story beats. You really have to tear into the scripts and tear them apart.

After you begin to understand more about scripts, then you can 'rite one. When you've finished it, try to read it as a viewer, rather than as an author. Compare it to the others you have read. Look for the good as well as the bad. You might even want to have someone else read and comment on your script. But if you do, make sure you trust them and respect their creative viewpoint. Then do the process all over again. This is how you will really learn to write.

There are far too many nuances of script writing to describe them all in this book. So I'll stick with the most important points of structure, action, and dialogue as they relate to animation.

There are two basic ways to write cartoon scripts (or any script, for that matter). One is the *master scene method*, the other is the *shot-by-shot method*. In the master scene method you simply use a slug line to set up the scene and the rest of the action is handled with description, without the mention of camera angles. In the shot-by-shot method, each shot is called out as you envision it. Different studios and producers prefer different methods.

In live-action movies and TV, the director shoots master scenes (a *full shot* of the entire scene), then *medium shots, close ups*, etc. Later, in the editing room, the editor, along with the director, splices these together.

In animation it's not done this way. Instead, a storyboard is drawn, indicating each of the camera angles and cuts (i.e., the sequence of visual shots, such as from wide to full to close, back to full, etc.) The animation is then drawn from this blueprint. So in animation, either the cutting is done by the writer via the shot-by-shot method, or if the script is written in master scenes then the storyboard man does the cutting as he interprets the script and draws the board. This gives the writer an important choice. Does he act as the director and call out all the shots, or does he just tell the story, and leave the angles and cutting to the storyboard man and director? If you feel you don't yet have a good sense of visual cutting, then perhaps you should write in the master scene method. If, on the other hand, you're good with visual cutting and pacing, try the shot-by-shot method.

Personally, I use a combination of the two methods. I use master scenes whenever I can, and only call out shots and angles when it will help convey the image I'm trying to create, or improve the dramatics and pacing. Years ago I used to call out every shot so that a storyboard man could practically draw a panel for every cut I called out and be done with it. This was a fine way to learn cutting, but it makes the script much too choppy for a good read. Remember, your script isn't just for the board man. It's for the story editor or producer to read and enjoy so he'll *hire you!*

The only other thing you need to know before you start to write is how to format a script. All scripts, animated, live, TV and film, are written on regular $8^{1}/_{2}$" x 11", three-hole punched paper. Always use Courier 12-point font. Margins vary, but a safe choice would be a top margin of one inch, bottom margin of $^{3}/_{4}$-inch, left margin of $1^{1}/_{2}$-inch and right margin of $^{3}/_{4}$-inch. The left margin is wider to allow room for the holes and brass fasteners, though many animation studios staple their scripts. Always number your pages at the upper right corner. To see how to format slug lines, description, character names, dialogue and transitions, just take a look at the Turtles script later in this chapter.

How To Begin Your Script

I have found a very simple method to begin writing a script. **I cut and paste my entire outline right into the script.** In order to take up the least amount of space, I reformat the outline to single-spaced, 10 pt. condensed type. This way the next scene to write is always right there at the end of what I've already written. After I write a scene I just delete that scene from the outline and the next scene is right there. This is also helpful because now and then you'll find you can use the exact words in your outline and you don't even have to type them again. You just move them to exactly where they should be and continue writing.

Most writers have a tendency to write long. There is an art to writing short, tight scenes, and it takes some time to learn. **One of the best ways to make sure you don't waste time (and money if you're being paid) by writing too long is to estimate the page**

count of your scenes <u>before</u> you begin your script. You do this by reading your outline, and doing the best you can to judge how many script pages each scene will be. I use increments of one half page. If I think a scene is going to take a quarter of a page to write, I'll count it as a half, which gives me a little leeway. And if I think a scene is just going to be a small fraction of a page I'll count it as zero (don't go trying to estimate pages in small fractions or you'll drive yourself crazy). Next, I make a notation after each outline slug line of the number of pages for that scene, along with the cumulative number of all the scenes up to that point. For example, if my first scene is three pages, I'll type "[3/3]" for that scene, meaning this scene should be three pages and there are three pages in the script so far. If I estimate the second scene to be $1^1/_2$-pages, I'll make a notation that looks like this: $[1^1/_2/4^1/_2]$. This means the current scene is $1^1/_2$-pages and total pages so far are $4^1/_2$. I'll keep doing this until I've finished estimating the entire script.

It's hard to guess how many pages a scene will take if you've never written a script before. So you might want to read a few scripts just prior to your estimation process in order to have some scene lengths fresh in your mind.

I've known writers who, because they failed to estimate their script, wound up writing 50 percent more pages than needed. Not only did they have to throw away dozens of pages of their work, they spent twice as long trying to figure out what to keep and what to cut.

If you don't know how long the producer or editor wants his series scripts to be, just figure thirty-five pages for a half-hour script, half that for eleven minutes.

If, after estimating your script length, the number of pages comes out too high, just go back and review the scenes, tightening up the longer ones until you come out to the right number of pages. If the total is too low, go back and increase the length of some of the scenes.

Your estimation skills will improve markedly over time. I've now written enough scripts to be able to often estimate to the exact page.

Once you begin writing your script, check your cumulative page estimate after writing each scene. Don't worry about one page, plus or minus. This will usually even out. But if you're obviously running long, and don't feel the material is overwritten, you can adjust by writing the next scene(s) shorter to compensate. Continue this process, keeping your eye on the target and your actual page count, until you've finished.

Editing Your Script

Almost no one writes a perfect script from page one. Many writers write a scene, then go back and rewrite it. They write another, then rewrite that. It's sort of a one-step-forward-one-step-back process. And it's the *wrong* way to write!

One of the best lessons I have learned about writing good scripts is this: **When you write, write. When you edit, edit. Never do both at the same time.**

Writing is the process of creating concepts and putting them down on paper or computer screen. Editing is the process of reading what's written, finding what's wrong with it, and rewriting to better communicate the concepts. Writing is a creative outflow, editing is a critical inflow (i.e. reading), and thus is somewhat of a "stop." At the very least it is stopping the bad writing. Thus, by wearing the writing and editing hats at the same time you will be starting and stopping and starting and stopping, never really getting going. When you get a good creative flow going you don't want to stop it, and the surest way to stop it is by editing yourself.

So wear your writing hat only and you'll get through the draft quickly. Then put on your editing hat and rework it from a critical point of view. Be as hard on your writing as you like, but don't ever invalidate yourself as a writer. Just realize that you'll get better as you write more.

There's a Catch-22 about learning to edit. In order to edit you have to know what makes a good script, but, being a new writer without much experience, you might not know what makes a good script. You'll have to pretty much fly by the seat of your pants. Fortunately, over the years I developed a very simple method of editing. Anyone can do it. It doesn't guarantee a great script, but I can assure you, your script will get better and better as you do it. Here's how it works...

After completing your first draft, simply read through it, making whatever improvements you feel you can along the way. Don't spend a lot of time on one scene. Just rewrite as best you can and move on. Do this with all the scenes until you have finished editing the script. Then do it again—and again. You'll find that the changes get smaller and smaller, and the script gets tighter and tighter. Just keep doing this until you have no more changes to make, or they are getting so nit-picky that it's obvious they aren't improving anything. Then you're done.

The more you write, the better writer you will become, the more you'll understand the proper elements of a good script, and the better able you'll be to edit your material. Of course, once you really understand the mechanics of writing you won't need much editing because you'll be able to get it right the first time. But this takes lots of practice.

If you're a new writer, I suggest you read this book before you write your script. Then, after you've finished the first draft, read the book again, this time from the point of view of learning what to edit. This will give you a fresh perspective from which to edit your script.

There is a lot more to be said about animated script writing, but let's take a break from the theory and see what a script actually looks like. The next thing you're going to do is step one of the Three-R method: **Read!**

On the following pages you will find the actual final-draft script for the "Mobster from Dimension X" episode of *Teenage Mutant Ninja Turtles*. I wrote this script in a modified shot-by-shot method.

"Mobster From Dimension X"

#9062-9606

Written

by

Jeffrey Scott

FINIAL DRAFT
April 8, 1996

FRED WOLF FILMS

CAST LIST[1]

GOOD GUYS:

1. LEONARDO

2. DONATELLO

3. RAPHAEL

4. MICHAELANGELO

5. SPLINTER

6. APRIL

BAD GUYS:

7. DREGG

8. MUNG

9. THE GLOBFATHER

10. FIRST GANGSTER

11. SECOND GANGSTER

12. THIRD GANGSTER

SUPPORTING CAST (in order of appearance):

13. PROFESSOR HUXLEY (African-American)

14. RONNIE HUXLEY (African-American, 6 years old)

15. MARINE GUARD (2 lines)

16. NEWS ANCHOR (2 lines)

17. SECURITY GUARD (2 lines)

18. MAN AT CONSOLE (1 line)

19. MILITARY LEADER (1 line)

---

1. Not all series require cast lists, and there is no real reason to do one on a sample script. The purpose of a cast list is to let the produceer know which actors will be working on a specific show, and how much his talent budget will be. Make sure your sample script doesn't have too many characters. There won't be time to develop them and it will show that you don't understand the business side of animation.

"MOBSTER FROM DIMENSION X"

<u>ACT ONE</u>

FADE IN:

EXT. UNIVERSITY - NIGHT

The campus is alive with faculty and students. PUSH IN on a
lecture hall and cut...

INT. LECTURE HALL - NIGHT

DR. ALVIN HUXLEY[2], a somewhat nebbish looking African-American
professor[3], is before a packed audience of academia. He is on the
dais, surrounded by a large computer. A small black sheet covers
something on the computer console. (Note: The computer console is
on a table with legs.)

> PROFESSOR HUXLEY
> Ladies and gentlemen, after ten years of
> research I am pleased to announce a
> breakthrough in computer bio-electronics.

Professor Huxley pulls away the black sheet, revealing a steel-
and-glass tank full of bubbling liquid at the focal point of the
computer. Suspended in the tank is a strange looking blob (about
the size of a pack of cigarettes), connected by wires to the computer. This is the PROTEIN COMPUTER!

> PROFESSOR HUXLEY
> The "protein" computer!

> AUDIENCE
> (various walla)

CAMERA PANS UP to the open skylight on the ceiling, high above.
PUSH IN on DONATELLO, looking down.

EXT. ROOF OF LECTURE HALL - CONTINUOUS

Donatello is staring down through the skylight. LEONARDO,
MICHAELANGELO, and RAPHAEL are with him. But they're not watching
the lecture, they're bored stiff.

---

2. In many scripts, the first appearance of a character is
capitalized.

3. Notice how sparse the description of Huxley is. Long
character descriptions are not necessary. The true character
will be exposed in dialogue and description.

> LEONARDO
> You don't really expect us to listen to
> this whole lecture, do you, Donatello?

> DONATELLO
> Shh! I'll miss what he's saying. Wow!
> Craneo-electronic reflex capacitors! This
> is fascinating!

> RAPHAEL
> No, this is **BORING!**

> MICHAELANGELO
> Yeah, I'd rather watch paint dry, dude.

BACK INSIDE THE LECTURE HALL - FAVORING PROFESSOR HUXLEY

> PROFESSOR HUXLEY
> And best of all it can be "linked" to
> the human mind.

Professor Huxley places a strange looking helmet on his head.

> PROFESSOR HUXLEY
> By simply thinking a thought, I can con-
> trol *anything* connected to the protein
> computer.

The lights go off and on.

> PROFESSOR HUXLEY
> Such as the lights!...

CLOSE ANGLE ON AIR VENT

as the air shuts off, then comes back on (as evidenced by the
little "telltale" attached to the vent grate).

> PROFESSOR HUXLEY
> ...the air conditioning...

WIDER ON LECTURE HALL

> PROFESSOR HUXLEY
> ...the electric doors![4]

As the doors open on either side of the hall four GANGSTERS
(two from each door) in three-piece suits and fedoras burst in,
carrying futuristic blasters.

---

4. Although in the outline the Professor controlled the
entire city, here I changed it to the simple devices in the
room. This was done so that I had something to build to
when Dregg later gets the protein computer. It also prevents
the later use of the device becoming redundant.

3

                              FIRST GANGSTER
                   Nobody move!

FAVORING A SECURITY GUARD

He reaches for an alarm button, but the gangsters fire their
blasters, frying the button, knocking the guard back.

BACK ON THE ROOF

                              DONATELLO
                   Uh-oh! We've got trouble!

                              RAPHAEL
                   What's the matter, pop quiz?
                              DONATELLO
                   No! Someone's trying to steal the pro-
                   tein computer!

BACK INSIDE THE LECTURE HALL

As the gangsters head for the dais, the Turtles drop through the
skylight, landing before Professor Huxley. The gangsters start
firing. The Turtles grab Huxley, dive away.

FAVORING DONATELLO

as another gangster pops up, blaster in hand. In one smooth move
Donatello spins his bo[5], knocking the blaster away.

MICHAELANGELO

rolls as another gangster fires, misses. FOLLOW Michaelangelo as
he knocks over a flag pole at the side of the dais. The gangster
has him covered. Then Michaelangelo stands, holding the university
flag like a bullfighter's cape.

                              MICHAELANGELO
                   Toro! Toro!

The gangster fires at Michaelangelo, who whips the flag away,
revealing a mirror on the wall behind it. The laser reflects off
the mirror, hits the floor before the gangster, knocks him back.

                              MICHAELANGELO
                   No bull!

FAVORING RAPHAEL

Several "academic types" duck in their seats as another gangster
fires his blaster at Raphael, barely missing.

5. Wooden staff, several feet long, used in martial arts.

                    RAPHAEL
          How 'bout a soda...jerk?

Raphael tosses one of his sais[6] at a soda machine. It slams right
into the coin slot. Several cans of soda fire out, spinning
across the floor, tripping the gangster.

THE FIRST GANGSTER

moves across the dais, pushes past Professor Huxley and reaches
for the protein computer tank. Leonardo suddenly whips his katana
blades and slices off the two legs at his end of the console
table. The table drops down on one side and the protein computer
tank slides away from the gangster.

FAVORING PROFESSOR HUXLEY

                 PROFESSOR HUXLEY
          The protein computer!!

He catches the tank before it slides off the table.

WIDER ON LECTURE HALL

The four gangsters retreat, running out of the hall with the
Turtles facing them, ninja gear in hand. Several university
guards appear at the other door, react to the Turtles.[7]

                  MICHAELANGELO
          Time to cut class, dudes.

And as the Turtles race out another door we...

                                              DISSOLVE TO:
EXT. TURTLES' LAIR ENTRANCE - NIGHT

PUSH IN on the sewer grate entrance as...

                    RAPHAEL (V.O.)
          Call me computer illiterate, but why
          would a bunch of mobsters want to steal
          a protein computer?

INT. TURTLES' LAIR - DONATELLO'S WORKSHOP - CONTINUOUS

                    LEONARDO
          I don't know. But ten-to-one they'll try
          again.

Suddenly Donatello's "Early Warning System" goes off!

---

6. A small trident, about 15 inches long, used defensively
against weapons like swords.

7. In the series, the Turtles are considered menaces by the
authorities.

>   DONATELLO
>   It's the Early Warning System!

Donatello moves to the computer, checks it out.

>   DONATELLO
>   The scanner is picking up traces of
>   transporter energy! That could only mean
>   one thing.

>   RAPHAEL
>   Captain Kirk just beamed down?

>   LEONARDO
>   No. Dregg is back!

>   MICHAELANGELO
>   But we trashed his Dreggnaut and
>   transported him to Dimension X!

FAVORING DONATELLO AT COMPUTER

>   DONATELLO
>   We'll know for sure once I've pinpointed
>   the beam-down location.

Donatello enters data into his keyboard, then the monitor screen
indicates a location in the city.

>   DONATELLO
>   Bingo! Let's go!

And as the Turtles rush o.s...

>   WIPE TO:

EXT. SEEDY END OF TOWN - NIGHT

Run-down old storefronts and warehouses. PUSH IN on the gangsters
hideout.

INT. HIDEOUT - CONTINUOUS

An ominous, shadowy figure is seated at a table, lit by a single
overhanging bulb. The First Gangster and his three accomplices
(the guys who tried to steal the protein computer) stand before
the table, facing the shadowy figure. Several more "hoods," holding
blasters, flank the four gangsters.

                          FIRST GANGSTER
                    (nervous)
               I had my hands on it, Boss, honest. If
               it wasn't for those freakin' reptiles...

                          GLOBFATHER
                    (deep, resonating)
               ENOUGH!

PUSH IN on the shadowy figure.

                          GLOBFATHER
               I want the protein computer, not excuses.

Suddenly the GLOBFATHER leans out of the shadow, revealing his
slimy green amoeba body stuffed into a three-piece pinstripe suit
and fedora. His face is an oozing mass of transparent green
slime, as are his hands.

                          GLOBFATHER
               No one fails the Globfather <u>twice</u>!

WIDER ANGLE

                          FIRST GANGSTER
               But...

The Globfather reaches out and touches the First Gangster's
shoulder, leaving a piece of slime. PUSH IN on the First Gangster
as the green slime begins to grow over him!

                          FIRST GANGSTER
                    NO!

FAVORING OTHER GANGSTERS

They watch in horror as the First Gangster is covered with living
slime, then turns into a blob of amorphous amoeba which oozes
across the floor.

                          OTHER GANGSTERS
                    (frightened gasps)

                          GLOBFATHER
               Anyone else who fails me will suffer the
               same fate.

The gangsters back away from the angry Globfather.

CLOSER ON GLOBFATHER

                    GLOBFATHER
          I was sent to this planet to get the
          protein computer by someone who's willing
          to pay dearly for it.

The Globfather opens up a large metal case filled with a dozen
alien-looking blasters. PUSH IN on the weapons.

                    GLOBFATHER
          Help me acquire it and I'll see that you
          get enough alien firepower to take over
          the entire city.

FULL ON GANGSTERS AND GLOBFATHER

The Globfather tosses the blasters to the gangsters.

                  SECOND GANGSTER
          You're the boss, Globfather.

                    GLOBFATHER
          Yes, I am! Now you're going to pay
          another visit to the Professor.

CLOSE ON GLOBFATHER

                    GLOBFATHER
          And this time I'm going with you to make
          sure there are no foul-ups!

WIDER ANGLE

The Globfather moves toward the door followed by his men.

                                        CUT TO:

EXT. GLOBFATHER'S HIDEOUT - NIGHT

The Turtle Van pulls up out front.

INSIDE THE TURTLE VAN

Donatello checks his instruments, looks out the window.

                    DONATELLO
          The beam-down point is inside that
          building.

Leonardo takes out his katana blades.

                        LEONARDO
              All right, guys, stay alert!

ANGLE ON HIDEOUT ENTRANCE

The Turtles enter, ninja gear at the ready. Like a SWAT team they
move to the front door, backs to the wall, two Turtles on either
side of the door. The others nod, indicating they're ready, then
Leonardo slices off the doorknob, Michaelangelo kicks in the door
and...

INT. HIDEOUT - CONTINUOUS

They burst in, take a dramatic ninja stance, hardware cocked and
ready.

                        TURTLES
              HIIIYYAAAHHH!!

As they look around, WIDEN to reveal the place is empty.

                        MICHAELANGELO
              There's no one here, dudes.

The Turtles relax.

                        RAPHAEL
              Yeah, but you've got to admit, that was
              one of the best entrances we've ever
              done.

                        LEONARDO
              You sure this is the right place,
              Donatello?

Donatello checks his hand scanner, points at the floor.

                        DONATELLO
              This is it, all right. Whoever beamed
              down landed right here.

FAVORING LEONARDO

He leans down, examines a slimy green streak on the floor.

                        LEONARDO
              What's this?

                        DONATELLO
              It looks like some kind of protoplasmic
              substance.

                    RAPHAEL
          It looks like somebody's in bad need of
          a hankie.

The Turtles react to an o.s. SOUND. They resume their ninja
postures. Leonardo silently gestures them to follow him. They
move toward the back of the place. A chair falls over in the
shadows, then another CRASH and a bottle rolls out of the shadow.
The Turtles dramatically kick a table away, get ready to pounce.

                    TURTLES
          Hiiyyyaaahhh!!

But they are shocked as...

THE FIRST GANGSTER/AMOEBA

slithers out before them.

                    MICHAELANGELO
          Eyew, gross!

                    RAPHAEL
               (holds his nose)
          I think the bus boy forgot to clear this
          table.

CLOSE ON FIRST GANGSTER/AMOEBA

A hideous face appears in the green slime.

                    FIRST GANGSTER/AMOEBA
               (bubbly sound)
          The...Globfather...

WIDER TO INCLUDE TURTLES

                    MICHAELANGELO
          Whoa! It's alive!

                    LEONARDO
          Did he say "Globfather"?

                    MICHAELANGELO
          Yeah. What does it mean?

                    RAPHAEL
               (still holding nose)
          Maybe he misses his daddy.

                              DONATELLO
                        (to gangster/amoeba)
                Is this Globfather guy a space alien?

FAVORING FIRST GANGSTER/AMOEBA

                        FIRST GANGSTER/AMOEBA
                        (faint, bubbly)
                Yes. Huxley's lab...computer...

The first gangster's face fades away into the slime.

WIDER ON TURTLES

                              LEONARDO
                I knew they'd go after the protein
                computer again. C'mon!

As they rush for the exit...

                                                      WIPE TO:
EXT. UNIVERSITY COMPUTER SCIENCES LAB - NIGHT

The building is surrounded by a chain-link fence with a guard
gate. Two armed National Guardsmen stand guard. A third is in the
back of a Humvee with a mounted laser weapon.

INT. COMPUTER SCIENCE LAB - CLOSE ON RC CAR - CONTINUOUS

From a close angle this radio controlled (RC) car looks real as
it races over the floor. Then it bangs into a shoe and stops.

WIDER ANGLE

to reveal the car has run into Professor Huxley's foot. Huxley is
working on his protein computer. Several other technicians in
white lab coats are in the lab. There is a national guardsman at
the door. Huxley looks down at the RC car.

                        PROFESSOR HUXLEY
                        (surprised)
                Ronnie?

The Professor's eleven-year-old African-American son, RONNIE,
comes out from under a lab table, holding an RC controller.

                              RONNIE
                Sorry, dad.

                        PROFESSOR HUXLEY
                What are you doing here? I thought you
                were with your mother.

>   RONNIE
>   She's working late at the med center.
>   Said I could stay with you.

>   PROFESSOR HUXLEY
>   It's too dangerous here. I'd better take
>   you home.

EXT. COMPUTER SCIENCES LAB - ON GUARD GATE - CONTINUOUS

A drab green sedan drives up, stops before the Guardsman.

INSIDE THE SEDAN

The Second Gangster is behind the wheel, the Globfather next
to him. Both wear Army uniforms. The Globfather has a General's
uniform and hat, his face in shadow.

The Second Gangster rolls down his window, revealing the National
Guardsman.

>   SECOND GANGSTER
>   This is General Patterson. We're here to
>   check out lab security.

>   NATIONAL GUARDSMAN
>   I'm sorry, sir, this is a restricted
>   area. I can't let you enter without a
>   pass.

FULL ON GUARDS AND SEDAN

Suddenly the back doors of the sedan swing open and two gangsters
step out with blasters.

>   THIRD GANGSTER
>   Here's our pass!

They fire, blasting the guardhouse. The guards dive away.

THE NATIONAL GUARDSMAN ON THE HUMVEE

opens fire with his laser, but the gangsters use their alien
blasters to return the fire. They hit the Humvee. The Guardsman
dives off as the Humvee explodes.

INT. COMPUTER SCIENCE LAB - CONTINUOUS

As they head for the door, Professor Huxley, his son, and the
others react to the O.S. EXPLOSION.

>   PROFESSOR HUXLEY
>   What was that?

The door opens and the Second Gangster and Globfather (still in uniforms) enter. The Globfather stops in a shadow.

> SECOND GANGSTER
> They're attacking the lab. We've got to get you and your equipment out of here, Professor.

> PROFESSOR HUXLEY
> Yes, of course!

As the Professor reaches for the protein computer tank...

RONNIE

fiddles with his RC controller and his RC car speeds across the lab floor, heading toward him. But it overshoots, hitting...

THE GENERAL'S FOOT

It flips over, tearing his pant cuff. Green slime oozes out!

WIDER ON LAB

> RONNIE
> Dad, look!

Huxley sees the green slime oozing out.

> PROFESSOR HUXLEY
> What's going on?

The Globfather/General steps out of the shadow.

> GLOBFATHER
> We're taking your protein computer!

Suddenly the doors burst open and four more gangsters appear with blasters, open fire, forcing back the Guardsman. The technicians put their hands up.

FAVORING PROFESSOR HUXLEY AND THE PROTEIN COMPUTER

The Second Gangster (in Army uniform) grabs Huxley as the other gangsters (not in uniforms) grab the protein computer. But before they can unhook it...

THE TURTLES

Drop down through the skylight again.

> TURTLES
> TURTLE POWER!!

They land before the startled gangsters. As the gangsters open fire, Leonardo swiftly cuts his katana blades through the air, deflecting the incoming laser blasts.

FAVOR RONNIE

He ducks a stray shot, then crawls under a lab table, hiding. And as the battle rages...

MICHAELANGELO

tosses his grappler[8] o.s. at...

ANOTHER GANGSTER

snagging his blaster muzzle. And cut...

BACK TO MICHAELANGELO

as he pulls on the grappler cable, yanking...

THE GANGSTER'S BLASTER

upwards. Its searing beam strikes a fluorescent light. BOOM! Then the gangster dives away as the light crashes to the floor.

ANGLE ON PROTEIN COMPUTER

Professor Huxley watches nervously as Donatello struggles with another gangster, using his bo to keep the gangster away from the computer. The gangster fires his blaster, hits near the protein computer tank, spilling some of the liquid out.

                         PROFESSOR HUXLEY
               No! You'll hit the protein computer brain!

As Donatello and the gangster continue to struggle, cut...

CLOSER ON PROTEIN COMPUTER TANK

As the firefight continues o.s., Huxley carefully takes the small protein brain out of the tank. He kneels down and removes the body from Ronnie's RC car, places the protein brain inside and replaces the body. Then he puts the car inside Ronnie's backpack.

ANGLE ON SECOND GANGSTER

firing his blaster. Raphael drops into shot before him, knocks his blaster away with his sais, then sticks his sai blades under the gangster's military shoulder patches and chest ribbons, rips them off with swift, sharp moves.

8. A turtle device consisting of a turtle shell with retractable cable.

                         RAPHAEL
              There's only one thing worse than imper-
              sonating an officer...

Raphael flips the gangster, slamming him into a 3' diameter
satellite dish attached to a computer. It breaks off, lands on
the gangster's back like a turtle shell.

                         RAPHAEL
              ...and that's impersonating a <u>turtle</u>!

ANOTHER ANGLE

Raphael turns, facing the Globfather/General.

                         GLOBFATHER
              You'll regret getting in my way, rep-
              tile!

The Globfather flexes his upper body, bursting out of his uniform,
revealing his entire body is just green protoplasm. Then the
Globfather grabs Raphael, who struggles with him.

                         RAPHAEL
              Get offa me you slime-bucket!

But every time Raphael tries to get away he just gets more
covered with the Globfather's slimy body, until the Globfather is
all over him.

WIDER ANGLE

The other Turtles watch as the Globfather covers more of Raphael
with his green, slimy body.

                         GLOBFATHER
              Once I cover you with protoplasm, you'll
              turn into an amoeba...just like me!

PUSH IN on Raphael as the green slime rises up around his neck,
approaching his head.

                                                    FADE OUT

                    <u>END OF ACT ONE</u>

ACT TWO

FADE IN:

INT. COMPUTER SCIENCES LAB - ON RAPHAEL - CONTINUOUS

Raphael is covered by the Globfather's slimy, green body. Only
his head is above the slime. The Globfather's head is beside
Raphael's.

                    RAPHAEL
          I think I need some help, guys.

The Turtles move closer, weapons ready.

                    GLOBFATHER
          Touch him and you'll all become amoebic
          blobs.

They stop! Michaelangelo gestures o.s.

                    MICHAELANGELO
          Dudes!...

ANOTHER ANGLE

The Globfather's gangsters rip the protein computer from its
connections. Two more gangsters grab Professor Huxley.

                    MICHAELANGELO
          They're getting away!

BACK TO GLOBFATHER AND TURTLES

The Turtles appear unsure what to do next.

                    LEONARDO
          But we can't leave Raphael!

Suddenly the Globfather separates from Raphael, leaving him with
a covering of green slime.

WIDER ON LAB

The Globfather exits with his gangsters and Professor Huxley.

ANGLE ON RONNIE

still under the lab table.

                    RONNIE
                (sotto)
          Dad!

WIDER ANGLE

Ronnie climbs out from under the table and grabs his backpack.
And as he runs out a <u>back</u> exit, cut to...

THE TURTLES

They move closer to Raphael but are still reluctant to touch him
as the green slime moves up his neck and over his face.

                    RAPHAEL
          If someone doesn't do something soon
          you're going to have enough Turtle jelly
          to last the rest of your lives!

                    LEONARDO
          Don't move, Raphael!

Leonardo raises his katana blades and swings them like a master,
shaving the green slime off Raphael's body. It falls to the floor,
forming a slimy puddle. Raphael is clean.

                    MICHAELANGELO
          Whoa! Teenage Mutant Ninja Barber strikes
          again!

EXT. LAB - CONTINUOUS

The Turtles appear in the doorway, scan the area. WIDEN to reveal
the Globfather and his men are gone.

                    LEONARDO
          They're gone!

                    RAPHAEL
          Probably headed back to their hideout.
          Let's go!

                    DONATELLO
          Wait a minute! What happened to the
          professor's kid?

                    MICHAELANGELO
          He wasn't with his dad.

BACK INSIDE THE LAB

The Turtles enter, look around. Michaelangelo spots a security
camera.

                    MICHAELANGELO
          Hey, dudes! Maybe the security camera
          can give us a clue.

The others move closer as Michaelangelo rewinds the security tape
VCR, then plays it. On the monitor we see a shot of Professor
Huxley taking the protein brain from the tank and putting it into
the RC car, then into the backpack.

> LEONARDO
> Professor Huxley put the protein computer
> brain into his son's car.

Michaelangelo fast-forwards the tape a ways, then hits PLAY. On
the monitor we see Ronnie grab the backpack and run away.

> RAPHAEL
> And the kid's got it!

> MICHAELANGELO
> Which means he's in big trouble.

> LEONARDO
> We've got to find him before the
> Globfather does.

> WIPE TO:

EXT. APRIL'S APARTMENT - NIGHT

to establish.

INT. APRIL'S APARTMENT - CONTINUOUS

April is at her computer, writing a story when a voice comes over
her Turtle Com.

> DONATELLO'S VOICE
> (muffled)
> April, you there?

She opens her desk drawer, removes the Turtle Com, on which is a
picture of Donatello's face.

> APRIL
> What's up, Donatello?

> DONATELLO
> An alien and some hoods just kidnapped
> Professor Huxley.

A shot of Ronnie (from video tape) appears on the Turtle Com.

> DONATELLO
> His son, Ronnie, has the protein computer's
> brain.

Donatello's face returns to April's Turtle Com.

> DONATELLO
> Have the police put out an All Points
> Bulletin on the kid.

> APRIL
> You got it!

Donatello's face disappears off the Turtle Com. April puts it down, picks up the phone, dials, then:

> APRIL
> Sergeant Murray? This is April O'Neil...

                                          DISSOLVE TO:

INT. THE GLOBFATHER'S HIDEOUT - NIGHT

The Globfather and his gang have the Professor tied to a chair. Several gangsters are at the master computer.

> SECOND GANGSTER
> There's something wrong, Boss. The protein
> computer isn't working.

The Globfather, who is wearing his three-piece pin-striped suit again, checks out the computer, sees that...

THE PROTEIN COMPUTER TANK

is empty!

FAVORING PROFESSOR HUXLEY

The Globfather turns to him, moves threateningly close.

> GLOBFATHER
> Where is it?

> PROFESSOR HUXLEY
> I...I don't know what you're talking
> about?

The Globfather calmly places his hand on the Professor's hand. The Professor watches in horror as the green slime oozes from the Globfather's fingers, crawling up his arm.

> GLOBFATHER
> If you don't want to become an amoeba,
> like that meddling Turtle, I suggest you
> tell me what you did with the protein
> computer brain.

PUSH IN on the Professor as he watches the slime creep up his arm.

                    PROFESSOR HUXLEY
                        (panicked)
              Please! Take it off!

                    GLOBFATHER
              Why should I? It gets lonely being the
              only intelligent blob of protoplasm on
              this puny planet.

As the slime creeps up Huxley's shoulder...

                    PROFESSOR HUXLEY
              All right! All right! It's in my son's
              backpack, hidden inside his radio-
              controlled car.

                    GLOBFATHER
              That's better.

                    SECOND GANGSTER
              How are we gonna find the kid,
              Globfather? We don't know what he looks
              like.

ANOTHER ANGLE - FAVORING TV SET

A THIRD GANGSTER watches a news broadcast.

                    THIRD GANGSTER
              Hey, Boss, look at this!

                    NEWS ANCHOR
              Professor Alvin Huxley's break-through
              "protein computer" was stolen from his
              lab this evening.

CLOSER ON MONITOR SCREEN

as the security video picture of Ronnie appears.

                    NEWS ANCHOR'S VOICE
              Anyone who has seen the Professor's
              son, Ronnie, should contact authorities
              immediately.

BACK TO SCENE

Huxley watches in terror as the slime moves down his chest.

                    PROFESSOR HUXLEY
          Please, take this off!

                    GLOBFATHER
          I think we'll leave it on to make sure
          you don't double-cross me.

The Globfather and his gang head for the door, leaving Professor
Huxley tied to a chair.

                    PROFESSOR HUXLEY
          No! Come back!

PUSH IN on Professor Huxley as he looks with terror at the green
slime. And as it continues to grow over him...

                                                  WIPE TO:

EXT. CITY - NIGHT

As the Turtle Van rolls down the street cut...

INSIDE TURTLE VAN

Raphael drives, with Donatello beside him; Leonardo and
Michaelangelo are in back.

                    LEONARDO
          That kid could be anywhere by now.

                    MICHAELANGELO
          Tell me about it. It's gonna be like
          finding a noodle in a haystack.

                    RAPHAEL
          You mean "needle," don't you?

                    MICHAELANGELO
          I was trying to be optimistic, dude.

Off Raphael's reaction we...

                                                  CUT TO:

EXT. THE CITY - NIGHT

As the Globfather's sedan rolls slowly down the street, HOLD on a
cluster of trash cans, then PUSH IN. Ronnie pokes his head up,
looks after the Globfather's sedan. Then he drops a skateboard on
the sidewalk and skates off the opposite way.

ANOTHER ANGLE ON RONNIE

As he crosses the street he's caught in a pair of headlights,
like a deer on the highway.

INSIDE ANOTHER DARK SEDAN

more gangsters react as they spot the kid.

                    THIRD GANGSTER
          There he is!

WIDER ON SEDAN

Ronnie makes a skillful U-turn on his skateboard, skates up the
side of a driveway, goes airborne and over a small wall, through
a parking lot. The sedan SCREECHES off after him.

IN THE PARKING LOT

Ronnie weaves in and out of the cars. He looks back as the sedan
follows. But when he looks forward again there's a shopping cart
in front of him. He slams into it, falls off his skateboard. PUSH
IN as the dark sedan stops, headlights illuminating Ronnie.

CLOSER ON RONNIE

He gets up. Then four gangsters enter, moving in on him. He backs
up against a brick wall.

                    RONNIE
          What do you want?

                    THIRD GANGSTER
          Just hand over the backpack, kid, and
          we'll leave you alone!

Ronnie nervously takes off his backpack, about to give it to the
gangster when...

                    MICHAELANGELO (O.S.)
          I've got a better deal, dude...

WIDER ANGLE

The Turtles surround the gangsters, ninja hardware ready.

                    MICHAELANGELO
          The kid keeps the backpack and we leave
          you alone!

The gangsters whip out their blasters, fire.

MICHAELANGELO

grabs Ronnie, covers him so he's out of the line of fire.

ANGLE ON OTHER TURTLES

Donatello jerks his bo up, knocking two blasters away. Leonardo does a high leap, grabs the blasters out of the air, then comes down in a back flip, landing on top of a wrought iron railing over the other Gangsters. He fires at the ground before them, forcing them back. Then...

THE GLOBFATHER'S CAR

SQUEALS to a stop, headlights flaring into camera.

FAVORING TURTLES

> DONATELLO
> It's the Globfather!

> LEONARDO
> Don't let him out of his car!

As Leonardo and Donatello rush o.s., cut...

INSIDE THE GLOBFATHER'S CAR

> GLOBFATHER
> This time I'll turn those turtles into
> mindless slime!

And as the Globfather grabs his door handle, cut...

OUTSIDE THE GLOBFATHER'S SEDAN

Raphael rushes into shot, thrusts one of his sais into the door handle, jamming it.

INSIDE THE SEDAN

The Globfather can't open the door. He reaches for the other side, but...

DONATELLO

slides his bo through the other door handle, jamming it.

BACK INSIDE THE CAR

> GLOBFATHER
> Open the windows!

ANGLE ON SECOND GANGSTER

He presses the electric window buttons. But before they can go down we cut...

BACK OUTSIDE

                   DONATELLO
           He's opening the windows!

Leonardo raises a katana blade and brings it down through the
car's hood. And cut...

UNDER THE HOOD

as the blade slices through the metal and severs the battery
cable, sparking.

BACK INSIDE THE SEDAN

the windows stop after dropping only an inch.

                SECOND GANGSTER
          We can't get out, Boss!

                  GLOBFATHER
           Maybe <u>you</u> can't...

PUSH IN on the Globfather as he turns into ooze, sliding out of his
suit, which collapses. FOLLOW the green slime as it flows through
the air conditioning vent. Then cut...

UNDER THE SEDAN

as the green slime oozes out and flows over the street, o.s.

ANGLE ON GLOBFATHER'S SEDAN

Leonardo is by the hood, with Raphael on one side, Donatello on
the other. They don't see as the green slime oozes past them along
the gutter, then up onto the sidewalk.

ANGLE ON RAPHAEL AND RONNIE

Ronnie spots the slime oozing toward them.

                    RONNIE
         Look!

                   RAPHAEL
         Either someone spilled the Jell-O mold
         or we're in big trouble.

Suddenly the slime rises up before them into the shape of the
Globfather. He reaches out a slimy hand toward the kid.

>   GLOBFATHER
>   Give me the backpack!

>   RAPHAEL
>   I'll keep the Jelly Green Giant busy,
>   you get out of here!

Raphael picks up Ronnie and helps him onto the fire escape above. And as Ronnie starts climbing, the Globfather tries to reach up and grab him, but Raphael picks up a trash can lid and slams the Globfather, sending a blob of slime splashing onto the nearby brick wall. And as the slime oozes down the wall...

>   RAPHAEL
>   Didn't anyone ever tell you you can be
>   fined for making graffiti?

CLOSER ON GREEN SLIME

It oozes down the wall and into the open end of a drain pipe.

ANGLE ON RONNIE

As he climbs the fire escape, PAN UP the drain pipe beside him, then cut...

HIGHER UP THE FIRE ESCAPE

As Ronnie climbs up into shot the green slime oozes out of a crack in the drain pipe, forming an arm. It reaches out and grabs for Ronnie, gets his backpack. Ronnie struggles, trying to get away. And as...

>   RONNIE
>   (screams)

>   FADE OUT

                    END OF ACT TWO

<u>ACT THREE</u>

FADE IN:

ON RONNIE AND THE GLOBFATHER'S ARM

sticking out of the drain pipe, holding onto his backpack.

                    RONNIE
          LEMME GO!

ANGLE ON TURTLES

                    LEONARDO
          He's got Ronnie!

And as the four Turtles leap to the fire escape and start climbing,
cut back to...

RONNIE AND THE GREEN ARM

Ronnie pulls out of his backpack, loses his balance, falls off
the fire escape, catching onto the railing.

                    RONNIE
          Help!

The rest of the slime comes out of the drain pipe and the
Globfather reforms into his humanoid shape, holding the backpack.
A moment later the Turtles climb into shot, stop before him. He
holds the backpack before them, taunting.

                    GLOBFATHER
          It's your choice, Turtles, the boy...or
          the backpack.

Then the Globfather leaps off the fire escape.

DOWN ANGLE ON STREET

The Globfather lands with a green splat, reforms into himself,
runs toward his car. Then cut...

CLOSE ON RONNIE

hanging from the edge of the fire escape. Suddenly several Turtle
hands reach into shot, grab him. WIDEN as the Turtles haul him
onto the fire escape to safety. Ronnie hugs Raphael.

> RAPHAEL
> Easy, kid. You're okay.

They react to the sound of CAR ENGINES, then look down at...

THEIR POV: THE STREET

as the three sedans race off into the night.

BACK TO THE TURTLES AND RONNIE

> MICHAELANGELO
> They're getting away, dudes!

> DONATELLO
> We've got to get the protein computer
> brain back.

> RONNIE
> What about my father?

The Turtles exchange a few concerned looks, then...

> LEONARDO
> Don't worry, Ronnie. We'll help you find
> him.

DISSOLVE TO:

INT. WAREHOUSE - NIGHT

The protein computer is all set up, with the protein brain back
in its tank. Professor Huxley is still tied up, with green slime
creeping over more of his body. The Second Gangster checks out
the computer, turns to the Globfather (who is back in his three-
piece suit and fedora).

> SECOND GANGSTER
> The computer's workin', Boss.

> GLOBFATHER
> Good! Our alien benefactor will be
> pleased.

CLOSER ON GLOBFATHER

He turns on a small, futuristic looking communication screen.

> GLOBFATHER
> This is the Globfather calling from
> Earth. Phase one complete.

Suddenly DREGG'S face appears on the screen!

                    DREGG
          Well done! You shall be rewarded
          handsomely.

INT. DREGGNAUT COMMAND BRIDGE - CONTINUOUS

We are back in Dimension X. The Dreggnaut is only a steel shell,
in mid-construction. Micro-bots work away: the electrical system
appears to grow before our eyes, forming webs of wires around the
frame as Dregg looks into his monitor screen. MUNG[9] is with him.
Globfather is on the screen.

                    GLOBFATHER
          Thank you, Dregg. Shall I commence Phase
          Two?

                    DREGG
          Yes. Once you've hooked the protein brain
          into the National Phone Switching Network
          I'll be able to control all earthly com-
          puters with my mind, including their mili-
          tary defense system. I'll conquer the Earth
          without lifting a finger!

                    MUNG
          But it will be days before the Dreggnaut
          is completed. How will we get to Earth?

                    DREGG
          Put all available micro-bots to work on
          the Vortex Transporter. We'll beam to Earth
          as soon as it's finished.

                    MUNG
          Yes, my lord.

                                              WIPE TO:

EXT. NATIONAL PHONE SWITCHING NETWORK - NIGHT

The place looks like an impregnable fortress with high concrete
walls, guard towers, etc. PUSH IN on a manhole in the street.

INT. CONCRETE TUNNEL - CONTINUOUS

Beneath the manhole. It is filled with hundreds of telephone
cables. One of the gangsters holds a flashlight as another snips
a wire. Then cut...

9. Mung is one of Dregg's alien underlings.

INT. GUARD HOUSE - CONTINUOUS

Two guards watch a bank of TV monitors, showing all of the entrances, exits and hallways. The monitors go black.

> SECURITY GUARD
> What the...?

He presses his alarm button, but nothing happens.

> SECURITY GUARD
> The alarm system's been cut!

They get up, rush for the door, but it's locked!

INT. HALLWAY - OPPOSITE SIDE OF DOOR

to reveal one of the gangsters has just shoved a steel bar across the door, blocking it. And as he moves off, cut to...

INT. MAIN SWITCHING ROOM - CLOSE ON DOOR

It suddenly explodes, blowing inwards. Two gangsters enter, wielding blasters. WIDEN to reveal the towering rows of main switching computers. The technicians at the switching computer console stand, hands in the air. Several more gangsters enter, carrying computer equipment. As they begin to hook it to the switching computers...

THE GLOBFATHER

shoves Professor Huxley into the room; he's still covered with green slime (more than before). He hands the protein brain to the Professor.

> GLOBFATHER
> Hook this up to the telephone switching
> computers and I might be nice and de-
> slime you!

The Professor moves to the main switching computer. He takes the protein brain out of the tank, then opens up the panel on the telephone switching computer.

INSIDE THE TELEPHONE SWITCHING COMPUTER

there are hundreds of circuits and wires. The Professor looks in through the open panel, reaches in with the protein brain in his hand. He places it onto the main motherboard. PUSH IN on the protein brain as it suddenly flows over the circuits and wires. It starts to make new connections, like a brain growing neurons! And as it grows over everything...

THE GLOBFATHER

sits down before the computer. He takes the Professor's control
helmet out of a box. Then he takes off his fedora, places it over
his slimy head. PUSH IN as the helmet glows with power.

                    GLOBFATHER
          Incredible! I can feel my mind connecting
          to millions of computers around the world.

                                                  CUT TO:

INT. APRIL'S APARTMENT - NIGHT

April is at her computer. She reacts as it suddenly crashes, her
screen going black.

                    APRIL
          Oh, great! What a time for my system to
          crash.

She takes out a notebook computer, turns it on.

                    APRIL
          Good thing I have a cellular modem in my
          notebook computer. Maybe I can find out
          what went wrong.

CLOSER ON HER NOTEBOOK SCREEN

As she types away we see a computer grid map of the world, with
glowing paths connecting all the cities of the world.

                    APRIL
          I don't believe it! The phone lines are
          jammed all over the world!

Suddenly the Globfather's expressionless face appears on her
screen, staring forward like an evil test pattern.

                    GLOBFATHER
               (creepy, synthesized)
          Warning, Earth beings! This system is
          under alien control. Any tampering will
          result in instant reprisal!

April's notebook computer goes black. She picks up her phone,
dials, then:

                    GLOBFATHER'S VOICE
                 (creepy, synthesized)
            Warning, Earth beings. This system...

April hangs up.

                         APRIL
                 This is crazy!

And as she picks up her Turtle Com...

                                                    CUT TO:

INT. THE TURTLE VAN - TRAVELING - NIGHT

April's face appears on the van monitor screen.

                         APRIL
                 Guys, it's April. Some maniac with a green
                 face is controlling every phone line and
                 computer connection in the world!

                        RAPHAEL
                 Sounds like our slimy amigo.

                       LEONARDO
                 The only place he could connect to all
                 of the phone lines is the National Phone
                 Switching Network.

FAVORING DONATELLO AND RONNIE

                       DONATELLO
                 I should be able to link up to him with
                 the van cell phone.

                         RONNIE
                 I wouldn't do that if I were you.

Donatello picks up a mobile phone, dials.

                       DONATELLO
                 I know what I'm doing.
                         (a beat)
                 It's ringing.

INT. NATIONAL PHONE SWITCHING NETWORK - CONTINUOUS

The Globfather (still at console wearing helmet) reacts.

                       GLOBFATHER
                 So, those Turtles think they can tap
                 into this network. Well, they'll soon
                 regret it.

PUSH IN on the Globfather as he concentrates. And as his expression turns evil...

BACK IN THE TURTLE VAN

Donatello reacts as the Globfather's face appears on his monitor screen.

> GLOBFATHER
> You've dialed the wrong number, fool.

Suddenly the fold-out-gun drops down.

> LEONARDO
> He's got control of our weapons! Get down!

Leonardo pushes Donatello to the deck as the gun fires, blows the opposite door off. Donatello rolls out. As Leonardo grabs him and pulls him back into the van...

THE TWO GUNS ON THE ROOF

suddenly aim upwards and fire, blowing...

A RADIO ANTENNA

off the top of a building. It falls, crashing to...

THE STREET

as the Turtle Van swerves, barely avoiding it.

BACK IN THE VAN

Raphael struggles with the steering wheel.

> RAPHAEL
> Now he's got control of the steering!

ANGLE ON TURTLE VAN

as it swerves back and forth down the street, knocking off a fire hydrant, side-swiping a parked car.

TIGHT ON RAPHAEL AND MICHAELANGELO

Michaelangelo helps Raphael with the steering. As Michaelangelo looks down at the wheel, gritting his teeth:

> MICHAELANGELO
> (struggling)
> This thing...won't turn!

                    RAPHAEL
               (looking ahead, o.s.)
          Ever wonder what a bug feels like when
          it slams into the radiator of a truck?

                    MICHAELANGELO
               (still looking down, straining)
          No! Why?

                    RAPHAEL
          'Cause we're about to find out.

Michaelangelo looks up, reacts in alarm to...

THEIR POV: THROUGH WINDOW

as they speed toward a huge truck coming right at them. The HORN
BLASTS!

BACK INSIDE THE TURTLE VAN

                    DONATELLO
          Kill the computer system! Quick!

                    RAPHAEL
          Whatever you say, Donatello.

Raphael whips out his sais and thrusts them down into the
dashboard. And as sparks fly, all of the van's computers shut
down, their screens going black. The steering wheel suddenly
frees up and Michaelangelo turns sharply.

THE TURTLE VAN

swerves away, just missing the big truck, which roars past. As the
Turtle Van stops, cut...

BACK INSIDE

The Turtles relax, sliding down and sighing.

                    MICHAELANGELO
          Whew! That was close.

                    LEONARDO
          How can we stop the Globfather if he can
          control any computer in the world?

                    RONNIE
          There's no reason more than one person
          can't control the...

33

                         DONATELLO
                    (cuts him off)
              Wait a minute! I think I just figured it
              out. We've got to get back to the lair.

Off Ronnie's annoyed expression we cut to...

THE STREET

As the Turtle Van makes a U-turn and speeds off...

                                              WIPE TO:

INT. NATIONAL PHONE SWITCHING NETWORK - NIGHT

The Globfather still wears the telepathic control helmet. Suddenly
the room begins to glow eerily, then there is a telltale flash
and Dregg appears, having been transported.

                         GLOBFATHER
              Dregg!

The Globfather rises, hands the helmet to Dregg.

                         GLOBFATHER
              Everything is ready.

Dregg takes the helmet, sits down at the computer console.

                         DREGG
              Very well. It's time to take control of
              this puny planet once and for all.

He places the helmet on his head. PUSH IN as Dregg smiles with awe
as he *feels* the control he has of the computers. Then he suddenly
senses something, reacts with alarm.

                         DREGG
              What's this?! The military is trying to
              regain control of the system!

INT. ARMY WAR ROOM[10]

Uniformed personnel are seated before computer consoles. There is
a giant map of the world on the wall. A GENERAL stands over a
COMPUTER TECHNICIAN.

                         COMPUTER TECHNICIAN
              I'm into the National Phone Switching
              Network, sir.

---

10. In some locations, such as an underground, windowless
war room, there is no indication of night or day in the slug line.

                    GENERAL
         Good! See if you can freeze the system.

As the Technician enters data on his keyboard, cut...

CLOSE ON DREGG

                    DREGG
         Think again, fools!

He concentrates, then...

BACK IN THE ARMY WAR ROOM

The computers go crazy, sparking, exploding. The General and other technicians react in alarm.

CLOSER ON COMPUTER TECHNICIAN

On the monitor before him a red alarm warming flashes beside an image of an orbiting satellite.

                COMPUTER TECHNICIAN
         We've lost control of our particle beam
         satellites!

ON PARTICLE BEAM SATELLITE - IN SPACE

It suddenly turns, aiming down at the planet below. It fires a blinding white beam. Then cut to...

EXT. A BIG CITY - NIGHT

The beam streaks down into shot, hits a towering mountain peak in the background, blowing the top off!

INT. ARMY WAR ROOM

The General and technicians look up as Dregg's face appears on their large wall monitor.

                    DREGG
         This is Lord Dregg! You shall be pun-
         ished for trying to resist...

INT. NATIONAL TELEPHONE SWITCHING NETWORK - CONTINUOUS

Dregg looks at the monitor screens. Several military leaders of various countries appear before him.

                    DREGG
        The nations of Earth have fifteen minutes
        to surrender, or next time I fire your
        satellite cannons your cities will be
        destroyed.

                                            CUT TO:

INT. TURTLES' LAIR

Donatello is working on a jury-rigged helmet, with all kinds of
wires and electronic parts on it. Ronnie is seated by the other
Turtles.

                    DONATELLO
        That ought to do it.

                    MICHAELANGELO
        What's it supposed to do, anyway?

                    DONATELLO
        It should allow me to tap into the main
        phone computer, giving me mental access so
        I can stop the Globfather.

                    LEONARDO
        Maybe you should try it out first.

                    DONATELLO
        Right. If I can turn the lights off with
        it we'll know it works.

Donatello puts it on, flicks a switch on the helmet. It lights up.
He concentrates. The lights don't go off, but the electric fan
turns on, blowing a stack of papers through shot.

                    RAPHAEL
        Close, but no cigar.

                    DONATELLO
        I can't seem to control it.

                    MICHAELANGELO
        Let me try, dude.

Michaelangelo takes the helmet, puts it on, looks at the light,
concentrates. Suddenly one of Donatello's computers shorts out and
explodes, showering them with sparks.

                        MICHAELANGELO
          Sorry.

                        DONATELLO
          I don't get it. Theoretically it should
          work.

                        RONNIE
          It will, but you've got to reduce your
          visual stimuli in order to concentrate
          your thoughts. Here, I'll show you.

Ronnie reaches for the helmet, but Donatello grabs it from
Michaelangelo.

                        DONATELLO
                   (ignoring Ronnie)
          Wait a second! I think I know how to do
          it.

Donatello puts the helmet on, closes his eyes, concentrates. The
lights shut off, then come back on.

                        MICHAELANGELO
          Way to go, dude!

ANGLE ON RONNIE

                        RONNIE
                   (sotto, discouraged)
          What am I hanging around here for? These
          guys think they know everything.

As he moves o.s. we cut...

WIDER ON TURTLES

                        LEONARDO
          Come on, we've got to stop the
          Globfather.

                        RAPHAEL
                   (looks around)
          Hey! Where's the kid?

                        DONATELLO
          There's no time to look for him. Let's go.

And as the Turtles exit (with helmet)...

                                        DISSOLVE TO:

EXT. NATIONAL PHONE SWITCHING NETWORK - NIGHT

PUSH IN and cut...

INT. MAIN COMPUTER ROOM - CONTINUOUS

Dregg is seated before the computer, wearing the Professor's
helmet, looking at the military leaders on his monitor.

                    MILITARY LEADER
                (grim)
            We have discussed your terms with the
            leaders of all nations. For the good of
            mankind, we have agreed to turn over
            command of the planet to you, Lord Dregg.

The Globfather and his gangsters react with delight.

                    DREGG
            At last, the Earth is mine!

Suddenly the Turtles burst in through a door, startling Dregg and
company.

                    LEONARDO
            Not today, Dregg!

As the gangsters open fire with their blasters, the Turtles dive,
roll, and cut...

CLOSER ON TURTLES

They huddle like a football team. Donatello puts on his helmet.

                    DONATELLO
            Block for me! I'm going to rush the com-
            puter!

Leonardo, Michaelangelo and Raphael kneel like linemen, then run
ahead of Donatello, right into camera, wielding their ninja gear.

                    TURTLES
            GO GREEN TEAM!

ANGLE ON GANGSTERS

They form a line of six gangsters, armed and ready. And as they
open fire...

THE TURTLES

drop face down, sliding over the floor, come to rest behind a computer in a messy pile.

              MICHAELANGELO
We've been blitzed, dudes.

              RAPHAEL
There's too many of them to tackle.

              DONATELLO
But I've got to plug my helmet into the
master computer to get control.

ANGLE ON DREGG

              DREGG
Once I vaporize a dozen cities you'll
see who's got control!

PUSH IN on Dregg as he concentrates. Then cut to...

A SATELLITE IN ORBIT

Its particle beam starts to charge up. And as the laser moves
into targeting position over Europe...

ANOTHER SATELLITE LASER

does the same thing, aiming down at North America.

BACK IN THE MAIN SWITCHING ROOM - ON TURTLES

              DONATELLO
I've only got sixty seconds to stop
Dregg before the particle cannons are
ready to fire.

              MICHAELANGELO
           (to Leonardo)
Go out for a pass, dude!

As Leonardo runs o.s...

THE GLOBFATHER AND HIS GANGSTERS

fire their blasters as they run toward Leonardo.

              GLOBFATHER
        Get him!

Leonardo leaps up as Michaelangelo passes his grappler,
trailing out its cable. Leonardo catches it, pulls the cable
taut, tripping all of the gangsters.

DONATELLO

rushes for the main computer, plugs in his helmet.

                         DONATELLO
              I'm in!

CLOSE ON DREGG

                         DREGG
              But you won't stop the satellite cannons
              while I've got control!

Dregg concentrates, then cut to...

A WHEELED COMPUTER VACUUM CLEANER

suddenly comes to life and races o.s.

BACK TO DONATELLO

He dodges as the vacuum device bashes into the side of the
computer, just missing him. And as it tries again, Donatello
dives over the computer.

                         DONATELLO
              Will somebody stop that thing! I can't
              concentrate!

MICHAELANGELO AND RAPHAEL

tackle the robot vacuum, comically wrestling it.

CLOSE ON DONATELLO

                         DONATELLO
                   (concentrating again)
              Got to shut down the satellites.

ANGLE ON SATELLITE IN ORBIT

as it shuts down and goes dark.

CLOSE ON DREGG

                         DREGG
                   (intense concentration)
              Your mind isn't strong enough, reptile!

BACK ON THE ORBITING SATELLITE

It turns on again, continues to aim its cannon.

BACK TO DREGG

                         DREGG
              My concentration is stronger! You can't
              stop me now!

ANGLE ON DOOR

as Ronnie enters.

> RONNIE
> That's what he thinks.

He drops his RC car to the floor, manipulates the controller. The car pops a wheelie and races o.s.

ANGLE ON STACK OF COMPUTER PRINTOUT PAPER ON FLOOR

Some of the top pages have slid over to form a ramp. The RC car speeds into shot, up the paper ramp and into the air.

ANGLE ON DREGG

Suddenly the RC car sails into shot, lands on the computer before him, racing over the buttons and keyboard. Sparks fly! The picture of the satellite on Dregg's monitor goes snowy.

BACK TO RONNIE

> RONNIE
> Donatello, now!

ON DONATELLO

as he concentrates...

THE ORBITING SATELLITE

changes aiming direction, then fires!

EXT. NATIONAL TELEPHONE SWITCHING NETWORK - CONTINUOUS

The laser beam streaks down into shot, blowing up the Globfather's empty sedans. BOOM! BOOM! BOOM!

CLOSE ON DREGG

> DREGG
> It'll take more than that to stop me, reptiles!

CLOSE ON DONATELLO

> DONATELLO
> How about this?

He concentrates...

ANGLE ON ORBITING SATELLITE

as it fires again.

INT. MAIN TELEPHONE SWITCHING ROOM

The laser blows a hole in the ceiling, then streaks down and
explodes on the floor behind Dregg, blowing him out of his seat.

ON PROFESSOR HUXLEY

Ronnie rushes into shot, reacts to the sight of his father as the
slime finally covers him completely.

                    RONNIE
          Dad!

CLOSE ON DONATELLO

                    DONATELLO
          Ronnie, get back!

As Donatello concentrates...

THE ROBOT VACUUM

races across the floor, stops before Professor Huxley. The vacuum
hose rises up, sucks the green slime off him. Then cut to...

THE GLOBFATHER AND HIS GANGSTERS

                    GLOBFATHER
          Let's get out of here!

But Leonardo and Raphael drop down before them.

                    RAPHAEL
          Not so fast, slimeball!

ANOTHER ANGLE

as the robot vacuum rolls into shot, stops before the Globfather,
sucks him up with its hose.

                    GLOBFATHER
          NOOOO!!!

FAVORING DREGG

He reacts as the Globfather is sucked away into the vacuum
and his gangsters retreat from the Turtles. Dregg holds up a
communicator.

                    DREGG
        Mung! Beam us back to Dimension X!

Dregg, the gangsters and the robot vacuum (with the Globfather
leaking out) are engulfed in glowing transporter energy.

                    DREGG
        I'll be back, reptiles. And next time I
        will not be denied!!!

An instant later they disappear in a flash of energy!

FAVORING PROFESSOR HUXLEY

Ronnie hugs his father.

                    RONNIE
        Dad!

Donatello takes off his helmet.

                PROFESSOR HUXLEY
         (to Turtles)
        Thank you for saving us.

                  LEONARDO
        Thank your son, Professor Huxley.

                  DONATELLO
        Yeah! We couldn't have done it without him.

Donatello tousles Ronnie's hair. Michaelangelo picks up the little
RC car and its remote control from the floor.

                MICHAELANGELO
        Dudes! If I had a cool car like this I
        could've tripped up Dregg, too.

Michaelangelo puts the car down, then manipulates the remote,
racing the car across the floor in wild circles. Then it suddenly
swerves at Michaelangelo. He tries to get away from it, but the
car hits his feet, tripping him. SPLAT!

                MICHAELANGELO
        Yaaah! Ooof!

                  RAPHAEL
        No doubt about it, Michaelangelo, you're
        a trip.

              TURTLES / PROF. / RONNIE
        (laugh it up)

                                  FADE OUT

                THE END

Chapter 8
Writing Description

Now that you've read an animated script and understand its form and content, it's time to look more closely at the two basic elements of a script: description and dialogue. In this chapter I'm going to discuss description.

Description (sometimes called action) is the telling of the physical part of the story. This includes all of the action that takes place, as well as the environment and what's in it, such as vehicles, characters, and anything else you might see on the screen. The description part of a script also includes any camera angles and moves, as well as notations of sounds or special effects which may be necessary to fully communicate your vision to the storyboard artist and animators.

Description is always written in third person, present tense. It is never written in past tense. Present tense gives scripts a certain immediacy. You're not telling a story that happened when you're writing a script, you're revealing it *as* it happens.

Perhaps the most basic thing to remember about writing description in any script is that for the most part it is simply representing in words what the viewer will see. It doesn't have to be said in impressive, flowery prose. Unlike a novel, it's pointless to say something in the description if you don't intend to see it. For example, consider this description:

```
Joe runs out of his room, wishing he'd left earlier.
```

The words "wishing he'd left earlier" are unnecessary, as there is no way to show this. It's an abstract concept that cannot even be shown with emotions due to the limitations of animation.

There are three basic elements to writing description. These are: *visualization*, *continuity*, and *pacing*.

Visualization

Movies and TV are visual media. In most instances, their pictures are more important than their words. But nowhere are pictures more important than in animation. This is especially true for children, many of whom watch cartoons long before they even know what the words mean. Many adults who watch animation—myself included—are enamored by the beauty of moving animation art. The pictures alone can evoke great interest and emotion. I am not for a moment discounting the value of dialogue in telling an animated story, but the scales definitely tip in favor of the visual.

This is why the cartoon writer must wear the director's hat to some degree. Specifically, you must be able to visualize what you're writing. You have to see it in your mind—but you have to do more than just see it. To be a good writer you have to choose the words that best communicate the images you see so that the reader—especially the artists and animators—will see exactly what you see. The better you are at visualizing, and the better you are at putting your mental images into words, the better toon writer you will be. If you can't see your cartoon in your mind before you write it, chances are no one will see it when reading your script. So think visually and do your best to paint with words the pictures you see.

People used to tell me they could "see" the animation just from reading my scripts. This is what you're shooting for, because this means that you, as a writer, have communicated clearly and effectively. Conversely, if you have a dull visual idea of what you're writing, the reader is going to get an unclear picture of your animation. This makes for rejected writing or, at best, very poor cartoons.

The more animation you watch the better you'll be able to think with animated images. I used to tell people that I always imagine in Disney animation. Why? Because imagination is free, and if you can afford to imagine anything, why not the best? This might sound like a joke, but there's a lot of truth here. If what you visualize in your mind is higher quality, what comes out on paper will also be higher quality.

One way to help your reader visualize your scene is the use of the shot-by-shot method, as I did in the Ninja Turtles script. Take a look at the difference in the following two scenes. The first is written as just description in the master scene method:

```
The coyote shoves the plunger down hard as the roadrunner
runs past the dynamite, flicking his tongue out. The
coyote reacts with surprise, then runs to the dynamite
and checks the connection. It's perfect. Uh-oh! KABLAM!
```

Following is the exact same sequence of words, only broken up into shots:

```
THE COYOTE

shoves the plunger down hard, as

THE ROADRUNNER

runs past the dynamite, flicking his tongue out.

THE COYOTE

reacts with surprise, then runs to the dynamite and checks
the connection. It's perfect. Uh-oh!

KABLAM!
```

Calling out the shots focuses the reader's attention on the character, breaking up the action into what might be called "visual bites." Thus, the purpose of slug lines and shots is to fix a visual image in the reader's mind, as well as to tell the board man what to draw.

Don't get stuck in the rigidity of script form. All of these techniques have one thing as their goal: to communicate the best cartoon. So feel free to be flexible with your script, but don't start bending the rules until you fully understand them.

So the first thing to do is *see* **your animation in your mind. The next thing is to find the words that best communicate what you see.**

The Importance of Communication

Now might be a good time to go over the subject of communication. But what exactly is communication? **It is simply getting an idea from one person to another.** As writers we do this with words. We craft infinite universes with nothing more. This sounds like a no-brainer, but there is actually a science to it, as well as an art. The art part takes years of practice and is subject to opinion. But the science part is very precise and very simple.

For a writer, a word is the building block of communication, so you sure better know what a word is or you'll find yourself out on the street like some gunfighter, your hands over your six-guns, not knowing what a bullet is. Words are your bullets!

But what *is* a word? **A word is a sound that has meaning.** This, of course, is the spoken word. The only difference with a written word is that it has a symbol or symbols (letters) that represent the sound and meaning. So a written word is a symbol of meaning.

The only reason we need words is to communicate meaning. If we could give people meaning without words we certainly would. This is called telepathy and is a much better form of communication because there are no multiple definitions and misinterpretations to deal with. Just pure ideas. However, last time I looked the networks weren't broadcasting telepathic toons.

We communicate with words, and words have meaning—and meaning is the beef! Meaning is what interests us. Meaning is what we are trying to communicate. Where is the meaning of your story? It's in the words.

So if you don't know the words, not only can't you sing the tune, you can't write the script, either. This is why a good vocabulary is so important, because the more words you know, the more meanings you can communicate, and the more nuance you can use to communicate them. Can you imagine a musician who didn't know all his notes?

This brings up a very important concept in the field of cartoon writing. Most cartoons are for children. In order to ensure that there is communication, **a children's writer must use the simplest words possible to convey his intended meaning.**

If communication is the moving of an idea from one person to another, and if we do this with words, and if words are just meaning, then if the recipient of the words doesn't know their meanings there is no communication. Thus, **a misunderstood word prevents communication**.

To use a more complex word in order to possibly get some subtler nuance is great for a novel or screenplay, but do it in a children's cartoon and you're gambling with confusion and might communicate no meaning at all.

The thing that most people forget about communication is that the intention of the communicator (writer) is to get his idea *duplicated* by the other person. You want them to have the very same meaning you have, so they must know the words.

The definitions of the words are utterly important to communication, and communication can be very precise.

After writing hundreds of scripts for kids I've learned to be very careful with the words I choose in dialogue (naturally, description only matters for the producers and artists). When I was story-editing *Dragon Tales*, Sesame Workshop's animated preschool series for PBS, our target audience was four. Even with my experience, it took me quite a few scripts before I was finally able to think and write with a four-year-old's vocabulary.

But just because you need to use simpler words to communicate to children doesn't mean you have to "write down" to them, or be condescending. Almost anything that can be said with fifty-cent words can be said just as effectively with five-cent words, though it may take a few more of them.

So choose your words wisely, especially for children. Know your audience and don't waste your time writing over kids' heads. I once spent hours struggling over a single line of dialogue for a children's cartoon. I finally nailed it. Boy, was it ever funny. Months later I saw a young kid watching the toon. That joke sailed right over his head, but he laughed like crazy when the character fell on his face. If you want to guarantee communication to any age audience, of any language, don't use words, use action.

I'm not suggesting you can't write funny jokes that go over some kids' heads. This is an effective way of writing animation. It worked superbly in *Jim Henson's Muppet Babies*. Some of the dialogue was on the sophisticated side so adults watching the show could enjoy it, while the physical schtick kept the kids interested. This kind of writing is called *crossover*, as it works for both young and old audiences.

There is, of course, a great deal more information on this subject that is vital to the writer, but provided I didn't use too many words that went over your head, I should have communicated the basic idea.

Continuity

Continuity means an uninterrupted succession or flow; a coherent whole. In script writing it means that there are no discrepancies in the cutting from scene to scene, so that everything flows smoothly for the viewer, both visually and conceptually. Thus, continuity problems are really just problems in logic.

An example of a gross continuity error would be if a character had his foot injured in one scene and in the next scene was shown dancing as if nothing had ever happened.

Continuity errors are easier to make in animation than live action because in animation (especially of the squash & stretch variety) we often stretch the laws of physics. By doing so, we set ourselves up to be inconsistent with these new rules. For example, if you describe a character who flattens when a piano drops on him, you'd better not have a safe fall on him in the next scene and bounce off his head.

Continuity errors are one of the most obvious signs of an inexperienced cartoon writer. Some of them are blatant, as with the injured foot. But some can be very subtle and thus hard for the inexperienced writer to spot. For example, you might have a super hero character in one scene straining to lift a car off someone, then, in a later scene he pulls up an oak tree with ease. In fact, pulling up an oak tree would be ten times harder than lifting a car. Four big men can lift a small car. It takes a tractor to uproot a tree.

This at once tells you that in order to avoid continuity problems you have to understand the subjects you write about. It helps to know about physics and other natural laws, as these are always present in real stories. It also helps to understand the unnatural laws created for squash-and-stretch cartoons.

Continuity errors are not just related to action. There can be errors in the continuity of characters. A character who is a jerk in one scene should not be a nice guy in the next unless something significant has changed him.

A simple way to ensure proper continuity is to read one scene at a time, asking yourself the question **"Is there anything about what just happened in this scene that doesn't make sense in light of what happened so far in the story?"** Your ability to answer this question will be governed by your knowledge of what you are writing about and your ability to be logical. If you find a continuity error you simply have to adjust an earlier or later scene, or in some cases both.

When you become experienced with continuity you can read through a script rapidly and the continuity errors will stick out like sore thumbs.

Pacing

Pacing is the speed at which a scene or story plays out. You could also call it the "energy level" of a scene or script. It has a lot to do with how well your cartoon is received by the audience, and a lot to do with good dramatics, emotions, and gags.

Pacing varies depending on what you are writing. For educational cartoons your pacing should be slow. If it's too fast, the information you are communicating to kids may not be received and understood. However, a car chase with the cars moving at twenty-five miles per hour would actually be a comedy. Thus, for action scenes the pacing should be faster. The pacing of comedy is a mixture. It's generally fast, especially for visual gags. There's often a lull before a gag to set up the anticipation. There's often a lull after a gag for character reactions (which can be as funny as the gag). The pacing of comedy is the most difficult and critical of all. This is especially true for the animation director. I've seen dozens of gags that work great in the script but totally fail on the screen because the animation was directed too fast and there was not enough time to fully get the humor, or even have time to laugh at it. (I'll talk more about comedy later.) Suspense often has very slow pacing, thus dragging out the tension of the scene.

Of course, the pacing changes throughout a script. In fact, it can change within a scene. The subject of rhythm has a lot to do with the proper pacing of scenes.

In animation writing, pacing is affected by the quantity of words used in description, the number of shots called for in scenes, and the amount of dialogue.

The pacing of a script is greatly affected by the number of words used. The more words you use the more it will slow down the pacing of the script, at least with respect to the reading of it (which is vitally important in terms of selling your script). **As a rule, if you can describe something with fewer words do so.**

Here are examples of identical pieces of action, one twice as long as the other:

```
Sam leaps fast off the building's roof, slapping leather
as he rapidly draws his Colts. He plummets through the
air, firing off several quick shots which blow down the
bandits before he finally lands on the dusty street.
```

That was thirty-eight words. Now see how it reads with nineteen:

```
Sam leaps off the roof, drawing his Colts, dropping the
bandits in rapid succession before landing on the street.
```

The same action was described in both. In the first example I added several "action adjectives" which one might think would give the impression of speed or excitement to the description. In fact, what gives the greatest feeling of speed to the scene is being able to read it in half the time. So try to use as few words as you can to describe what you want the reader to see. But use enough so that he or she *can* see it!

Another thing that can happen if you use too many words to describe your scene is that your script can actually come out short. Using too many words will make your scenes appear to be longer, while the extra words, in fact, don't take up any more screen time. The above scene is only about 3 seconds long. The last thing you want when you turn in a script is to have the story editor tell you to go back and add more pages to bring it to length.

Cartoon pacing is generally fast. This is true for action like *Batman*, squash-and-stretch antics like *Bugs Bunny*, and even sitcoms like *The Simpsons*, with their rapid-fire jokes.

A simple rule to remember about pacing is to **make sure that the pacing of your script is as fast as it can be without detracting from what you are trying to communicate.**

Cutting is a part of pacing. A cut is the transition from one visual angle or perspective to the next. How you choose to cut from one scene to another, one angle to another, or from one character to another, affects the pacing of the script. Each slug line and shot you call out indicates a cut of some kind, regardless of whether or not you use the words CUT TO. The number of cuts (shots) you use creates a rhythm, like a drummer pounding his bass drum. This could be totally wrong for a quiet dialogue scene, while in an action sequence it might create a fast-paced, heart-pounding moment.

But description accounts for only half of your script. The other half is in the dialogue.

Chapter 9
Writing Dialogue

GOOD DIALOGUE IS HARDER TO WRITE than good description. Once you figure out how a scene will unfold it's not that difficult to describe what happens. But figuring out what a character will say in that scene isn't so obvious.

This book is not the place to go into a full dissertation on film and TV dialogue. Much of what needs to be known about dialogue writing is gleaned from years of experience, as well as reading novels and watching movies and TV. To a lucky few, it comes naturally. So instead of delving too deeply into the principles of dialogue, I am going to stick to the subject of cartoon dialogue.

Different types of animation require different treatments of dialogue. For prime-time toons, which are really just animated sitcoms, the dialogue is just sitcom dialogue. However, squash-and-stretch toons, like *Roadrunner* and *The Pink Panther*, don't have any dialogue at all. In between, there are many types of cartoons with as many types of dialogue, including action, comedy, educational, and preschool, among others. However, there are a few basic rules that will help you with any dialogue you write.

There are only two ways to really perceive a person's character: by what they say and by what they do. It is through actions and words that we learn what a person is about. Thus, **actions and dialogue define character.**

This at once tells you that **good dialogue must come out of the *personality* of the character who is saying it.** You wouldn't expect Homer Simpson to say "Don't have a cow, man!" Neither would you expect Bart to say "Doh!" This gives us one of the most basic rules of dialogue: **It should never be interchangeable.**

The test for this is simple: If you can give a line of dialogue to another character in the script then it obviously hasn't come out of the intended character's personality. It will thus seem flat and uninteresting. Well developed characters have unique ways of looking at life and unique ways of expressing themselves. This should come out in the dialogue whenever possible.

In the above *Ninja Turtles* script, notice that most of Donatello's dialogue comes from his more serious "techie" point of view, whereas most of Michaelangelo's dialogue comes from his comical "screwy-surfer-party-dude" character.

As noted earlier, when you're writing to a younger audience you have to be careful with the words you use in your dialogue. I always try to use the simplest words possible to say what needs to be said. If you have any doubt as to what words are acceptable to a certain age group you can get vocabulary word lists used in schools. But if you do use such word lists be careful; many kids don't know all the words they're supposed to.

Another thing to consider in writing dialogue for preschool kids and for educational material is repetition. Children may not understand something they hear the first time, but as they hear it again and again they slowly get it. Don't be afraid to repeat yourself in preschool material—just do it in a creative way.

With an older audience you need to make your dialogue more interesting and unusual to keep their attention. The bottom line is, **know your audience and make sure your dialogue is *real* to them.**

One of the most important things that any artist must learn is the ability to assume the point of view of their audience. This allows the artist to ensure that his communication is being received by the viewer. If you can't hear or see from your audience's viewpoint you'll never be sure that what you're trying to convey is really being conveyed. **The better you know your audience the better you'll be able to communicate to them.**

You may have seen how animators get into the character they're drawing, then look in a mirror at their wacky expressions. This helps them envision what they need to draw. This can also work for the writer. My wife has come into my office many times asking, "Are you talking to me, honey?" In fact, I was acting out the characters I was writing, both physically and with words. When I was writing the *Muppet Babies* series I learned to do the voices of all of the main characters. My kids still ask me to do Piggy and Kermit (though Gonzo is my favorite).

The more you can become the characters you are writing the better you will be able to create their moves and dialogue. Know your characters well, even if it means strutting around the room like a sponge in square pants!

There is a tendency in writing dialogue to want to make it hip. Anyone can write, "Jerry, look at that great skateboard," but it sounds much cooler to say "Dude! Scope the phat wheels!" Using contemporary slang references can make your writing seem much more current, but don't forget that this same dialogue may mean absolutely nothing in a just a few years. Studios want their cartoons to have a long shelf life. Look at Disney's features. They're a gold mine, and Disney re-releases them to theaters or video every seven years or so. One thing that can instantly date a cartoon is dialogue that is no longer meaningful. So be aware that there is a balance between hip dialogue and that which can survive over time and allow your toon to become a classic.

Again, animation is a visual medium. You don't want to spend too much time with what is euphemistically known in the toon business as *talking heads*. Other than animated sitcoms, you don't want to have your animated characters carrying on excessively long conversations, especially in cartoons for a younger audience. Two pages of non-stop dialogue, without some action to break it up, is too long. You don't "tell" stories in animation, you "show" them. If you need pages of dialogue, even in an action series like *Batman*, then chances are you haven't paced your story properly or are revealing too much at one time.

Never have dialogue for dialogue's sake. If you can see it in the action then do so, and don't explain it in dialogue. This will go a long way toward optimum pacing. Long speeches are guaranteed to slow your story down. Use only as much dialogue as need-ed to get your idea across, then move on. Short speeches keep the pacing fast and hold the audience's attention more effectively. **Dialogue should be as short as possible to get across whatever's necessary for the development of the story.**

"Actions speak louder than words" is very true in animation. **Show it, don't say it,** is a good, simple rule to apply whenever possible.

Dialogue Checklist

Below is a list of some of the main things that can be wrong with dialogue. You can study it to learn the correct elements of dialogue, or you can use it after you've written a script to check for problems.

- **Out of character**
- **Without character and thus interchangeable**
- **Does not further the story or character development**
- **Bland, ordinary, or uninteresting**
- **Inappropriate (for character, story, audience)**
- **Unnecessary ("When in doubt, leave it out!")**
- **Not funny (when it's supposed to be)**
- **Redundant**
- **Goes on too long**
- **Unclear (does not effectively communicate what is intended)**
- **Reveals something that would be better shown than said**
- **Describes action we can see (e.g. "Look! The bus went off the cliff!")**

Chapter 10
How to Write Funny Stuff

WHY DID THE ANIMATED CHICKEN cross the road? Because there was a big truck coming and cartoon violence is funny stuff. But what happens when that big truck tire hits that wide-eyed chicken? Figuring that out is where the fun is!

There's a term in our industry called cartoon logic. It means that no matter how wild something is, there's still got to be at least a little bit of sense, or physics, to it. An example of this would be a character running through a wire fence and suddenly sliding apart into a pile of slices. The logic goes sort of like this: if it works for a salami, it works for a toon character. This kind of logic is great fun, but it has, at its foundation, something that is not very funny at all—an understanding of the way things work, or logic. There's that word again. *Logic!* It may sound like a dry, boring, mathematical subject that has nothing whatsoever to do with humor. But, believe it or not, logic is at the root all of humor.

Humor is based on illogical sequences. You're not supposed to step on a rake head and have the handle *thwak* you in the face and react with a silly expression. It's not a logical thing to do, and that's why it's funny. The smarter the person who steps on the rake the more illogical, and thus the funnier it is!

It's not logical for a coyote to run off the edge of cliff, stop in mid air and look at the camera with dread—so we laugh. When was the last time you laughed at a man turning on the faucet and having water come out? Probably never—because it's perfectly logical. Yet it's not logical to have the water come out of his ears, and so we laugh at it.

This, by the way, tells you why you have to know your audience before you can write humor for them, and why they have to be educated. They have to know what's logical before they can understand, and laugh at, what isn't. This also tells you why physical comedy, such as slapstick, gets the most laughs. You don't have to be a Harvard Ph.D. to understand it.

Something happening where it's not supposed to, when it's not supposed to, in a way it's not supposed to, are all illogical, valid approaches to comedy. Conversely, things *not* happening when, where, and in a way they're supposed to are also funny. However, just being illogical doesn't make something funny. A man trying to cut grass by praying to the gods is tragic. A man trying to cut grass with a toenail clipper is funny. You have to be somewhat logical in your illogic. Start with something logical, like cutting grass with blades, then twist that into something illogical in order to make it funny.

To make dialogue funny you can set up a logical question or idea, then surprise the audience with an illogical (thus unexpected) response. For example, in my Turtles script, Michaelangelo, when referring to how hard it's going to be to find the kid, tells Raphael, "It's gonna be like finding a noodle in a haystack." When Raphael questions, "You mean *needle*, don't you?" Michaelangelo surprises us with his illogical answer, "I was trying to be optimistic, dude." It is illogical to think that a noodle in a haystack is going to be much easier to find than a needle.

When plotting a story, whether drama or comedy, make sure it's logical. When you're writing gags, make sure they're as illogical as possible.

There are two basic ways to make things funny in animation: visuals and dialogue. Writing funny dialogue is an extremely difficult thing to teach. But there are a few simple tips that may help.

Always try to put the funny concept of a speech at the very end. This may sound like a no-brainer, but it is possible to ruin the rhythm of a funny line by putting a few words after the gag. Take Woody Allen's classic line, "I always keep a bullet in my pocket in case someone throws a bible at me." This is a wonderful 180-degree spin on the not-at-all-funny concept of people being miraculously saved from a bullet by a bible in their pocket. It is superbly illogical, and thus brilliantly clever. But all you have to do to ruin it is put a word or two at the end, such as, "I always keep a bullet in my pocket in case someone throws a bible at me in church." With those two extra words the humor is lost. It's not because the word church cannot be funny. It's because the funny concept has been bypassed. The funny concept should be the only thing the viewer thinks about before laughing. Nothing else.

This is also useful in dramatic dialogue. **For real drama you want to end a speech or scene with the most dramatic concept being communicated.**

Visual comedy sequences are often called *sight gags*. A man's pants falling down is a sight gag. Charlie Chaplain and Buster Keaton were masters of the sight gag. If the Olympics gave awards for such nonsense they would both have a dozen gold medals, but so would Bugs Bunny, Goofy, Droopy, and many other famous toon characters. Sight gags work on the principles of illogic laid out above. Squash-and-stretch animation relies almost entirely on the sight gag. As a sitcom relentlessly hits the viewer with funny dialogue, so a squash-and-stretch toon hits the viewer with an unending stream of visual gags.

Sight gags emerge out of the environment that the characters find themselves in. This is why it's so important when writing the premise of a cartoon for the writer to choose the best possible location. An empty grass field wouldn't be the best place to locate a series of visual gags because there are so few props. A prop is anything that a character can use. In a grassy field all you've got is grass. Of course, if you're clever, and look deeper, you may find a few more things to play with. In the grass there are ants. Under the grass you might have gophers, sprinklers, or other bugs. It may be not be impossible to have humor on grass, but it's not the ideal environment. The ideal environment has loads of props around for fun and games.

Always think about the best location before laying out a gag scene. However, if the constraints of the story you're writing demand a certain location, then you must examine, to the best of your understanding, everything that could possibly be in that environment. Don't stop at the walls or floor. Look right through them. There may be pipes or wires or rats or people in the next room. All of these things are potential sources of humor.

For a fun drill, try to make a list of places that are full of fun props, such as a hardware store or a bowling alley. Next pick several places that are less obvious, like a coin-op laundry or a phone booth, and find all the props that might be there. This shows you again how important it is to be familiar with people, places, and things in life. If you've never been in a coin-op laundry you won't know what's there, and won't know how much fun you could be missing.

Not all gags come from the environment, though. Depending on what kinds of characters you're writing, you can likely get visual gags from them as well. Just as dialogue, funny or otherwise, comes from your characters, so can physical humor. Take Disney's Goofy for example. Though much of his humor came from the props in his environment, plenty also came from the wacky way in which he dealt with those things. His nose might twist into a spiral, his eyes might bug out, his arms and legs might get tied into a pretzel. Though this was physicality, it was really part of Goofy's personality.

Emotions can also be a source of physical humor. A waterfall of tears that fills up a room or anger that turns a character's head red hot with steam screaming from his ears are character derived.

A character's clothing can, like the environment, generate humor, such as a hat that keeps falling down and covering the eyes while driving, pants that keep falling down, or shoelaces tied together.

If you want a great example of how physical humor can come from character think of all the funny things that the Seven Dwarfs did in Disney's *Snow White*. These all came out of character.

There is an old tried-and-true way to make the most out of any visual gag. It is to build on the gag, escalating the humor a second and third time, then capping it with a funny twist at the end. For example, if you have a hungry cat trying to steal a snoozing canary out of a cage, he might first try the direct approach, reaching into the cage and getting his paw bitten as the canary wakes up. His second attempt might be a sneak attack by using a tiny acetylene torch to cut the bars behind the snoozing canary. This time the canary might be wise to the attempt and have placed a dummy canary on the perch, so he now jumps out from behind the seed bin and shoves the acetylene torch into the cat's mouth, inflating his head with flame. On his third try, the cat (bandaged, of course) goes all out. He wheels a barbecue under the cage and lights the coals. Ha! He'll cook the little yellow pest right where he swings. Then, just as the "canary" is turning red hot the real canary taps the cat on the shoulder, smiles, and flies off. The cat realizes something's up, takes a closer look at what's in the cage and realizes it's a stick of dynamite with yellow feathers glued on it.

KABOOM!

That was three gags in succession. To go past that would be overdoing the scene. But you could still put a *capper* on it. A capper is a final gag that caps the scene, often as a twist on the original intention. For example, with the cat and canary bit, a cute capper might be to see the cat eating paper cutout birds from a nature magazine. This caps the sequence with a gag that shows the change in the cat's intentions. He's lost the game and has settled for something less than his desired lunch.

Chapter 11
Feature, Internet, and Sample Scripts

S INCE DISNEY'S *The Lion King*, feature animation production has exploded in Hollywood. Every major studio has gotten into the market in a *big* way, spending anywhere from twenty-five to 150 million dollars for full-length animated features. However, before you get too excited and think that there's a feature out there with a blank "Written By" card waiting for your name, remember that this is a small industry. If every big studio produced two animated features a year it would mean only about fifteen scripts. It's a *very* competitive market for writers.

The holy grail of the Hollywood screenwriter is the million dollar spec screenplay sale. Spec is short for speculative, which means "engaged in risky business on the chance of quick or considerable profit." Thus, a spec script is one that a person writes on his or her own time—the risk—with the hopes of selling it to a studio—the quick and considerable profit. I have to confess to writing a spec or two with that goal in mind. Considering the fact that animated feature budgets can go upwards of $100,000,000, a million bucks for the script isn't out of the question.

Before you decide to rush out and write an animated feature spec script I need to throw a pail of ice cold water on you. Most animated features are written in house, meaning at a studio under the guidance of studio executives. This is true at all the major studios. I just did a quick, informal survey among the cartoon writers that I know and discovered a very interesting fact: to the best of my knowledge, as of this writing, no spec animated screenplay has ever been sold or produced. Even if I am wrong, and one has been sold, it means there are so few that even a working professional like myself hasn't heard about it.

If you've got your heart set on being the first to sell such a script, good luck. Just remember that selling your spec will be like winning the lottery. So prepare for rejection. If you're willing to spend five dollars on paper instead of a Lotto ticket, and pick 25,000 words instead of six numbers, then by all means go for it. Someone is going to sell an animated spec one day and it might as well be you.

Assuming you're still interested, there are several things to think about. First, choose the right story. Before you just dig an idea out of your bulging idea file or dream up something that sounds really cool, think about your audience, because I assure you, the studio exec you're going to try to sell your stuff to *already has*!

I'm not going to tell you that you can't sell that story you always wanted to write, but if you want to increase the odds of selling your project you have to find a story that a studio will want to buy—and they want to buy what sells. The first thing to do is look at what the public is buying.

This brings us to the audience. There are three distinct audiences for animated features: children, adults, and what is called "crossover" (in which you hope to appeal to both children and adults). Interestingly, there doesn't seem to be much of a teen audience at present. Apparently teens feel animation is kid stuff and would rather try to sneak into R-rated movies (though I suppose some teens enjoy watching racier animated features such as *Beavis & Butthead Do America* and *South Park—Bigger, Longer and Uncut*).

An example of children's features would be *Swan Princess* or *The Goofy Movie* or Disney's *Winnie the Pooh*. However, most animated features these days are attempting to cross over. There are really two types of crossover features: truly crossover stories like Disney's *Beauty and the Beast*, which work as well for adults as they do for kids, and the type of crossover features which the producer *hopes* the children's parents will like enough to maybe spread some good word of mouth. These aren't true crossovers, but really just a children's features with some added gags to keep the parents from falling asleep.

The reason so many producers are trying to make crossover features is that animated films are so expensive that they generally have to get a crossover market to make their money back. The liability is that you can sometimes miss the children *and* the adults and wind up with something in the middle that no one wants to watch.

Perhaps if budgets were reduced then animated features could be directed at more specific audiences, including teens and adults. I, for one, have always felt that the adult feature animation market will someday break wide open in the U.S., as it has on prime-time TV, but there hasn't been similar success in features yet. Mark my words, though. The huge Japanese anime market will someday cross the Pacific and *American Anime* will be born.

The story content of animated features that sell well is amazingly predictable. That's because most (though thankfully not all) animated features are based on classical material or historical characters, as five out of Disney's last six features and so many of the new releases from the other studios were.

One of the reasons for this might be that classical stories have a built-in pre-sold quality. We're all familiar with them and want to see them again and again. If you've got a great take on a classic that hasn't been done in a while, that's a safer way to go. On the other hand, *Toy Story* was certainly a fresh idea, so don't look at this as an ironclad rule.

Though it means risking some money, another way to help sell an animated feature is to *option* a piece of existing material—a children's book, novel, old movie, even the use of a living or dead celebrity likeness. This, like a classic, makes your story more familiar and "user friendly."

A buzzword you often hear bandied about in Hollywood is *high concept*. You could define high concept as a particularly clever or unique idea which, summed up in a sentence or two, creates an interesting image. An example of a high concept animated movie would be *Toy Story*. The one-sentence pitch might have been: In a bedroom full of living toys, the arrival of a child's new space action-figure causes his "old favorite" cowboy doll to jealously get rid of the intruder, only to learn the true meaning of friendship.

As you can see, it is not so much the plotting or character relationship that makes this high concept, but rather the unique arena—living toys. Personally, I don't believe that every story has to be reducible to one sentence. But if you can't sum it up in a short paragraph then you can bet it's not high concept.

Another thing to consider when choosing a story for an animated feature is the medium. We now have several choices of how animated feature stories can be told: conventional cel animation, CG (computer generated animation), paper cutout, clay, or in many cases, a combination. Hardly any features these days are done purely in cel animation. Disney has put at least one CG scene in all of their features since *The Little Mermaid*. DreamWorks's *Prince of Egypt*, which was generally cel animated, had a multitude of "miraculous" CG effects. *Toy Story* is an example of full CG that worked wonderfully because it was not only exquisite animation but had a terrific story as its basis.

The difficulty of choosing CG as the medium of your animated feature is that there are only certain stories that lend themselves to this form. As of this writing, human characters are only marginally believable in CG, whereas anything inanimate, such as dolls, robots, or toasters, work quite well. Even bugs and aliens can be acceptable. But if your story is primarily about human characters I'd stay away from full CG until the state of the art improves.

Will Vinton, the Academy-Award winning producer of the clay-animated theatrical short, *Closed Mondays*, made Claymation a household word. Claymation is stop-motion animation using clay for the characters, hardware, and environment. His latest TV production, *The PJ's*, is produced in Foamation, which uses foam characters.

The *South Park* movie is an example of CG animation made to look like paper cutout. The *South Park* series and feature have proved that it doesn't matter how you animate your project so long as the content is entertaining.

You should pick the medium that best suits your story. For example, most squash and stretch characters lend themselves to cel animation, as do stories with realistic human characters. Stories with objects as characters or geometrical life forms (like bugs or aliens) can work well in CG. If your story is very quirky you could use paper, clay, or one of the many other forms of animation.

There'$ one e$pecially $ignificant $ubject I always$ $tre$$ writer$ $hould con$ider fir$t before $tarting a $creenplay. Wanna gue$$ what it i$?

That's right—money! Or in Hollywood parlance, budget. A budget is how much money a production company has decided it can afford to spend on a project and still have a chance of making some profit. If you ignore the budget on a project you're writing you can have your idea shot down in a "Hollywood second" (the time it takes the word "No" to get from a studio exec's lips to your ears).

It's likely you'll be pitching your idea to someone who is going to be thinking about how much it's going to cost. You don't want to be caught with a $200 million idea when pitching to a company with $20 million to spend. Of course, knowing what an animated feature is going to cost is like knowing how much a gray suit costs. Depends on who makes it, and whether it's sold in Frostbite, Alaska, or Beverly Hills.

Any scene can be animated inexpensively, but our audiences today are used to some pretty spectacular stuff. So if you call for something spectacular it's either going to cost a lot, or look like doo-doo. I'm not suggesting to have your animated feature budgeted before you pitch it, but if you're going to call for lots of amazing visual effects you must at least have an idea of what ballpark the studio is playing in.

Writing an Animated Feature

Once you've chosen your idea, it's time to write an outline, or as they're often called in Hollywood, a *treatment*. A treatment is an outline of your story, including a description of most, if not all, of the scenes, the major characters, and possibly a few examples of choice dialogue. Where an outline lays out all the beats, a treatment can sometimes be more of a description of a movie, as if you're selling it rather than telling it.

A feature treatment is similar to a television outline. However, feature stories are longer and thus have a more expanded story structure and more extensive character development. There are several good books on film story structure which could help the animation writer with general story construction. I strongly suggest you read several of these books and glean from them the information that feels workable to you—but beware! You may find some of the concepts contradictory, which only means that different writers have found different techniques that work for them. Toon writing is not calculus, so use what makes sense to you and don't worry about the rest. The important thing is to find anything that helps you to start creating and organizing your thoughts.

There are three possible reasons to write a feature treatment, all of which you should be aware of before you start writing. The first, and most obvious, is so your story is laid out for when you eventually write the script. This would actually be more of a beat outline. The second reason for writing a treatment is so that you have a well thought out, coherent story that you can pitch to a prospective buyer. I'll discuss how to pitch your story in a later chapter. The final, and perhaps most important reason to write a great treatment, is to have something to leave behind when you pitch your story. To this end, your treatment should be an interesting read, not just the dry beats written down in order. It's a sales tool, and as such, anything within it that might help sell the story, and sell you as a writer, is valid.

A feature treatment can be anywhere from ten to thirty or more pages. Any shorter than ten and it will probably fall into the category of a *presentation* or synopsis rather than a treatment. A presentation is something that just presents your story concept in a summarized fashion without going into every scene. You can write a presentation before you write a treatment, and you can, if you're good, pitch your story from a presentation. The problem is that, if you haven't worked out all the story beats and *charac-*

ter arcs, you may be caught flat-footed when an exec asks you a question about your story or characters. So unless you're an established writer or are pitching to someone who knows you very well, I would write a full treatment.

The form of an animated feature screenplay is identical to a live-action feature screenplay. The content is almost the same, but there are always two things that must be done in any good animated feature script: First, you must remember that it is a *visual* medium. Thus, the story should emphasize, where applicable, aesthetic vistas, breathtaking action, and, ideally, events that either couldn't be done in live action (though almost anything can with CG) or would cost zillions. Second, the animated script generally has a bit more "directing" in it. Again, this is because animation is such a visual medium and often needs more description.

An animated feature screenplay looks pretty much the same as the *Ninja Turtles* script in Chapter 7. Although this is a TV script, the form is close enough. You can vary it slightly, leaning toward more of a master scene approach, but it's really a matter of choice rather than rule.

Live-action features are generally considered to be one page of script for each minute of screen time. You won't go wrong if you use this rule for your animated feature. The reason feature scripts are one page per minute and TV cartoon scripts are closer to 1 $\frac{1}{2}$ pages per minute is because motion-picture productions have more money and time to turn a script page into animation. There is more time to explore the emotions of characters, more time to direct an exciting action sequence, and more time to milk the gags. With the hectic pace of television cartoon production, there is little time for all this, so they try to cram more action and fun into every second of screen time (probably to keep the kids hypnotized so they won't change the channel).

There is a great deal more to feature writing, but because the structure and content of animated feature screenplays are so similar to live-action screenplays, the best way to learn more about the subject is to study general screenwriting. But no matter what form of animation you're interested in, there is one thing you absolutely must write...

Writing a Sample Script

Despite the difficulty of selling a spec script, you won't be wasting your time if you write a good one. Why? Because the real value in a good spec screenplay or TV script comes from using it as a *sample*.

A sample is a script written with the intention of giving it to someone as an example of your work. It's purpose is not necessarily to sell, but rather to show the producer or story editor that you are good enough for them to take a chance on and give you a script assignment.

Very few animated features are conceived by a writer, but rather, the concept comes from someone at the studio, such as a producer or executive. They only hire a writer once they decide to make it. If these people have read your sample script, and liked it, they might just pick you to write their feature screenplay. This is where a good sample script is worth its weight in gold.

A spec animated feature is always something that's for sale if someone wants it, but a spec TV script may not always be possible to sell. For example, if you write a spec script for a series that subsequently goes off the air, you'll never be able to sell it. But you could still use it as a sample, at least until that series becomes so dated that no one cares about it anymore.

In choosing which animated series to write your sample for, the first thing to take into consideration is your skill. What are you best at writing? Comedy? Action? Preschool? Whatever it is, write your sample for that genre. The second thing to think about is what you most like to write? Why isn't writing what you're passionate about the most important thing? Because, if you sell a script you're in the game, and then you can write what you love. However, if you write what you love, but aren't good at, you may never get in the game at all. A good rule to remember is, **first write what *they* want, then write what *you* want.**

There's another important rule when it comes to writing sample scripts. **Never write a sample for the show you want to write for.** This may sound ridiculous at first, but upon further examination it will become clear. If you write a spec *Simpsons* script and submit it to the *Simpsons* staff, they, knowing more about the *Simpsons* than anyone on Earth, will see every little thing that's wrong with your script. Thus, they will probably come away with the feeling that you cannot write for the show. However, if you submit a *King of the Hill* script to the *Simpsons* show, they probably won't have as much of a working knowledge and will be more likely to simply see what's funny in your script. If they think it's good they might just give you a shot at a script.

It's a good idea to write a sample TV script in as many genres as you are capable of writing well. In other words, write a half-hour action-adventure, a half-hour animated sitcom, an eleven-minute reality show, and a seven-minute squash and stretch toon. The more types of samples you have the more shows you can submit to.

Don't make the mistake of thinking that any good script will get you work on any show. Many producers and network execs are extremely myopic when it comes to genre, and many feel that, even if you've written a good comedy sample, you may not be able to write action. So have them all.

Of course, television and film are not the only playgrounds for animation writers. There's a vast new market unfolding that may someday require more cartoon scripts than at any time in our short entertainment history! Can you guess what market I'm talking about? Let me give you a hint.com

Writing Animation for the Internet

As of this writing, the Internet is the frontier of animation. No one knows for sure exactly how it's going to work in terms of distribution, but everyone is certain that the Internet is going to explode as soon as the bandwith increases. Even though I've worked on Internet toons, there isn't much useful information I can give you in this area because by the time you read this the market will have morphed into something entirely different.

At present, animation on the Internet consists of very short, very simple, and very inexpensively produced cartoons. Being short and inexpensive, there will be a lot of them. I believe this will open new vistas of opportunity for cartoon writers, especially neophytes. Remember, the less money at risk on a script the more likely producers are to take a chance on a new writer. So look to the Internet for a good way to break into toon writing. You may not get paid much, but who knows? Those few pennies of stock options might someday be worth a million bucks!

As for the techniques of writing Internet animation, the market is just too young to have any hard and fast rules yet. Most of what they're buying and broadcasting now is edgy, irreverent comedy for around the eighteen to thirty-year-old market. Because the scripts are short there is no time for character development or story arc (unless you're writing serialized stories that continue over time). Thus, Internet series are very simple in form.

The only rule is "there are no rules." Anything goes. It's virgin territory, and you've got just as much chance of staking a claim to it as anyone else.

Although I can't say much with certainty about this new and wonderful medium, I do believe that in the near future many more websites around the world will begin to use animated cartoons just like newspapers use the funny pages—to lure people to their sites or their advertising. There could be lots of animation writing in the future for those who learn to effectively write short animated cartoons.

The best way to know what's currently happening is to just go online and search for the hottest Internet toon sites. Contact the sites and see what they're buying, or find out what studio produced their stuff and ask them. And if all else fails, create your own cartoons and put them on your own website.

There's one more small animation market and that's direct-to-video features. The budgets are sometimes very low, though I've heard of some going as high as $8,000,000. I'm sure Disney's are even higher. So you might want to check into the studios' various home video units.

Now that we've looked at TV script writing, animated features, the Internet, and video, what else is there? If you're looking for the big game, the big money, and the really big challenge, the next chapter is for you!

Chapter 12
Creating an Animated Series

INSTEAD OF WRITING A SAMPLE cartoon script with the hope of getting work on someone else's series, many people choose to go for the "grand slam" and create their own animated series. If this is the game you want to play, here are some pointers that may prevent you from falling into the holes that are waiting for you.

Over the years, many people have contacted me with animated series ideas which they've dreamed of selling. Some of these ideas were, I'm afraid to say, terrible. Others weren't bad creatively, but were nonetheless impossible to sell. This is because it takes more than just a good idea to sell a series. There are several elements that must be present before a series concept is going to be seriously considered.

When you're setting out to create an animated series the first thing you need to ask is, "Who is my audience?" There are distinct demographics to consider when choosing your audience. With respect to the youth market they are: Toddlers (0-3), Preschoolers (2-5), Kids (6-8), Tweens (9-12), and Teens (13-15). There are also various adult ranges.

Many people make the mistake of laboring over an idea they like without carefully considering the age of their audience. What they often wind up with is a show that cannot be sold because there is no audience for it. An example of this might be a series directed at teens who, demographically speaking, aren't watching TV.

So before you begin to create your series make sure you know what audience it is being created for, that this audience does, in fact, exist, and that all of the elements of the show work for that age group.

I certainly don't want to tell you what kind of show to create. I also don't want to suggest that there is a simple formula for creating good series. Many new shows are totally unique, and don't fit any mold. *South Park* wasn't like anything else on the air, but it became a huge hit. There are no hard and fast rules about how to pick a winning series concept. But there are some factors that, if considered, may give you a better chance at selling your show.

There are two basic ways to come up with series ideas. One is to look at what's on the air (the follow-the-leader method). The other is to just ignore what's being bought and create exactly what you want (the leader-who-gets-followed method). Being a leader is always harder than being a follower, but always has a bigger payoff. *ER* became a smash-hit and *Chicago Hope* soon followed. Right after *Pokémon* went through the roof, *Digimon* came out close behind. There are generally more followers than leaders. You'll have to decide who you are.

If you're a trendsetter, you don't need my help. Just go for it! But if you're a trend surfer, perhaps the most important thing you can do to increase your chances of selling a series is to find out what the broadcasters are looking for. It can be terribly discouraging to spend months creating a show only to discover that everyone in the industry is looking for something totally different. Unfortunately, it's not easy to find out what networks are looking for. This is really the job of an agent. Of course, the Catch-22 is that you can't get an agent until you've created a good series concept, but you can't find out what to create unless you have an agent. Fortunately, there are ways around this dilemma.

One way to choose a concept for a series is to look at what's getting high ratings on the air. The problem with this method is that it's possible that, if there are several such shows already on the air, you may have already missed the wave, and that type of show may be on its way out. However, it's a good bet that if there is a *new* hit series on the air, other networks will be looking to buy a show from within that same genre. After *Rugrats* became a huge hit, several new "baby" shows soon followed in its wake.

The pendulum swings in the animation industry, so you'll find boys' action is hot for a while, then it fades and comedy is hot. Sometimes buyers will all want pre-sold ideas, like popular toy products, then a few years later everyone wants fresh ideas created by newcomers. If you have a great series idea, but they're not buying it right now, just put it on the shelf and wait till the pendulum swings back your way.

Another way to create a series is to option an existing property. You might find a successful, but not hugely popular, series of children's books, or a new comic book and, for a small option payment, secure the rights and develop it into a series. The reason I say "not hugely successful" is that, if a property is a smash-hit, the chances are good that a major studio is going to buy it for a very high price. You've got to be clever and look for properties that have a following in a niche market that the masses haven't caught onto yet. Maybe a property that was successful thirty years ago is ready to be refreshed. *Men In Black*, for example, was a relatively obscure comic book before it became a blockbuster movie and animated series.

Existing properties can be found in the publishing market (books, comic books, comic strips), in the toy market, in the gift or greeting card market, and elsewhere. You might even find a property that is hidden within another property. *Muppet Babies*, for example, started out as a single scene within a live-action Muppet movie.

Let's assume you've got a terrific idea for an animated series. What do you do with it?

Developing Your Concept

Once you come up with an idea for a series, or option a property, you have to develop it. In TV-*ese*, developing means expanding a concept into a fleshed-out series, complete with format, characters, and story ideas, capable of lasting for several years on television.

Sound complicated? *Nah!*

A series, like life, is really an amazingly simple thing in terms of structure. It is comprised solely of characters and an environment. Nothing else. If your characters—their goals, jobs, motivations, etc.—are properly laid out, then *they* will embody what your series is about. This may sound too simple, so let's take a quick look at it.

Let's use the animated *Batman* series as an example. If you fully describe who the characters are, both the good guys and bad, and what their goals are, then what else is there "about" the series to describe (other than the environment and its hardware)? How Batman uses his weapons? This is really part of his character. Which villains he goes after? This is determined by his motivations and theirs. Why he does what he does? When he does it? Where? To whom? All are determined by Batman's personal motives. There's nothing there other than characters and environment.

This tells us at once that **the characters are the heart and soul of any series**. It also tells us why the hardest things to do (and teach) are creating and developing good characters—because it's *all* in the characters.

It is the characters that the audience is interested in. It is the characters that make them feel and think. It is the characters that make them laugh or cry. It is the characters that will ultimately bring them back again to watch another episode. (Or not!)

What is a character? With respect to animation, a character is a person, animal, or other living entity, who acts and reacts to other characters and things in a unique way. Every character, no matter how simple, has a point of view—a unique way of looking at and dealing with life. Although a person's point of view can be very complex, it doesn't have to be in order to make an interesting character.

Most good cartoon characters have simple yet precise points of view. Wile E. Coyote simply wants to catch and eat the roadrunner. He's very clever, very, very persistent, and very, very, very unlucky. Goofy was just a goofball and utter klutz, who was totally oblivious to the fact.

Series with human (or humanoid) characters tend to have slightly more complex characters than these, but they are still not very complicated. The Ninja Turtles are good examples. Although the characters may have developed a little more depth as the animated series evolved, you can define each in a short sentence. Leonardo is the caring leader. Donatello is the more analytical and technically minded one. Raphael is the sarcastic jokester, and Michaelangelo is the carefree surfer-dude.

All you need in terms of a character's point of view is enough personality so that he or she can act and react to the world in a unique (with respect to the other characters in the show) and interesting way.

There are two basic types of characters in animation. Real ones and cartoony ones. Real characters in animation, such as Batman or Bart Simpson, are treated pretty much the same as they are in live-action. Cartoony characters, on the other hand, such as Daffy Duck or SpongeBob SquarePants, are entirely different animals.

With respect to cartoony characters, the basic rule is *there are no rules*. If it's funny, it's okay. Cartoony characters are as broad ranging as our imaginations. Anything is fair game for a wild and crazy cartoon character. Just give them a silly point of view—like Johnny Bravo's overblown Elvis-tinted ego—and they're off and running.

Realistic characters, on the other hand, have some basic elements that, if understood and developed properly, can make them much richer and more interesting. Perhaps the simplest way to look at any real character is as a contrast of *need* and *want*. To define these two terms so we can differentiate them, *need* is a lack of something that is required, such as air or food. *Want* means to desire greatly or wish for, as to want a thick chocolate malt. Need is intimately related to survival, whereas want has more to do with happiness or personal gratification.

With respect to characters, need is usually represented as something the character requires in order to become a better person. For example, an alcoholic needs to be sober; a greedy person needs to learn to be more giving. Want is usually expressed as something the character desires, which he thinks will make him happier. In fact, it is always the need which, if fulfilled, will truly make the character happier (just as it is in real life).

In Disney's *Beauty and the Beast*, the beast wanted to become a good looking young man again, but he needed to learn to see the beauty within himself and others. In *Toy Story*, Woody wanted to remain the favorite toy (i.e. be loved as a best friend), but he needed to learn how to be a true friend and thus become worthy of such love. It is the balance and contrast between need and want that makes an interesting character.

Cartoony characters, unlike real characters, don't necessarily have a conflict between their needs and wants. Take Wile E. Coyote again. He wants only one thing—the roadrunner. The thing he needs is brains, but this is simply an excuse to create humor, not a real character flaw that is going to be explored.

The exploration of a character's needs and wants is generally better suited to longer stories, such as novels or features. In animated series, need and want can be problematic.

A character arc is essentially the path of change a character takes in the course of a story. In terms of need and want, the character often lets go of his want and fulfills his need, ultimately becoming a better and happier person. In almost all animated series there is no real expression of character arc in the stories. Sometimes you may see an arc over a period of an entire season, or it might even take three or four seasons. Some shows have no arc whatsoever. The reason for this general lack of character arc is that, if the main character were to fulfill his need, the series would be over. Although you can explore a number of ways in which your character stumbles and recovers due to his basic need-want conflict, you cannot fully resolve it. This point is also valuable in terms of secondary characters, because there is nothing stopping you from fully resolving their character conflicts.

As a general rule, **the younger the audience the shallower the characters, and the more their needs and wants converge.** Children, after all, are too busy learning about life to be interested in, or understand, any of life's weightier character problems.

The above is a very simple and cursory view of the makeup of character and character arc. There is much more that can be learned about the subject. But what I have laid out should give you enough of an understanding to get you started developing and writing animated characters. Why is it enough? Because most cartoon characters, save for those in feature films, are as shallow as the 2-D cels they're painted on.

In our world of vast media conglomerates with their unquenchable thirst for dollars, one thing that you may want to consider when creating a series is its merchandising potential. A *toyetic* property is one that will lead to a demand for lots of toys and ancillary products. *Toy Story* is the *ne plus ultra* in a toyetic movie. *Teenage Mutant Ninja Turtles* was an equally toyetic cartoon series.

One can still create a series simply for its intrinsic entertainment value, but many studios need licensing revenue to make a profit. These studios will definitely respond better to toyetic projects.

It used to be that only animation writers created new (non-pre-sold) series. More recently it has become the norm for artists to both develop and sell series. If you are a writer, you might want to consider partnering with an artist who can bring your writing to life. It is, after all, a visual medium. An artist can bring an entirely new dimension to the written word. Alternatively, if you are an artist who has created a series, you may want to consider partnering with someone who can bring more structured story and character to your artistic creation, and thus look for a good writer. Ultimately, animated television series are a combination of writing and art. Thus, by packaging these two elements together at the inception, one can enhance the concept and increase the chance of a sale.

Speaking of *package*, this word has a unique meaning in the entertainment industry. A package is two or more of the creative *elements* of a project already put together. An element is one of the creative principals of an entertainment project, such as a writer, director, animator, producer, or actor. Packaging means bringing together these creative people to enhance the project *before* you sell it.

The more and bigger elements you have signed to your project, the more powerful your package becomes. If you can tell a studio that Tom Hanks has agreed to do the voice of your lead character, you're a lot closer to selling your project. Similarly, an award-winning composer or animator attached to a project can help considerably. Anyone with creative credentials can be an asset to your project.

The reason packaging is so important is that each element of a package gives greater assurance to the buyer that the project will be a success. If you, as a neophyte writer, bring in a wonderful series concept, there's still no guarantee that the studio can turn it into a hit. But if you've already got a name actor and artist attached, you're closer to the target.

Of course, getting name talent attached to a project if you're a no-name yourself isn't easy. But if you're clever and persistent, you might be able to find some talented people who, when attached to your project, can help you sell it.

So now you've got some idea of the ingredients needed to make an animated series. The next step is to mix these ingredients in your creative blender and turn them into something that can be sold.

Chapter 13

Writing a Presentation, Bible, and Pilot

THE BASIC STEPS OF ANIMATED TV series development are concept, presentation, *bible*, and *pilot*.

The concept is just the basic idea for the series, summed up in a sentence or two. Once you have it you've got to mold it into something sellable. This brings us to the presentation.

An animated series presentation generally consists of two parts: the written presentation and the artwork. The written presentation can be any length, but is generally from five to fifteen pages, double spaced. It describes what the series is about, and who the characters are, so that the reader will become interested in it and want to know more. Although it's possible to sell a series from a presentation, the purpose of a presentation is usually not to sell the series, but to get a *development deal*. When a network or studio makes a development deal they usually pay for a bible, pilot, and maybe some additional artwork. So in order to get them to give you a development deal you want to excite them about the property. This is the purpose of the presentation's written material and art.

The presentation art can be as simple as a single drawing of a character, or as elaborate as a fully rendered painting of a scene from the series. If money is no object, then more artwork can be done, and even three-dimensional sculptures can be made of the characters. I once made a presentation that included a full bible and $25,000 worth of artwork, sculptures, and toy prototypes. But you don't need all the bells and whistles to sell a series. I once made a two sentence, off-the-cuff pitch while walking out the door. Oddly enough, I sold the two-sentence pitch and not the $25,000 one, which goes to show you that it really comes down to the basic concept.

How to Write a Bible

In the beginning was the word. Then it was edited.

If you're thinking about playing Cartoon God and creating an animated world, or you've already done so and want to get it into the proper form, here's what you need to know.

A bible is a complete description of a series. Like the one you find in so many motel room drawers, an animated series bible has four basic parts: the world, the characters, the stories, and the format, which describes how all of these things interrelate to form a coherent series.

THE WORLD: An animated series bible lays out the time and place of the series, including important locations that are an integral part of the show. As part of the world, a bible might describe significant vehicles and other hardware to be used on a continuing basis.

In writing the bible for *Jim Henson's Muppet Babies* I described the nursery in which the babies lived, including such key elements as the bookshelf, Rowlf's piano, Piggy's vanity, and the window seat with toy drawer. All of these elements were key to the environment and designed to allow the babies to play out stories within the nursery.

In most series there are recurring locations and props. Examples would be the living room and backyard play area in *Rugrats*, as well as their Reptar wagon. In *PB&J Otter*, there is the dock and the boats along it. In the case of the *Muppet Babies* we only had the nursery. The rest of the babies' world (except for occasional forays into the basement, attic, and kitchen) were all in their imaginations.

THE CHARACTERS: Most bibles go into some detail about who the characters are, including their backgrounds, their goals and motivations, their emotional tone, their look and dress, and perhaps most importantly, how they relate to other characters within the series.

In the *Muppet Babies* bible each of Jim Henson's muppet characters had to be described as toddlers. What would Kermit be like as a baby? How would Piggy's total self-absorption manifest at four years of age? What kind of jokes would a baby Fozzie tell? And how would the familiar interrelationships of the grown muppets translate to little kids? All of these had to be determined and described.

THE STORIES: One of the most important things the buyer wants to know about a series is whether it will yield a lot of good stories. Thus, a bible contains anywhere from a half dozen, to an entire series worth of story ideas. These are not full stories, but either springboards, which are just a paragraph notion, or premises.

Stories in bibles need to be excellent examples of what episodes will be like, and must show how all of the elements of your series will come together. Generally, it is one of these story ideas that will be used as the pilot episode.

THE FORMAT: There are basically two parts to the format. The first part deals with the content of the show. What is the series about? How do the characters work into the stories? What is the theme of the series? Is it comedy? Action-adventure? All of these questions and more need to be answered in the format.

With the *Muppet Babies*, for example, the format described how each episode would begin in the nursery where the babies would find themselves facing some problem. Through a succession of four or five independent story elements, each imagined by a different muppet character, the problems would slowly be confronted and resolved. The theme of the show was imagination. We wanted to show how wonderfully imaginative kids could be, and how they can solve their physical and emotional problems by imagining possible outcomes. This theme also bled over into the second part of the format, which is context.

Context is not the setting (which is included under the World), it's the artistic and physical form that the production will be set in. How long are the episodes? Will it be cel animation, paper cutouts, CG, or clay? Is music an important part of the show? What is the age of the intended audience?

For *Muppet Babies* I specifically noted in the bible that the babies' imaginations should be expressed in various artistic techniques depending on the character. For example, when we told stories from the point of view of Animal's imagination, to express the fact that he was the youngest of the group we used crayon backgrounds. For Gonzo, the weirdest of the babies, we often used strange and incongruous photographic or live-action backgrounds, such as clips from 1950s B-movies. I also described a song element in every story, as well as a never-before-done thirty-second comical tag that came *after* the final credits.

Other questions that could be answered are: Who is your intended audience? Is there an educational curriculum? Is there an interactive element?

There are many ways to structure a bible, so don't worry about it being properly formatted like a script. The most important thing is for it to be well thought out and written professionally. I generally start with some kind of short overview of the series, so that the reader gets a quick picture of what the show is all about. This might include a cursory description of the main characters and the general environment and format. Next, I get right into describing the characters in more detail, each with their own section. I follow this with sections on the world and hardware (if any). I then put all of this together by fully describing the content portion of the format, after which I might have a page or two on the context, if appropriate. Next come the story ideas. And finally, I add a very short page to summarize and possibly excite the reader one last time.

An additional (and optional) part of a bible is the *backstory*. A backstory is a description of events that take place prior to when the series begins. Perhaps the best example of a backstory is Superman's. Because it was such a wonderful story, the backstory was told in the first *Superman* movie starring Christopher Reeve, even though it was never shown in the *Superman* TV series from the 1950s.

Regardless of whether it's used in the series or not, knowing the backstory serves to help the writers (and buyer) understand the characters and their motivations. Knowing, for example, that Superman was found and adopted by George and Martha Kent may give rise to story ideas involving the Kents, or to personal motivations or reactions in Superman himself.

With regard to its physical form, a bible can be anywhere from fifteen to thirty pages or more. As with presentations, many bibles contain artwork of the characters, locations, hardware, or other vital story elements. This is not necessary but, as noted, if you can draw, or afford to pay someone who can, artwork can help to effectively communicate the essence of your animated series, especially if the designs are unique and fun. Finding artists is pretty easy. If you don't know any you can go to the nearest art school and usually find some students who will work for peanuts. If you have the funds, you can get a copy of the *LA* or *New York Work Book*, which lists professional artists and illustrators of all kinds. You can even search out artists on the Internet. Find the style you're looking for and give their reps a call.

On some occasions, a writer may want to do a bible and/or pilot as part of the pitch. The plus side of this is that the buyer knows exactly what he's going to get, so you may be able to bypass the development process if you hit the mark. This is especially important for new writers entering the business, whom a buyer may not trust to deliver a quality bible. The down side is that it pretty much carves your concept in stone, and if it's not exactly what the buyer is looking for you may not get a chance to develop it further. In general, though, I recommend that new writers take the time to write a full bible for a series they want to sell.

The best way to understand what a bible consists of, technically and creatively, is to read one. I've included one for a series I created. If you happen to be into extreme sports, or extreme milkshakes, you may have seen a funny looking, yellow-haired character with sunglasses smiling at you from the waxy container of a *Wacky Willie Extreme Shake*. Wacky Willie was the brainchild of dairy marketing whiz Shane Donavan. He needed a character to adorn the cool milkshake he had created and, with the help of artist Eddie Young, created Willie. To everyone's surprise, the shakes sold like hotcakes (there's a simile that'll give you indigestion). It turned out the kids buying the shakes liked his little character so much, Shane decided to expand Willie's horizons. He found an agent, who found two producers, Karin Levinson and Kathy Porter of Whirlwind Pictures, who found me. Just like everyone else, I immediately fell in love with Willie and his lightning bolt eyebrows and agreed to create an animated series around him. Thus, *The Extreme Adventures of Wacky Willie* was born.

The Extreme Adventures of
Wacky Willie

Created By

Jeffrey Scott

Whirlwind Pictures, Inc. / By Jeffrey Scott, Inc.

IMAGINE FERRIS BUELLER in Bermuda shorts, sunglasses, sandals, and with a shock of yellow hair that makes Bart Simpson's look like it needs Viagra.

You've just imagined Wacky Willie, the coolest 14-year-old ever to *ollie into a frontside slider.*[1]

Willie lives in sunny Southern California, in a suburban seaside community called *Burrito Beach,* named for its big waves which, if you're not careful, can wrap you up like so many refried beans.

Ordinary kids in Burrito Beach endure school, suffer through their homework, and hang at the mall.

Sure, Willie and his friends go to school and do their homework. And sometimes they even go so low as to hang at the mall. But unlike ordinary kids, Willie and his friends haven't surrendered to the dull routine of life. They've found "the way."

They've found *extreme sports.*

Definition of an EXTREME Sport:

A recreational activity that is out of the ordinary, thrilling, and has an element of risk involved

Willie's definition of an EXTREME Sport:

ANYTHING HE DOES!

Just how extreme is Willie?
Read on...

1. For the uninitiated, this means to make your skateboard virtually fly off the pavement and onto a stair rail, then slide down the rail, balancing on the belly of your board. [These footnotes appeared in the original bible.]

Extreme Characters

The most extreme thing about *The Extreme Adventures of Wacky* Willie is its characters...

Wacky Willie

Willie is *extremely* cool!

He's a twenty-first century mixture of Bart Simpson and Ferris Bueller who's totally addicted to *the rush!*

What's *the rush*? It's that totally alive, totally in the moment, exhilarating feeling one gets from extreme sports. And Willie can't get enough of it.

Unfortunately, Willie's need for extreme goes waaaaay beyond sports, and gets him into more than his share of *extreme* trouble. It's not that he's a bad kid. It's just that he can't stop himself from going "over the top" in everything he does.

A normal kid might skateboard down a steep hill and think it was pretty cool. Not Willie. He'd have to "expand the envelope" and skateboard down the face of a hydro-electric dam—more than likely shorting out the power in the city in the process. If his friends made a bet to see who could eat the most pizza, Willie would simply <u>have</u> to win, and stuff an entire mega pizza into his little tummy, then blow "pepperoni chunks" all over the place. Or if Willie was playing the lead in a school play of "Camelot," he'd switch his lance for a pair of boxing gloves, then tease his hair out so he looked like "Don King Arthur!"

Get the picture?

Willie's Achilles' heel is that he doesn't know—or want to know—where to set his limits. Like Michael J. Fox in *Back to the Future*, who couldn't let anyone tell him he was chicken without proving he wasn't, Willie just can't let someone even suggest he isn't capable of doing something extreme. Sometimes this gets him into *major trubs*[2].

Willie preaches what he practices, and is as extreme with his words as he is with his actions. He's always embellishing the truth to fit his own extreme point of view, and often expresses himself with cool sayings, like:

2. Big troubles.

Dictate Your Destiny!

Willie's way of saying "be the master of your universe."

Immortality Now!

used as an exclamation—like *Banzai!*—when Willie's about to do something really extreme.

What's the RUSH?

two meanings: first, spoken as an admonition when someone's being impatient and not very Zen ("Have another taco, bro. What's the rush?); second, used as a question when asking what it is that makes something exciting ("So you jump off a bridge with cords tied to your ankles. But what's the ruuush?").

I've Got The Urrrrge For Surrrrge!

Willie says this when he gets an "extreme attack."

E=Xtreme²

(pronounced *E equals extreme squared*) This is used to show great admiration, usually for something or someone that's extremely extreme.

Willie's focus in life is *the rush*. But to have extreme fun one sometimes needs extreme "funds," so to earn a few *Benjamins*[3], Willie does what he likes to call "extreme odd jobs," like cutting lawns by surfing on a lawn mower, or painting curb numbers with brushes attached to his skateboard. Or he might wax cars by putting some polish on a poodle and dangling a chicken taco over the car on the end of a stick. Willie'd get a quick wax job and the poodle would get a snack.

But don't get the idea Willie's a slacker. On the contrary, Willie puts out twice the "kilowatts" of kid energy compared to others kids. In fact, he's actually a very responsible dude. He's just more clever than the average kid.

I guess you'd have to call Willie *recklessly in control*.

In contrast to his extreme antics, Willie lives in an ordinary, small stucco house, in the seaside community of Burrito Beach, with his mom, Doris (a nurse), his dad, Mitchell (an accountant), his sister, Mary (a pest), and his pet chameleon, Bungee.

But more about them later. First you need to know about Willie's buds...

3. Hundred dollar bills.

The Extreme Team

Hanna

Hanna is *extremely* competitive.

Next to Willie, she's the best on wheels, be they inline, skateboard, BMX, or otherwise. She's equally *spankin'*⁴ on surfboards, snowboards, and bungee cords.

Hanna is also extremely cute. And she has a big crush on Willie. So it drives her crazy that he's more into the *rush* than into her. But he can't help it. Hanna's been a neighbor since they were kids and Willie thinks of her as a sister. When he does get around to thinking about Hanna, Willie is usually distracted by something extreme.

Hanna will do anything to get Willie's full attention. She tries hard to out-extreme him in various ways, hoping it might turn his head. But it doesn't. It just turns him onto the rush again. She tries to hang out now and then with taller, cuter jocks, but that doesn't work either.

Then there are those times when she gives up in frustration, and is just herself, and Willie suddenly notices her. But Hanna doesn't get it, so she instantly tries to impress him again, losing the moment. In her frustration she falls back on the thing she loves second best to Willie, and that's extreme sports.

Roland

Roland is an *extreme* worrier.

He's also Willie's best friend. Roland is into trying as hard as he can and using the best equipment and <u>having</u> to win.

He's too much in his head and worries way to much . . . about his grades, about his future, about girls, about getting pimples, about breaking his leg. It's probably because Roland's folks are *Mr. & Mrs. Rich N. Perfect*, and put pressure on Roland to be the best in school and in sports so he can get into a top Ivy League college.

Roland's dad is a lawyer in a big firm and expects Roland to be the same. He thinks extreme sports are a waste of time and tries to discourage Roland from doing them. But it's just this that drives Roland to do things more and more extreme.

4. Good.

Maui

Maui is *extremely* weird.

She's a 14-year-old, native Hawaiian girl who only recently moved to Burrito Beach when her jet pilot dad was transferred to El Toro Air Base.

Maui learned her love of extreme from her dad, and her love for spiritual stuff from her native Hawaiian mom. The result: Maui can talk to dolphins, "tap a vein" on a surfboard, or channel a departed Hawaiian spirit god (though no one quite knows for sure who she's really talking to).

Maui loves extreme sports because they make her feel closer to nature. Soaring like a bird, swimming like a fish, barrel-rolling like an F-16. Of course, being Hawaiian she's the best at surfing.

Most people at Burrito Beach Junior High think Maui is the *freakyfreak of the week*[5]. Even Hanna and Roland think she's a bit of a *lunachick*[6]. But Willie knows that she's onto something. Not sure what, but something. It's Willie's understanding and acceptance of Maui's weirdness that makes her so loyal to him. But more than Willie, Maui likes Wheels. No, not the kind on skateboards...

"Wheels"

Wheels is *extremely* intelligent.

He got his nickname because a genetic birth defect confined him to a wheelchair. But that hasn't stopped him. He's better in his chair than most guys are on a skateboard. He can do spinners, wheelies, and is a killer at basketball and street hockey.

Wheels is a bit of a geek, as evidenced by his horn-rimmed glasses and *dirt chin*[7]. He dreams of being the next Bill Gates and Steven Jobs rolled into one. Thus, he's always in his garage working on the next invention he plans to patent, like his X^2TREME SNEAKERS with retractable inline wheels and jets, or X^2TREME BOOGIE MOWER on which a rider can surf and cut the lawn at same time, or his X^2TREME BODY BALL, a six-foot diameter clear Plexiglas ball you strap yourself inside and ride down a mountain or off the end of pier!

As Roland is always looking for mechanical means to improve his extreme skills, he's happy to be the "test pilot" for Wheels's inventions, even though he usually winds up making face prints on the ground and getting a *grill*[8] full of grass.

---

5. Someone who is really strange.
6. A girl that exhibits behavior that is out of the ordinary for the given situation.

7. Untidy chin with small amount of facial hair.
8. Face; especially teeth and mouth.

Though they're really complete opposites, Maui and Wheels like each other a lot. It's probably a yin & yang kind of thing. Go figure!

When Willie and his tribe need to know when a movie's playing, or a juicy tidbit from their principal's rap sheet, or how to rig up a bike helmet with infrared for night snowboarding, Wheels gets *on da wires*[9] and has the data in a nanosec. Very resourceful guy!

One reason Wheels is so resourceful is that his dad, Fred, owns FRED'S DETERIORATED EQUIPMENT REPOSITORY, which everyone in Burrito Beach knows is just an ordinary junk yard. Wheels lives with his dad at the junk yard, where he gets all the stuff he needs for his wild inventions. Willie and his tribe have even made a jury-rigged BMX track through all the junk.

Bungee

Bungee is extreeeeemely slow.

He's Willie's pet chameleon. He's so slow you can barely see him move. When Willie holds out a piece of banana and calls, "Here boy!" it could take Bungee half an hour to crawl a few feet and get it.

Being a chameleon, Bungee changes to the color of whatever he's on. This can be a real pain when Willie's trying to find him, or when he's camouflaged as a hot dog and Roland puts mustard on him and tries to scarf him down.

Most of the time Bungee just hangs out on Willie's shoulder, his eyes moving in two different directions at the same time as he scopes out the place.

Bungee reacts with his eyes. They show his emotions. Like the extreme team, he likes to try new things. For instance, he might sip a cola, then let out a loud burp that makes his eyes spin. Or he might check out Willie's new CD game player and get spun around in circles and flung onto the TV screen just as the villain explodes! Or he might stalk a pair of red dice, thinking they're ladybugs or something, and shoot his long, sticky tongue out and eat them. Then he'd probably move his eyes around, make a face and spit them out, rolling a seven!

Though Bungee doesn't talk, Willie talks to him when he needs to "think out loud." His eyes will appear to react to Willie's words, and Willie will take meaning from them, though it's really just his own realization.

9. Signed onto the Internet by means of a modem.

Mary

Mary is an *extreme* pain in the ass.

She's Willie's 16-year-old sister. Her attention is fixed on one thing—finding a boyfriend. There's just one problem: She's not very cute. Make that two problems: She's not very smart either.

Mary is always buying the latest, greatest cosmetic or wardrobe accessory that's advertised to make her gorgeous and get the guys. But they never work. At least on her.

She hates Willie because he's so happy with himself in contrast to her, and because girls are attracted to Willie without him even trying. What's he got that she doesn't, anyway? After all, they're from the same gene pool.

It's probably her jealousy of him that causes Mary to constantly try to get Willie in trouble. She knows what he's really up to, and tries to tell their folks or his teachers. But it always backfires on her, making her look bad and Willie look good. And he doesn't even resent her for it. That pisses her off even more.

One way Mary tries to get back at Willie is through Bungee. She hates the disgusting little creature and often tries to get rid of him. But he always manages to survive, then turns up in her underwear drawer to get revenge.

In Willie's eyes, there's only one redeeming thing about Mary. She's got a *driver's license!* This makes her *extremely* valuable to Willie and his tribe. She'd never in a million years offer to give them a lift to school or an extreme event, but that doesn't stop Willie. He always manages to con her into taking him wherever he wants to go. Like the time Willie faked a call from the high school "hunk," pretending to ask her to meet her at the diner, which just "happened" to be the same place Willie was going. Poor Mary. She just can't understand why guys keep standing her up.

Willie's Parents

Doris and Mitchell are *extremely* ordinary.

Mitchell is an accountant. He eats, sleeps, and breathes numbers. Extreme to him is a hexadecimal calculator. Whoa!

Doris is a nurse. Not the exciting kind, like in an ER. She takes care of old people in a nursing home. Extreme to Doris is listening to some old codger pass gas to Beethoven's 5th.

Doris and Mitchell are oblivious to Willie's extreme world, and will contrast it with their dullness and obtuseness. But they're a happy couple. Always smiling. And Willie loves them.

Other Extremely Strange People

There are several other important people in Willie's world. Like...

Ernie, the Eye-Tec Patrolman

Ernie is *extremely* unlucky.

He's the clumsy neighborhood patrolman who drives around in his Eye-Tec patrol car. Ernie always wanted to be a real cop, but didn't make the cut. Probably because he's too overweight, too slow, and too dumb.

His big goal in life now is to nab Willie! That's because when the snooty neighbors complain about Willie's extreme activities, try as he might, Ernie can't do anything about it.

Ernie's so intent on getting Willie that he's always plotting against him, taking his attention off his work, allowing homes to be robbed, mail boxes to be vandalized, or cars to be broken into.

Captain Jim

Captain Jim is *extremely* out to lunch.

And that's not because he owns *Titanic Taco*, the local Health-Mex taco joint. It's because 40-year-old Jim is a lifetime surfer who's run into the pier pilings one too many times. Ouch!

Jim is a carne slinging, air-guitar playing, air-headed philosopher. His take on the universe is so skewed you can't help but wonder if the guys in the white coats are going to come in any second and wrap him up like a burrito.

Everyone on the Extreme Team loves Captain Jim, and they often hang out at his taco place. Jim drives a "woody" and is such a buddy that he'll sometimes shut down the shack to go surfing or snowboarding with his Extreme Team buds.

Despite his flakiness, Jim is Willie's quasi-mentor. Although his cosmic ideas are always off the wall, they often give Willie a great idea.

Wacky William, Senior

William is *extremely* old.

This is Willie's 99-year old great grandfather who lives with Willie and his folks. Willie calls his great grandfather "Ace" because William Senior was a pilot in World War One. He loves to tell Willie all about his adventures in the sky with Baron von Schtruddle, his affairs with French girls, etc. Trouble is, William Senior can barely remember his name, let alone century-old memories. So he often contradicts himself, and no one knows for sure what's true and what isn't.

William Senior is totally bald, except for the ring of white spiky hair around his temples that gives us the impression he probably looked a lot like Willie when he was a kid. He likes to brag that Willie got his love of "the rush" from him, because he was into such extreme stuff as croquet and eating straw hats.

Everyone else thinks William Senior is just senile, but Willie knows he's really a pretty hip cat. For example, William Senior likes to joke that he was hoping when Y2K came he, like the computers, would go back to 1900 and start over again.

Principal Ferret

She's an *extreme* neurotic (she's also extremely *bugly*[10]).

Principal Ferret (or Warden Ferret as the students like to call her) tries to run Burrito Beach Junior High like a correctional facility. To her, everyone is up to something. Especially Willie.

No extreme sports slacker could possibly maintain a B+ average in her school, so Willie must be cheating. That's why she's out to prove that Willie cuts class, cheats on tests, that his notes from his parents are forged, that he was skateboarding down the hall, that he's got head lice. Anything that will get him kicked out of school. Trouble is, she can never prove a thing, and always winds up with egg on her face...or worse!

Warden Ferret is always pulling Willie into her office and giving him the third degree. Nothing bothers her more than Willie's Zen-like confidence and cool. *"Will you take those glasses off!"* she's often heard shouting. But Willie never does. Even when she makes a school rule that sunglasses are forbidden just to spite him. But he still doesn't take them off. (Truth is, he never *will* take them

---

10. Short for "butt ugly."

off. He even sleeps and showers with them. In fact, Willie likes to say, "My future's so bright I need shades just thinking about it!")

Principal Ferret's goal (besides getting Willie) is to turn Burrito Beach Junior High into the exemplary school of the nation. That's why Willie's free-spirited antics are so upsetting to her. Seems every time there's someone from the school board there, Willie manages to make her look bad.

Coach "Doobs"

He's an *extreme* (expletive deleted).

Coach Dubowski (they call him Coach *Doobs*[11] and he hates it) is Willie's PE teacher. He's an ex-Marine with a pot belly. He hates Willie because Willie isn't a follower and team player like the rest of the kids. Willie's a maverick who wants to do sports only one way—*extreme*.

Anthony "Diesel" Truccanti

Diesel is an *extreme* egotist.

He's Coach Doobs's star athlete. You know the guy. Too good looking. All buff and no brains. He thinks extreme sports are for slackers. He's into REAL sports like football, baseball, and basketball. Diesel and his lettermen flunkies often challenge Willie and this friends to one-on-one, or a game of tackle, figuring they'll cream them. But it never turns out that way.

Diesel is one of those smiling "Yes, ma'am," kiss-ass polite kids who looks and acts perfect on the outside, while under his sheepskin-lined jacket he's really a self-absorbed, egotistical, do-anything-he-can-to-win, cheating, lying wolf.

Diesel also hates Willie because Hanna likes Willie, and Diesel likes Hanna, and Diesel isn't used to taking back seat to anyone, especially a "wimp" like Willie. So Diesel tries to win Hanna's affection, but she always goes for Willie, making Diesel look like a big fool. This gets Diesel really *lit*[12] and makes him an eternal adversary to Willie and the gang.

11. Bad, lame (from dubious).
12. Angry.

Where It's At, Dude

Most of our stories will take place within the city limits of Burrito Beach, in such locations as...

Willie's House

Willie's house is extremely ordinary. Cheesy times ten! That is, except for Willie's bedroom. It's totally *phat*,[13] as bedrooms go. Cluttered with extreme sports posters, lots of trophies, computer and peripherals, electric guitar and amp, super-loud stereo, and a closet full of sporting clothes, like wet suits, shorts, sandals, etc.

Willie's second-story bedroom window has an *extreme egress rig* for stealthy getaways. It goes something like this: 1) skateboard ramp out window; 2) slalom down roof; 3) frontside slider along rain gutter; 4) grab onto telephone pole support cable; 5) slide through trees (grab apple for quick nutrition), and; 6) drop off onto sidewalk and skate away without the *rents*[14] being the wiser.

Fred's Deteriorated Equipment Repository

As noted, it's Wheels's dad's junk yard. This is not only one of the tribe's favorite hangs, it's where Wheels builds all his extreme gizmos. It's also where they jam. Wheels has rigged up the biggest speakers ever seen (six feet in diameter), for ear-busting rock 'n' roll.

Burrito Beach

Bodacious waves. Lots of girls in bikinis and boys in jams. A big pier with a Ferris wheel and carnival games. Lots of surfers. It's *the* hangout in summer.

Titanic Tacos

It's the hottest joint on the beach. The building is painted black and white to look like a ship, and slants on an extreme angle as if it's sinking. It's even got portholes, four smokestacks on the roof, and a big, blinking neon sign that says *Titanic Tacos—Sink Your Teeth Into Them!*

The inside of the place is also on the bias, including the booths, counter, and kitchen. Captain Jim serves Health-Mex, soft tacos, shark pizzas, iceberg shakes, and other cool comestibles.

13. Awesome, great.
14. Parents.

The Mall

The music store's okay, but otherwise it's a boring *hang* for Willie and company. So they spice it up by body-slaloming (skateboarding around panicked pedestrians), doing front-side sliders down the escalator, and best of all, outmaneuvering the guards.

Burrito Beach Junior High

It's a typical junior high, with bland buildings that make it look like a prison. Nothing extreme about it. Just plain Dullsville.

"Da Hill"

The tallest hill in Burrito Beach. It's *the grail*[16] for local extreme sports enthusiasts. Ordinary kids are terrified to ride it. But not Willie and his buds. It's a rush for them. They do it on skateboards, inline blades, street luge, and BMX. Da Hill runs right through Ernie's neighborhood and ends at a cliff overlooking the beach. There's a sign at the top that says NO SKATEBOARDING ALLOWED! And Ernie often waits at the bottom like a spider in a web. A very dumb spider!

What It's All About

Willie, Hanna, Wheels, Maui, and Roland make up the Extreme Team. They hang together, face life's problems together, do extreme sports together, and are pretty much inseparable.

Although they get into the same kind of fun and trouble as most kids, they're focused on just two things: *extreme* sports and *extreme* rock 'n' roll.

Extreme Sports...

Willie and his tribe do their extreme sports in whatever venue is appropriate. When they can't get away from Burrito Beach they surf or skate or ride their tricked out BMX bikes.

But if they can *stack some chips*[17] and find a ride to the mountains or the desert they love all extreme sports, like **snowboarding, para-surfing, wind surfing, rock climbing, para-sailing, bungee jumping, jet skiing, wakeboarding** (surfing behind a boat like water skiing), **four-runners, dune surfing**, etc.

16. The ultimate in anything.
17. Save some money.

Willie and the gang are also into what they call **X²treme Sports**. Cutting edge stuff, half of which they invent themselves just for the rush of it. There's **body bowling** (where you get inside a large sphere and roll down a mountain), **rocket skating, canyon surfing, skyscraper rappelling** (with window cleaning for extra $), **geyser jumping** (where you sit on an active geyser in your wet suit and wait for it to rocket you into the sky), **BMX polo, skateboard rodeo, skateboard hockey, inline street dog sledding, dam skateboarding** (á la Hoover), **mall slalom** (blading around panicked shoppers while avoiding the guards), **skateboard laser tag.** And the list goes on...

Extreme Rock 'n' Roll...

Willie and the others play their music in Wheels's dad's junk yard garage. Their music is as extreme as their sports. It really rocks! And their instruments are as tricked out as their sports equipment.

Willie plays a purple Fender. Hanna is lead singer. Roland plays the electronic keyboard. Maui plays electric bass. And Wheels plays a makeshift set of "junk drums" made from every spare part and old broken thing you can imagine—hubcaps, washing machine drum, pots and pans, not to mention some real drums and cymbals—all wired up to a synthesizer to make them sound really cool.

When it came to naming the band it was a no-brainer. They're *Willie & The Extremes.* Though Roland is always thinking of bigger and better names, like *Rockin' Roland and the Bungees* or *Roland's Burrito Beach Blues Band.* But his names never stick.

A Fully Extreme Format...

The Extreme Adventures of Wacky Willie is a half-hour comedy series about the contrast and conflicts of ordinary, day-to-day teenage life versus the primal urge to make life more exciting and oneself more important. The way Willie and his friends do this is through extreme sports and extreme fun.

Life is simple for Willie and his Extreme Team. You scrounge a little bread so you can have a little fun. Then you do it again. This is the *Circle of Life* for a teenager.

Although Willie and his friends are extreme in the ways they live and play, they are not extraordinary. They are real teens. Their goals, motivations and actions are those of any young teenager who looks back on childhood and ahead to growing up. It's just the way they are manifested that is more comical and extreme than usual.

The theme of the series is *LIFE IS AS EXTREME AS YOU MAKE IT*. And Willie knows how to make it $E=Xtreme^2$

Willie and his buds will use their heads, their hearts, and their chutzpah to meet the everyday challenges of life in unique, exciting, and funny ways.

They hang at Titanic Taco, the mall, Willie's bedroom, school, or the junk yard, looking for their next *rush*. They might have to make some money to get to the mountains, or buy some new skateboard trucks, or make entry fees for a big event. They might have to deal with a bully who thinks extreme sports are for extreme wimps. They might have to overcome conservative parents who "just say no" to extreme. Whatever the challenge, Willie and his tribe will face it and surmount it with intelligence, humor, and above all, a fully extreme attitude toward life.

Extreme Stories...

Our stories will be a blend of everyday teenage experiences and extreme sports. Though we can do any ordinary teen story, following are a few *extreme* examples...

A + B = C U L8R

Willie has been practicing for months for the big BMX contest. But there's one problem. The qualifier is on the Friday before the event, and so is Willie's big algebra final. If he misses the test he flunks, and if he flunks he's got to redo the class. An extra year of algebra? No way! So Willie develops an elaborate scheme to have a kid disguise himself as Willie and sit it on the test while the real Willie goes to the event. But Willie isn't the kind of kid who cheats, so he rigs it up with a cell phone so he can "call in the answers." This becomes problematic when Principal Ferret gets suspicious and tries to find out what

Willie's up to. With Willie, Hanna, and Roland at the event, and Wheels and Maui back at school trying to hold down the fort, Murphy's Law prevails as everything that can go wrong does. It's only Willie's extreme cool that allows him to nail his algebra final, win the bike riding event, and get back to class in time to make Principal Ferret look like a fool!

Rush For The Money

When Captain Jim can't pay the balloon payment on Titanic Taco's mortgage, the bank threatens to turn the place into a parking lot. Willie and the gang try to help Jim raise some money, but the guy's so off kilter in the brains department that he just can't make anything go right. Then Willie discovers that there's a senior surfing contest that weekend, and the prize is just enough to pay off the balloon. Trouble is, Jim never was able to win a surf contest in all his years of surfing because, though he'd often reach the finals, his love of the rush always caused him to go too far and screw up. Now Willie and his buds have to build up Jim's confidence, and get him to focus on winning, not *rushing*. Jim makes it to the finals, but Willie notices that he's just not the same guy. He's lost something. At the last minute Willie tells Jim to do what's in his heart. So Jim does an incredible maneuver, making an even more incredible wipe out. And he loses the prize money. When the banker comes to take his deed, the gang can't believe Willie betrayed Jim. But Willie has another idea. He gets everyone on the beach to mount an extreme protest, letting the banker know that any establishment that replaces Titanic Taco will be boycotted. The banker has no choice but to extend Jim's loan. Jim keeps his taco joint, and his self-esteem, knowing that he didn't compromise his love of the rush for the almighty buck.

You May Already Be A Sucker!

When Ernie the patrolman wins a skiing vacation he thinks he's headed for a weekend of fun and relaxation. But it turns out that Willie & Co. are headed up to the very same mountain for a snowboarding event. Ernie tries to hide the fact that he's taking his first skiing lesson and belongs on the beginner slope. Instead, he attempts, as always, to catch Willie. But Willie winds up the hero as he saves the lodge from an avalanche caused by Ernie...who winds up in a full-body cast.

Ace In The Hole

Willie's Mom and Dad are at work, so Willie and the tribe are hanging with 99-year-old William Senior (AKA Ace). When Ace has a sudden pain, his life begins to flash before him (he says it's in black and white because his memory started before color film was invented). Ace figures it's the end. Willie is about to call 911 when Ace suddenly stops him. "No," he says, "They'll just take me to the hospital." Ace wants one last *rush* before he goes. Willie reluctantly agrees. But they'll need some money. Ace has a few bucks. The others put their cash together with his and come up with $50. Ace promises they'll get their money back, and on the way out scribbles a note, reading aloud as he does: "Doris: Kids took me. Gotta *ruuusssssh* before I croak. Please leave them fifty $. Grandad." Then he tapes it to the fridge and leaves with the kids.

Ace insists on reliving his war experience, so they go to the local municipal airport and rent an old biplane. When Doris comes home she reads the note. But it reads differently on paper. When Doris reads it aloud it sounds like this: *"Doris: Kids took me. Gotta rush! Before I croak leave them fifty grand. Dad."*

She thinks it's a ransom note and calls the FBI. When a photo of William Senior goes out on television, someone at the airport recognizes him and calls the Feds. Suddenly Ace and the kids find an FBI helicopter chasing them. William Senior thinks the Feds are Baron von Schtruddle and gets into a comical dogfight. Once they land, it turns into a high-speed pursuit with the Extreme Team outrunning the FBI on skateboards and BMX. And Ace is right with them!

Ace is really digging the rush...until he feels that pain again. Willie has no choice but to surrender. The Feds surround them. And Doris and Mitchell arrive a moment later. They realize it was all a misunderstanding, and a moment later an ambulance arrives and takes Ace away.

Later, at the hospital, Ace is hooked up to monitors. Everyone looks grim as they think it's the end for great granddad. Then we'll hear a LOUD FART and the old man wakes up. The doc says he's fine. It's just a bad case of gas.

Extreme characters

Extreme humor

Extreme music, and

Extreme sports, in an

Extremely spankin' series

that'll hook 'em

and cook 'em

from 4 to 14.

What's the ruuuussssh?

The Extreme Adventures of
Wacky Willie

How to Write a Pilot

The final part of the development process is the pilot script. A pilot is the first episode written for a series. Generally, the studio or network will pick one of the premises in the bible for the pilot episode.

If you're creating your own series and are going to write a pilot, there's one mistake you really want to avoid. Most non-professionals who write pilots for their series ideas pick an *origin story*, in which the characters and/or format come to be. An example of an origin story is how little Kal-El was sent to earth from Krypton, was adopted by George and Martha Kent, and went on to become a mild-mannered reporter and superhero.

99 out of 100 times the network *doesn't* want an "origin" pilot.

They almost always want a random story that could be aired anywhere in the series. The reason for this is twofold: First, even if an origin story works very well, subsequent stories might be difficult to come up with. The last thing a network wants is to buy a series concept that doesn't work when put to the litmus test of episodic writing. The second reason is that it raises the question of whether those viewers who miss the origin story will be able to understand the rest of the episodes. Buyers want to make sure that the series is perfectly understandable, and a random episode helps them see this.

If you're writing a spec bible, you might want to consider writing a pilot as well. If you don't sell the series, you've still got a sample script. If the script is really good, it might help sell the series. The more you can do to build confidence in the buyer, whether he's a studio exec who might option your property or a network exec who might buy it, the better.

A pilot is usually written just like an ordinary episode. That's why I didn't include a pilot script in this book. However, there are a few additional things to keep in mind when writing a pilot:

Try to establish as much of the format and characters as you can in the pilot episode. Don't focus too narrowly on one character or aspect of the show. This can be done in a later episode, once the audience knows the show. When you're trying to sell a show to a network exec, you want to reveal as much of the show as you can in the pilot.

By the way, not all pilots run as the first episode of a series. Sometimes they're held back and aired later. Don't write your pilot from the viewpoint of it being the first episode aired.

The pilot is more important than the bible. Why? Because even though the bible is the foundation of the series, and even if it reads like gangbusters, it's the pilot that determines whether or not the concept will ultimately translate into a good series.

When you write a pilot, don't be surprised if the format needs some tweaking. When you begin to bring all of the elements of a series together in a pilot it's not unusual to discover that some dynamics of the show you created don't work that well in action. Don't be afraid to drop what doesn't work and add what's needed. Sticking to the bible because it's the bible is a good way to not sell your show. On the *Dragon Tales* series I co-developed for Sesame Workshop, the format was still being revised after a dozen scripts had been written.

Thus, another purpose of a pilot is to further develop the series, get the bugs out, and make sure it can translate into good stories, character relationships, action, and/or comedy.

By now you should have a good idea of how to write a script, presentation, or bible. But that's only half of the game. Now comes the hard part. How are you going to sell it?

PART III

SELLING YOUR ANIMATED PROJECT

Chapter 14

HOW TO GET AN AGENT

Believe it or not, up until the mid-1980s there really was no such thing as animation agents. My first agent was the William Morris Agency. I signed with them after having already written 150 animation scripts, and they didn't even attempt to get me any animation work. They wanted to represent me for live-action writing only.

Today, with prime-time animation being so popular, practically every agency in Hollywood represents animation writers. However, there are only a handful of companies that represent animation writers and artists exclusively, and even fewer of these who are willing to take in new clients. But take heart! If you're clever you can get them to read your script, and if it's good, you're on your way!

Do I Really Need an Agent?

Yes and no!

Back in the mid-1980s one could argue that an animation agent wasn't necessary. I did very well without one. Today the market is entirely different. In the 1980s there were only a few animation studios, so you didn't have to go far to find out what shows were being done and where. Today there are hundreds of animation studios worldwide. It can take a great deal of effort to find out what they're doing and what they need. Animation agents do just this.

Some studios won't read scripts or take pitches without an agent submitting the material, others will. It's definitely easier if you have an agent, but not a disaster if you don't.

Where Do I Find an Agent?

If you have a great prime-time animation or sitcom script, you might try one of the big agencies, like CAA, ICM, and William Morris, or the dozens of mid-size and smaller agencies. For a list of these agents go to the website of the Writers Guild of America, and click on their *List of Agents* link. They list hundreds of agents, from nearly thirty states, as well as foreign agents. They also indicate which agencies will consider new writers, which require a reference, and which won't give you the time of day. Another source of agency names and numbers is the *Hollywood Agents &* *Managers Directory*, a semi-annual publication that can be purchased as a book, on a disk, or as an online subscription service at *www.hcdonline.com*. The best way I've found to get a list of animation agents is to call the WGA (323-951-4000) and ask them to send you the latest copy of the *Directory of Animation Writers*, which is issued by the Animation Writers Caucus. This directory lists over three hundred WGA members who are also animation writers. After each writer's name is their agent, and the agency's name and telephone number. By checking the writer's credits you can determine if the agent handles prime-time animation, Saturday morning, preschool, cable, or any other type of animation writing.

How Do I Choose an Agent?

Beggars can't be choosers, and new writers are definitely beggars. Unless you have a positively fantastic sample script, it's not going to be that easy to get an agent. But being a writer isn't an easy thing to win at, either, and if you've gotten this far through the book the chances are you're probably going to follow through. So here are some things to look for when trying to choose an agent:

1. Who do you know?

Before you try to do it the hard way, be sure to check if you know someone who has an agent, or knows one, and might be willing to recommend you to this person. Again, it's "who you know" that really breaks down barriers in this business.

2. Will they read scripts from new writers?

Many agencies won't even read new writers. When you look through the lists of agents noted above, be sure to check which ones will accept new clients without referrals.

3. Do I need an agent that specializes in animation?

If you want to write for prime-time animated series you'll do fine with an agent that doesn't know much about the animation industry as a whole. The big, prime-time animated series are treated just like live-action sitcoms, and any good TV agent can and does work with these shows. However, if you want to write any other kind of animation you better find an agent who knows the industry. A good animation agent knows which studios are doing feature and TV animation, knows the people who buy shows, what they are looking for, and also knows enough about the industry as a whole to make good decisions about what kind of samples to write, who might be looking for a writer like you, and what shows to work on to enhance your career. In general, it is best to find an agent who specializes in animation.

4. Am I better off at a big or a small agency?

There is no concensus about the best size of an agency. Some say that you can get lost at a big agency and are better off being a bigger fish in a smaller pond. Others believe that big agencies, having more and bigger clients, have more clout. Both of these views are correct. The fact is, when you're starting out, be happy to get *any* agent. If, by some miracle, you have a choice between a big or a small agency, measure some of the other factors listed here to help make your decision. The most important factors should be the agent's belief in you and the agent's knowledge of the animation industry.

5. How important is an agent's personality?

The agent-client relationship is a tough one in most circumstances. There's a lot of pressure, not the least of which is that you may be depending on your agent to find you work when you're in dire need of money. It really helps if you like and respect your agent. However, if you're looking for your first agent and there's only one who'll take you, unless the guy's a blood-sucking vampire, sign on the dotted line.

The above may help you decide if you have to choose between two or more agents. But in reality, the chances are high that your first agent will choose you. And if they do, count your lucky stars.

What Do I Need to Have to Get an Agent?

A terrific sample script, a lot of persistence, and a little luck. Getting your first agent is a lot like selling your first script. It's not easy, but there are some precise steps that, if followed, will eventually work.

Just as you need a sample script in order to get your first script assignment, you need one to get an agent.

The sample script is your calling card. You can be short, tall, male, female, pimply, smell bad, or have eyebrow rings, but if you have a good sample the doors will open.

How Do I Get an Agent to Read My Script?

The steps necessary to get an agent to read your script are actually the same as those to break into the business without an agent. I'll go into it in more detail in the next chapter, but the basic steps are as follows:

1.   Make a list of the agents you want to contact.

By culling the agent lists you should be able to put together a list of several potential agencies. Consider things like the location of the agency, whether you want an agent who knows the whole animation industry or just prime-time animation, whether you want a big or small agent, and whether you know an agent or know someone who does.

2.   Contact the agents.

There are several ways to contact an agent. In order of best to worst they are: calling, e-mailing, writing, and faxing. Calling is best, but is the most difficult because most agents are simply too busy to take your call. E-mail is second best, but you might find it hard to get e-mail addresses. One way around getting a personal e-mail address is to get the general e-mail address of the agency, then send a message to the specific agent via the webmaster. They will most likely forward it for you. Letters and faxes are equally as good, but their failing is that they are easy to toss into the trash and not answer. E-mail, on the other hand, is so easy to answer that you're more likely to get a response.

Be courteous and professional in your communication. Keep it short and get to the point. Most importantly, say something interesting and creative!

Here's a little trick about getting any important person on the phone. Don't! That's the secret. ***Don't* try to talk to the important person. Talk to his or her *secretary!*** Nine out of ten times you don't need to talk to an agent to find out everything you need to know. This, by the way, is true for anyone, including producers, story editors, presidents of the United States, etc. So don't forget to apply it! You can get it from the assistant. You can always get the assistant on the phone. They're the one who answers it! Though they're very busy, they're generally very friendly people who are willing to talk. Don't make the mistake of asking for Mike Super-Agent and, when he doesn't take your call, giving up. Mike's assistant can tell you what Mike is looking for. After all, it's his job to know everything that Mike is doing and thinking. He can tell you what Mike wants, doesn't want, and whether Mike will read your script. If you are friendly and get to know Mike's assistant he might even want to do you a favor and help you along.

3. Promote yourself to the agents.

They sell soap by telling people how good it is. Whether you like it or not, it's your job (especially before you have an agent) to sell yourself by pointing out how good you are. You must promote yourself. You don't want to be obnoxious or false about this, but you don't want to be a total unknown to the person to whom you're talking. Find something about yourself or your products that are worth bragging about. Perhaps you took some reputable writing courses, or went to a good film school, or wrote an award-winning short story. Anything that can make you, as a writer, more real to the agent is worth communicating, if only that you believe in yourself and love cartoon writing.

4. Find out what the agents need and want.

Some agents are specifically looking for certain kinds of writers. They may want sitcom writers, or preschool writers, funny writers, Internet writers, female writers, etc. Find out what they want or need and see if you can fulfill this. Most likely they'll say all they want is a fantastic script. Needless to say, you're going to tell them that yours is terrific—and it better be!

5. Give them what they need and want.

Having found out what they want, simply give it to them. However, if they want an action sample and all you have is a comedy, giving them what they want may mean revising your script, or writing a brand new one.

6. Follow up.

You can't just send an agent a sample script and forget about it. If they eventually say "No thanks," you can't just drop it and move on, either. If you do you'll lose a valuable opportunity for feedback. If they *pass*, be sure to ask them what they didn't like about your sample and how you might improve it. Get all the feedback you can. This is really just an extension of step #4 , as you're clarifying what they want by getting them to tell you what they didn't want about your script.

Never pester anyone, but be persistent. If you have to, write another sample and send it back to the agent. By continuing this process, again and again if necessary, you will improve as a writer and improve your knowledge of what agents are looking for. Don't forget, it's the people who give up that widen the road for those who don't.

What Should I Expect If I'm Lucky Enough to Get an Agent?

Or, more realistically, what NOT to expect.

1.   Don't expect your agent to be calling you every day.
They might during the "honeymoon" period after just signing with them, but honeymoons don't last long.

2.   Don't expect them to be working to sell your stuff every day.
The squeaky wheel may get the oil, but the imminent deal gets the agent's attention, and most agents have many clients. Money talks in this business, so if you're stuff is selling you'll get lots of calls from your agent. If it's not, you won't—and when you're not working is when you'll want your agent to be calling the most.

3.   Don't expect to be thrilled with your agent.
When they call and say, "I just got you an assignment at Disney," you're going to love them. When you call them for the eleventh time and they say, "There's just nothing out there," you won't be liking them much at all. This is the business.

4.   Don't expect your agent to suddenly get you a lot of work.
It can take months of slowly cultivating contacts and sending out your scripts to finally get an assignment. You may feel like you've made a great victory by getting an agent—and you really have. However, the real victory isn't even getting an assignment. The real victory is getting the call for *more* scripts from the same producer or editor. This means they like your work and you've made a relationship, and as anyone will tell you, this is a business of relationships.

5.   Don't expect your agent to do it all!
I do most of the promotion for myself, and make dozens of calls and e-mails every week. In fact, it is my efforts or contacts that get me most of my work. I use my agent for PR, handling problems, helping to collect money, and, now and then, for getting me some work.

Chapter 15

How to Break into Toon Writing without an Agent

THE ODDS ARE AGAINST YOUR BEING able to get an agent when you first try. Don't feel bad. It's to be expected, and it's not the end of the world. Remember, I get 90 percent of my work myself. You can get 100 percent.

What I'm going to suggest you do is actually very easy, but it does take a degree of talent, and a lot of persistence. There are five simple steps to breaking into the business. These steps are similar to those used to get an agent. I can tell you from experience that, if done with intelligence, creativity, and persistence, these steps will (if anything can) get you into the business.

Step #1—Find People to Contact

Who do you contact? How do you find them? That reminds me of the famous line in Hollywood, "It's not *what* you know, it's *who* you know." This is true in any business. People feel most comfortable hiring their friends. The first thing you want to find out is if you know anyone in the business, or know anyone who knows anyone. Maybe your gardener also cuts the lawn of some producer. Don't be afraid to ask around. The leads are there. You just have to find them. If you do, don't be too proud to use the contact.

If you don't happen to have a friend in the business—and even if you do—you've got to contact as many producers and story editors in the business as possible. To do this, I suggest you get a copy of the *Hollywood Creative Directory* (www.hcdonline.com) or the *Animation Industry Directory* (www.animationmagazine.net), both of which have listings of animation production companies. The *Animation World Network* (www.awn.com) also lists some production companies.

Step #2—Contact Them

One important thing to remember is the value of e-mail. If you can find people's e-mail addresses I strongly suggest you use them. E-mail is so easy to read and answer that it greatly increases your chances of getting a response. Get the producers or story editors on the phone if you can, or get their assistants. If you can't, use e-mail. Ask someone's assistant what projects they have in production and for the names of the producers and story editors of those shows.

Step #3—Promote Yourself to Them

Let's say you've put together a nice long list of people to contact. You call them, write them a letter, or send them an e-mail and introduce yourself. If you have any kind of writing credit or other relevant experience, such as a film school education, mention this. Above all, be creative! Don't forget you're a writer. You need to stand out from the next guy. Try not to be dull on the phone, and don't write a dry résumé with facts and dates. Be funny! Be different!

The secret is to contact as many people as possible. Believe it or not, the key to succeeding is simply persisting with your promotion. The more people you contact, the more phone calls you make, the more letters and e-mails and scripts you send out, the greater your chance of success.

Step #4—Ask What They Need and Want

If you're talking to a producer or a story editor (or their assistant), find out as much as you can about what they need and want. Will they accept story pitches without agents? Will they read a sample of your work? What genre would they prefer? If you've already written a sample, and it turns out not to be the genre they're looking for, you might still want to send it to them, explaining that it's just a sample of your writing. Tell them it's not the only genre you write in, and that you'd love to write for their show as well. After they've read your sample, and are interested, then decide whether writing a spec script for their show, of one of a similar genre, would be wise.

The questions you ask, and the answers you get, will be different depending on whether you're using these steps to get an agent, get a pitch meeting, sell a script, sell a series, or whatever. Once you find out what they need and want, the next step is easy.

Step #5—Give It to Them!

Well, it's easy in theory. It's not always easy to give them something so right that they buy it, or buy you. I have asked execs what they want, then crafted a series to fit their needs, only to find out that what I did was not exactly what they were looking for. This, too, is just part of the game. If you don't get it right, learn from your mistakes, ask better questions, write better material, and do whatever it takes, again and again, until you win.

If they want a certain type of sample script, write it for them. If they're looking for a certain type of series, develop one and pitch it to them. If you're lucky enough to be given a story pitch meeting, do your best to pitch them what they want.

Don't give them what *you* want instead of what *they* want. The secret to my success has been that I have always given people exactly what *they* want, not what I thought they wanted, or thought they meant they wanted, or should want. This may sound like an artistic compromise, but only by first writing what *they* want will you someday find yourself in a position where you can write what *you* want. The artist who knows his paintings are great art but can't sell them may be a Van Gogh at some future date, but he'll starve today.

I constantly hear producers and story editors say, "There aren't enough good writers." So even without an agent, if you do Steps 1-5, your sample script is good, and you don't give up, you should hit pay dirt.

There is one other way to possibly break into animation writing, and that's via the Internet. Although it's virgin territory and, as of this writing, unmapped and in a constant state of flux, it seems pretty clear that animation on the Internet is going to be booming over the next several years. Thus, there may be opportunities to get in on the ground floor of animation writing by doing some spec toons for the Internet. There may even be producers willing to pay a little for scripts. Although you won't make much money this way, having a produced toon on your credit list may add to your credibility when looking for an agent, assignment, or series sale. It's also a terrific calling card, because all you have to do is give someone the URL (web address) and they can see your cartoon. If you want to try to write for the Internet, just get online and search like crazy for who's doing animation, then do the above five steps.

Now, let's say you lucked out and, with or without an agent, got yourself a meeting with a producer or creative exec to try to sell a story or series. What do you do now?

Chapter 16
How to Pitch Your Project

"THIS BABY'S ONLY GOT 10,000 miles on it and was driven on Sundays by a little old school teacher."

Ah, the pitch!

People have been selling things to people since Eve sold Adam the apple. As much as most of us dislike it, writers have to sell their wares as well, and the pitch is the way we do it.

Let's assume you've got a series concept for the next *Simpsons* or a feature idea that'll out-gross *The Lion King*. You'll have to sell it. You're going to do this by setting up a pitch meeting with a producer, studio, or network.

But how exactly are you going to pitch it?

I don't script my pitches. If I'm selling a TV series concept I use my presentation or bible. If I'm selling a feature idea I use my outline. My written pages are the bases of my pitches and are what I leave behind after the pitch is over.

Pitching your idea, whether for a series or feature, shouldn't take more than twenty minutes. Longer than that and you'll put the buyers to sleep.

Anything you can do to get the buyer to visualize and like your idea is fair game. Having artwork or toy prototypes or a minute of video can only help you sell your project. If you can afford them, use them. If you can't, don't worry about it. The most important thing is the concept. The artwork and goodies are secondary.

The most important thing about pitching is to be prepared. Sitting in front of someone and reading your idea off the page is no way to get them excited. To really sell someone on your idea you want them to not only get the story, but to be as enthusiastic about it as you are. The way to do this is to be spontaneous, and the way to be spontaneous with your pitch is to drill it. Read over your written material until you really know it, then drill your pitch over and over until it becomes second nature. Don't memorize it, just *know* it. This will not only allow you to relax and feel confident, it will give you the freedom to really get into your pitch and act it out. You should communicate the excitement of your story and characters. If it's dramatic, say it dramatically. If it's funny, say it in some funny way. Put emotions into your pitch. Be enthusiastic. Bring it to life. You want the buyer to feel your passion.

Another important thing to remember while pitching is that you can't just give your pitch by rote, paying no attention to the person to whom you're pitching. You have to be in good communication with the buyer, and that means not only getting your ideas across to him or her, but also watching their reactions and facial expressions. You want to spot it quickly if they don't understand or don't agree with something you've said. If a buyer doesn't understand what you're saying and doesn't stop to ask, you're sunk.

After the pitch is over it's important to be prepared for questions. You'll always get them. It's quite embarrassing when an exec asks you a question you can't answer. Know your project inside out. If it's series, know its intended audience and be prepared to pitch some story ideas.

When you're through with your pitch, be prepared to leave something in writing. It's best if the material you leave is a little more detailed than your pitch so that when they read it they are getting something new.

The last thing to be mentioned about pitching is the ever-present pass. In Hollywood-ese, a pass means "No, thank you!"

You're going to get them—that is, if you even get a pitch meeting. Odds are, most of your pitches will be passed on, as mine are. Don't let this discourage you. It's part of the game. Just because someone doesn't like your idea doesn't mean it's not a great one. The classic Hollywood pass story is owned by none other than George Lucas. As I heard it, six of the seven studios passed on *Star Wars* until Fox finally said yes. Good thing George didn't give up or we would never have enjoyed it, and he would never have become a billionaire.

Regrettably, I've got a pretty good pass story of my own—only I was the one doing the passing. When I was working at Stephen J. Cannell Productions a gentleman came to my office to pitch me a project. He illustrated the pitch with old Japanese footage of robots and leaping characters in skin-tight suits, corny explosions, and frenetic action. I just didn't get it, so I passed. He went on to sell it to Fox Kids. In fact, he went on to *own* Fox Kids!! The show was *Mighty Morphin Power Rangers*. Go figure!

Just remember that pitching is like shoving nickels into a slot machine. You're going to go through a lot of rolls until you hit a jackpot. The answer is to just keep pitching. The more you create and the more you pitch the better chance you'll have of selling something.

It's as simple as that.

Chapter 17

How to Prosper in Toon Town

BEFORE YOU RUN OFF HALF-COCKED with that shiny new animated six-shooter of yours, here are a few pieces of advice that will help you live long and prosper in this business.

It would be foolish to think you could become a good animation writer without first understanding a little bit about creativity, especially considering cartoon writing is one of the most creative forms of writing there is. Fortunately, creativity is not as ethereal as some might lead you to believe.

The reason most people think creativity is such a mysterious thing is probably because "authorities" have written so much on the subject that it begins to look pretty complex and unfathomable—left-brain versus right-brain, the unconscious, chemical reactions, gifts from God. The list goes on and on. There are great gobs of confusing theories on the subject of creativity and its origin. Some psychiatrists have suggested that creativity and madness are similar, and that to be really creative you must be somewhat loony tunes! Sounds to me like they've been watching too many cartoons—or maybe not enough!

If you've bought into any of this gobbledygook then you may have already begun to shackle your creativity. Why? Because, by simple observation, creativity can be seen to be totally unlimited. Any conclusion you draw about creativity—where it comes from, why you have it, why you don't, what drug makes it better, which one makes it worse—becomes a creative limitation. Don't think about creativity, just create.

Here's some simple examples. I've known writers who think they can only be creative in the early morning. I've spoken to others who think they have to have a drink to loosen them up creatively. I've heard of some who believe they have to wait for moments of creative inspiration, without which they just can't write.

Although these considerations may work for these writers, I never agreed with any of them. I simply chose to believe that I could create at any time, on any subject. That's what I've been practicing my entire career. So you're free to believe you can only get good ideas after deep breathing and yoga, or after sex, or whenever, but you're only going to limit your creativity.

Creativity begins with getting an idea, and there are an infinity of ideas. All of us are inherently creative. We get new and unique ideas all the time. The writer's job is to communicate ideas in such a way that they maintain the interest of the reader or viewer.

Interestingly, the most common question I'm asked as a cartoon writer is, "Where do you get all your ideas?" My first response is usually the line I gave to Gonzo in the "Romancing the Weirdo" episode of *Jim Henson's Muppet Babies*:

```
          GONZO
     All good ideas come from my nose. Though now
     and then I get a pretty good one from my
     elbow.
```

Seriously, I get my ideas from the same places everyone else does: travels, social encounters, day-to-day experiences, movies, TV, books, newspapers, dreams, past lives. That's right. Ideas can come from anywhere, even past lives. Whether or not you believe in the phenomenon is not the issue. What's important as a writer, is to be willing to experience *anything*. Because if you can't confront an idea I can guarantee you that you won't be able to write about it.

The fact that I was open to the concept of past lives gave me the opportunity to get a great story idea. Many years ago I vaguely recalled a past life experience about being in some kind of slave mine. The most oppressive thing about it was that the mine was only four feet high, so that everyone had to work while crouching over. This made it hard to dig and even harder to escape. I didn't think much of it at the time, but a few years later a producer asked me if I had any ideas for an animated feature. I started looking closer at my slave mine "experience," and it blossomed into a fascinating story about a slave society that knew only of their mine world. There was no outside world to them, nothing to life but eating, sleeping, and digging. In fact, they had a myth that told them to never dig up—up was hell. Then, while digging in the mine, the young hero of the story uncovered an object which spoke to him, telling him that his freedom would be found in the world above. He defied the rules and dug upward until he broke through to the surface of the planet, where he discovered that his people were being unwittingly forced to mine fuel for the starships of an evil empire. Our young hero wound up helping to free his people from bondage. I wound up selling the screenplay, which was released in 1984 as *Starchaser: The Legend of Orin*, the first 3-D animated feature ever made.

Moral of the story: Your mind is a virtual gold mine of ideas.

How do you find those few sparkling gems in that mountain of dull ore between your ears? The first thing you have to do is start digging. More specifically, you have to get your ideas flowing.

When I started out as a story editor at Hanna-Barbera, a woman came into my office one day and in the middle of our conversation said, "There's no such thing as a shortage of ideas." That idea struck me like a dart in the forehead. *Poing!* I agreed with it instantly. It's proven to be true ever since.

Here's a practical drill that will not only demonstrate that there are an infinity of ideas, but will help open up your creative flows anytime they're stuck. Wherever you happen to be, look around and find an object. Make up an idea about it. It doesn't matter whether the idea is good or bad—we're just looking for ideas. Now look at another part of that same object and get another idea. Do this over and over until you've realized that you can keep doing it indefinitely. I'll give you an example. I'm looking at the telephone on my desk—

Idea #1: I discover my phone is magically connected to heaven.

Idea #2: The man who made the buttons on the phone has secretly made one of them out of C-4 explosive.

Idea #3: The government has figured out a way to listen to me via satellite, even when I'm not talking on the phone.

Idea #4: There's a gremlin inside the phone who secretly adds expletives to my conversations without my hearing—or knowing!

Idea #5: My phone number is a winning Lotto ticket number.

Are you getting the idea? I could do this forever. And we're just talking about a mundane telephone. Imagine if we chose something interesting to develop ideas about! The purpose of this drill is to teach you that getting ideas is really the easiest thing in the world. The trick is getting funny ones, or brilliant ones, or ones you can sell. However, in order to find these you've got to get the brakes off your idea machine.

Writer, Know Thyself!

What is a writer's first and most important tool? Computer? Paper and Pencil? Eraser? Wastebasket? It's none of these. A writer's most important tool is his mind.

Of course, everyone knows that. Perhaps, but very few people truly understand what their mind is made of.

You wouldn't think much of a professional auto racer if he didn't have a clue about engines and drive trains. Without such an understanding he would be at the mercy of his mechanics. He'd be driving a mystery down the track, not knowing what was going on with each whir and click of the engine. Was that chatter a gear properly changing . . . or a clutch about to blow?

Similarly, a writer without an understanding of his mind is at the mercy of any "breakdown" or stray thought that wanders past.

What is a mind? Our minds, by practical observation, are made up of countless images of our past experience. We all have stored away in our minds, to greater or lesser degree of availability, everything we have experienced in the past. If you don't believe it just try this simple experiment: Recall the earliest time you rode a bicycle as a child! Can you recall what color the bike was? Did it have two wheels or three? Can you recall the environment through which you rode? What were you wearing at the time? Where were you going? Were you happy or sad?

It's likely you haven't looked at these past images in a very long time. Perhaps you just looked at them for the first time since they were recorded in your mind. If I hadn't asked you to look at them you may have never contacted them again. Regardless, they're still all there, like data in a computer, neatly stored in your memory bank, filed under childhood, cross-filed under bike, color, number of wheels, time, date, emotions, and just waiting for you to put attention on them and bring them back to life.

This is the most useful tool of a writer—a file cabinet full of images of a lifetime, your very own experiential database. The more experience you have, whether of things you actually did or movies you watched, books you read, stories you heard, the more you have to draw on.

I didn't know I wanted to be a writer when I went to college, but I knew I was going to do something creative. I also knew that accumulated experiences would be the building blocks of my eventual creation. For my first two years at UCLA I was an undeclared major and took courses in everything—math, physics, music, photography, logic, debating, computers, history, and geology. This turned out to be quite valuable input for my creative database, and I've continually drawn on this material in my writing.

You've probably heard that most great writers have led fascinating lives. Hemingway lived in France, Florida, and Spain, fought wars, fought bulls, battled marlins and men in bars. This all makes for good story material, but don't worry. As a cartoon writer you don't have to experience something in order write about it (although I do feel a bit of regret about never having stood under a falling grand piano).

Bad Habits and Other Things to Watch Out For

When you were a kid, growing up, did you ever say to yourself, *I can't write*, or *I can't draw*, or *I'll never be as good at* _____ *as my dad?* That little voice inside your head—the one that says, *I'll never think of a good idea*, or *Writing is so hard*, or *This idea sucks!*—is the killer of creativity. We all know we create with our minds, and that they're much like computers. But did you know that by thinking a simple thought like *My ideas stink* you've just programmed your mental computer with a piece of software that is going to affect all of your writing?

You create and write with thought, and if you think you're a lousy writer, guess what—*you are!*

Did you ever tell a child that the drawing they just did is terrible? They'll stop drawing for a month. But tell them it's terrific and they'll shower you with artwork. The point here is that we're all just kids under our aging skin, and we work the very same way. If you think thoughts like, *I can get lots of ideas and they're going to be good,* you've programmed yourself to do just that. Sound too easy? It's worked for me, and I haven't had a shortage of good ideas yet.

Criticism can kill an artist quicker than a hollow point. Don't be fooled by "constructive criticism," either. It's often really a few drops of hemlock in your wine. Yes, it's important to listen to what people have to say about your writing, and often a great way to learn, but if their criticism makes you feel bad it's not constructive, it's an attack! If someone tells you all the reasons why your script stinks and they're *right*, after the initial disappointment you'll actually feel a bit better, because you'll see what you have to do to correct it. If comments just make you feel worse, then I'll bet you dollars to donuts they were calculated to do just that. Don't buy it! Or you'll be buying a coffin for your creativity.

"In the beginning was the word, and the word was good." Why was it good? Because the writer liked it, and for no other reason. Remember *that* when you write! If you think it's good, it's good. That's the truth. If a producer or story editor thinks it's bad then that's *their* truth. It doesn't mean your writing is bad, it only means you have to adjust it if you want to sell it to *them*. Don't worry about whether it's good enough. It's obviously the best you can do at the moment. You can always write better. Each script you write should be better than it's predecesser because you'll have had more experience.

Some Helpful Pointers

Want a great trick to make you feel like a better writer? Just watch some bad movies or TV episodes, or read some bad scripts. Then tell yourself (as you probably already have a million times) I can write better than this s—-! *You can!*

If you're jammed and feel overwhelmed while writing, you probably just need to get what you're creating out of your head and into the real world. Take paper and pencil and start drawing out your ideas, or diagram them. If I'm trying to figure out a complicated scene, like how to get a hero out of a difficult trap, I usually just draw a picture of it first. Then it flows much faster when I write it.

By the way, if you've ever had writer's block or blank page syndrome, don't bother going to a psychiatrist (even though they've probably already classified them as mental disorders and are prescribing Prozac). You can get the flow going again by simply starting to write anything. Good, bad, indifferent. It doesn't matter. Just get the flow going. Then go back and improve it as necessary. What you must avoid at all costs are those sneaky little self-invalidating-bio-software ideas like, *God, am I ever going to be able to write again?* Just write! Trust me, it will come, but you've got to start. Otherwise you'll just sit there in wait mode. That's when those devilish, self-invalidating voices will creep in. Once you start validating yourself and your creative ability, you'll turn that trickle of ideas into a raging river. Believe that you are the master of your thoughts and you will soon begin to control them better. Eventually, your ideas will jump through hoops for you like a well trained dog.

Ever since I started writing at Hanna-Barbera I have always tried to be a professional. A professional is not just someone who makes a living at a given job or profession. A true professional is someone who learns as much as possible about his work, does the best he can at producing that product, isn't satisfied with mediocrity but only with top quality products, is willing to spot his mistakes and correct them, and demands this of those around him as well. I have always striven to be as professional as possible in my writing. It's not just what you do. It's also the way you feel about it, and believe me, it feels good when you can produce high quality products that others want to buy.

One of the best tricks for writing faster and getting more done is to set targets. I remember hearing my father say that five pages was a good day's work. However, this seemed quite arbitrary to me. I decided to see if I could do better. After my second year running the *Superfriends* series I got up to five pages an hour! I did it by making a game out of it. I'd set a very stiff target—but one I knew was possible—then I'd start writing. I started with one page an hour. Then two. Then four. I still made sure to never sacrifice quality. If it was no good I'd throw it away. Don't believe that time has anything to do with quality. It doesn't. Good is good, whether it takes five minutes or five months.

A surefire way to slow your production down is to stop and start. When you write you get into another space. Call it creative space or imagination or the "zone" or Aunt Beauregard. It's not the same space that holds your chair and your body. You have to get into it, which you do when you start to create. Once you're in it, you begin to create the people and events of your story in that space. The more you get into it the more real the characters and things become, and the better you can see and hear them. If you stop after a few pages and take a break, you're leaving this space and must then take time to get back into it. When you're in it, and the writing is flowing, *don't stop!*

I can't tell you how many times I'd stop after writing a long scene and say, "That's enough. I can stop for the day." Then I'd immediately tell myself to start the next scene quickly, before I agreed with myself and stopped. Once into the next scene I'd easily ride it out. Several pages later that scene would end and I'd hear that voice again. "Hey, ten pages. Not bad! That's twice what Dad used to do. You can stop now." I'd persist through this and the process continued.

When you finish a scene there is a tendency to get into the "end-ness" of it and want to end your writing. Starting, as with a blank page at the beginning of a script, is harder than continuing, and a heck of a lot harder than ending. Each time you finish a scene give yourself a little *push* into the next scene. The more you write, the better writer you'll become, and there is a correlation between one's production and one's morale. The more you produce, the better you'll feel.

Here's a tip that cannot be repeated enough. *Keep it simple!* I'm still learning this one. The biggest mistake writers make is making everything too complicated. Take a look at the best books and movies and you'll discover an amazing fact: you can usually describe the story in a sentence. What makes the writing good is time spent on character, conflict, and comedy. An excessively complex story leaves no time for these. I suggest you chant this each day before you start writing: *keep it simple keep it simple keep it simple...*

One of the most emotionally dangerous traps laying in wait for the writer is having just one project to sell. If it is rejected, your entire creative existence has been rejected. Life can feel pretty dismal when the one thing you've sunk your heart and soul into is unwanted. This is why actors who go on only a few interviews are emotionally crushed when they aren't hired. If you have three or four projects, say a spec script, a series idea, a novel, and a children's book, then when you get a pass on one you've only been told 25 percent of your life is worthless, and you've still got a majority of your creative energy that hasn't been negated.

Here's a tip that will save you from riding the show biz emotional roller-coaster: Be sure to keep that day job! One of the deadliest traps a writer—or any artist—can fall into is hoping that their art will feed them. It's extremely hard to keep focused on writing when you're worrying about bills. The best way to buy quality creative time is to have a job that keeps you secure. A few hours at the computer in the evening will be much more rewarding than a full day of desperate writing. It's also a fact that show biz is one of the most competitive businesses in the world. There simply isn't room for everyone to succeed. Don't give up, just keep that day job.

Over the years, many people have expressed their concern about having their ideas stolen and have asked me what they can do to protect them. They register their scripts with the WGA, copyright them, ask people to sign non-disclosure letters, etc. All of these are valid ways to protect copyrighted material. Do them if it makes you feel better. Personally, I don't bother with this. I just pitch my ideas freely, and no one has ever stolen one yet. Rather than worry about my ideas being ripped off, I just create so many ideas that I can afford to lose one or two. I have so many ideas in my idea file that I constantly see them coming out in the movies or on TV. No one's stealing them. It's the nature of the business. People are constantly coming up with contemporary, clever ideas. When you create one, it's possible someone else will also have thought of it. Don't worry if you lose one. Just create three more!

We've all heard stories about that person who wrote their first script and sold if for umpteen zillion dollars. Though new writers sometimes succeed in writing a great script, it's quite rare. It can also be a terrible self-inflicted barrier to strive to do so. The fact is, it takes a lot of practice to do anything well, especially writing. My first script was pretty ordinary, but I kept writing and they got better. Skills are improved through practice. As a new writer, you set yourself up for a huge loss if you're just trying to sell the next *Lion King* or the next *South Park*. Be willing to start out small. Do it one step a time, and get each step down pat before taking the next. It's a slower but much surer ladder to success.

Don't spend too much time rewriting your material over and over. Personally, I learn a lot more by writing *many* scripts rather than trying to rewrite each one to perfection. It really comes down to arithmetic. If you write four scripts in a year, rather than spending four years on one script, in the same period of time you will have had the experience of writing sixteen scripts instead of one. I assure you that you'll be a much better writer with sixteen scripts under your belt.

Here's a short one: Better to be too short and leave the reader wanting more, than too long and leave the reader snoring. And on that note...

Epilogue

YOU SHOULD NOW HAVE A PRETTY good idea of how the animation writing business works, as well as how to create, develop, and write an animated series or screenplay. Knowledge, though, is only valuable in practice, so *use* this data. Create a series. Write a sample cartoon or a spec animated feature. Who knows? With a little creativity and lot of hard work you might just build a successful career as an animation writer. If you do, don't forget to tell me. After all, that's why writers write (or should): to create a positive effect on their audience. That's certainly why I wrote this book. It wasn't to make money, but to pass along my experience to those who aren't fortunate enough to have had a story editor for a father. I get no greater pleasure than to help people. So by telling me your successes, no matter how small, you'll repay me ten-fold for any help I've given you.

Needless to say, there's more to toon writing than I was able to cover in this book, so if you have any questions or comments feel free to send me an e-mail. You can find my current e-mail address at my website: www.jeffreyscott.tv. Keep your questions few and brief, and please don't ask me to read your material. My lawyer won't let me.

And now it's time to say, *"That's all folks!"* I like to end all of my written works with something inspiring, if at all possible, so I spent some time searching for just the right words to end this book. Then I realized that the perfect words were already written by Jim Henson in a letter he sent me after I left the *Muppet Babies* series, thanking me for making him laugh. I will end this book by giving to you the simple but profound words that Jim gave me . . . words I've tried to live by ever since:

Go forth and do good things!

Biography

JEFFREY SCOTT WAS BORN Jeffrey Alan Maurer in Hollywood to Norman Maurer, creator of the world's first 3-D comic book, and Joan Howard Maurer, daughter of Moe Howard of the Three Stooges.

At age eleven, Jeffrey began his creative career by acting in motion pictures, including two Three Stooges films produced and directed by his father. At age seventeen, he wrote his first screenplay for what was to be the final film of The Three Stooges, but the production was canceled when the producers failed to successfully replace ailing stooge Larry Fine.

After receiving a Bachelor of Arts degree from UCLA, with a major in Motion Pictures and Television, Jeffrey worked for four years inking comic books, including such classics as: *Mickey Mouse, Donald Duck, Coyote & Roadrunner, Daffy Duck,* and *Woody Woodpecker.*

Following comic books, Jeffrey created several pieces of fine art, including an American Flag made of one hundred seventeen crisp U.S. one-dollar bills, one of which is hanging in the Gerald R. Ford Library.

Tired of people misspelling and mispronouncing Maurer, and because his fiancée was going to change her maiden name, Jeffrey decided to change his last name as well. After marrying Sonya "Sunny" Kroch at the Hotel Bel-Air in Los Angeles, they became Mr. & Mrs. Jeffrey Scott. (If you're a sucker for mushy love stories you'll appreciate the fact that Jeffrey met Sonya in the 5th grade and it was love-at-first-sight in both directions!)

Over the course of his writing career, Jeffrey has written over six hundred animated television scripts for such series as: *Superfriends, Pac-Man* (Hanna-Barbera Productions); *Jim Henson's Muppet Babies, Spider-Man, Dungeons & Dragons* (Marvel Productions); *Plastic-Man, Thundarr the Barbarian, Mega Man* (Ruby-Spears Productions); *The Littles, Hulk Hogan's Rock 'n' Wrestling, Wacky World of Tex Avery, Sonic the Hedgehog* (DIC Enterprises), *Teenage Mutant Ninja Turtles, Zorro, James Bond, Jr.* (Fred Wolf Films); *Duck Tales, Tale Spin, Winnie The Pooh* (Disney); *Dragon Tales* (Columbia-TriStar/Sesame Workshop); and *Mr. Baby* (Wild Brain).

Jeffrey's animation writing has been recognized with three Emmy Awards and the Humanitas Prize.

Jeffrey has also worked freelance and as a staff writer in live-action television, including scripts for *The Misadventures of Sheriff Lobo* (Universal), *Mr. Merlin* (Columbia), *Wake, Rattle & Roll* (Hanna-Barbera), and *The Powers Of Matthew Starr* (Paramount). He has also written screenplays for Paramount, Columbia and Will Vinton Studios.

Following the family tradition, Jeffrey managed the worldwide rights to The Three Stooges from 1988 through 1994, including the development of motion pictures, television and licensing. He executive produced, wrote, and starred in *The Three Stooges Live-Stage Show* at the MGM Grand Hotel in Las Vegas.

Toonography

(i.e. Jeffrey Scott's animated TV and film credits)

2001

MR. BABY † ‡
Wild Brain

Dog & Phony Show
20,000 Leaks Under the Sea
No Baby Is An Island
Old MacBaby Had A Farm
Invasion of the Baby Snatchers
Nightmare on Smarmy Street
The Big Baby's Birthday

RECOGNITION & REWARDS ‡
Trainingcape.Com

One-hour animated edutainment
program for the Internet

2000

CHRISTMAS IN DUCKPORT ‡
Lyrick Studios / Suzy's Zoo, Inc.

One-Hour Animated Special

JACK HAMMER, P.I. ‡
Trainingcape.Com

Three-minute animated Internet script

THE UNBEARABLE LIGHTNESS OF BEING...A JERK ‡
Trainingcape.Com

Three-minute animated Internet script

LI'L GREEN MEN ‡
Warner Brothers Entertaindom / Jinx
(3-D CGI Animated Internet Series)

Take Me To Your Happy Meal!
We're Being Invaded, By George
Tattoo Barada Nikto
I Did Not Have Extraterrestrial Relations With
Those Li'l Green Men, Ray & Tony
One Small Step For Guppies

WESTOONS
Animationsstudio Ludewig, Hamburg

The Smell of Danger
Quicksilver, Quick Steel
Doppelganger
Grizzly
Soldier of Misfortune
Dark Spirits
Deadly Survey
A Crude Plan
The Eagle's Eye
Knockout

JAMES MARSHALL'S "FOX OUTFOXED" ‡
HIT Entertainment, London

Animated Series Bible
Fox Goes Fishing (pilot)

MR. BABY † ‡
Wild Brain

Animated Series Bible

Series story-edited by Jeffrey Scott are indicated by †.
As of this writing all credits are produced unless indicated by ‡.
For an up-to-date list of credits go to www.jeffreyscott.tv

Building Blockhead (pilot)
Driving Mr. Baby (pilot)
One Small Stumble for Smarmy
Yo-Ho-Ho And A Bottle of Milk
A Few Good Babies
That Championship Baby
A Fistful of Plungers
Tooth Or Consequences
Horsing Around
Jungle Bungle
Wolfgang Amadeus Baby
Lights, Camera...BABY!
The Golf War
Rock-A-Bye Wrestler
The Curse of Tutankbaby
Tyrannosaurus Wrecks
Calling Dr. Baby
Counterfeit Fitness
Go West, Young Baby
Mr. Baby for President
Smarmy Wars
Frankensmarmy vs. Babyzilla
Mr. Babysitter
Mr. Babyface
A Lad In The Lamp
What About Baby?
Double-O-Baby
Go, Baby, Van Go!
The Baby Man of Alcatraz
Business is BOOM-ing!
Smarmy Goose Stories
A Smarmy Cartoon
Stage Frights
Just Plane Fun
Pest Intentions
Hot L Smarmy
Mr. Baby in Toyland
Tour de Farce
Superbaby vs. The Evil Ice Cream Man
The Sheriff of Naughtyham
Baby Formula One

1999

DRAGON TALES †
*Columbia-TriStar / Children's Television
Workshop / PBS*

Quetzal's Magic Pop-Up Book
My Emmy Or Bust!

My Way Or Snow Way
Don't Bug Me!
Roller-Coaster Dragon
Much Ado About Nodlings
The Great White Cloud Whale
Ord Sees the Light
The Ugly Dragling

ALPHABOAT ‡
*AlphaBoat Prods. / Children's Television
Workshop*

**Co-Created by
Executive Producer**

Series Bible

**THE EXTREME ADVENTURES
OF WACKY WILLIE ‡**
By Jeffrey Scott, Inc. / Whirlwind Pictures

**Created by
Executive Producer**

Series Bible

DISNEY'S PB&J OTTER
Jumbo Pictures /Disney Channel

Opal's Magic Mud Party
Leave It To Munchy
A Very Surprising Party

1998

DRAGON TALES †
*Columbia-TriStar / Children's Television
Workshop / PBS*

A Picture's Worth A Thousand Words
Emmy's Dream House
Knot A Problem
Pigment of Your Imagination
The Great Siesta Fiesta
Calling Dr. Zak
Staying Within the Lines
A Smashing Success
No Hitter
Good-bye Mr. Caterpoozle
Follow the Dots

Ord's Unhappy Birthday
Max's Comic Adventure
Sky Pirates
Zak & The Beanstalk
Do Not Pass Gnome
Sounds Like Trouble
The Big Cake Mix-Up
Frog Prints
A True-Blue Friend

WE THE PEOPLE ‡
Cinetopia

One-hour Edutainment Video

1997

WACKY WORLD OF TEX AVERY †
DIC Entertainment

"EINSTONE" segments:

The Ugh-Lympic Games
Is There A Doctor In The Cave?
Look Who's Ughing
A-Hunting We Won't Go

"GHENGIS & KHANNIE" segments:

What's Yours Is Mayan
Himalaya Down And Die
A No-Etiquette Barbarian In King Arthur's
Court
Dances On Lions
Donkey Conqueror

"MAURICE & MOOCH" segments:

Run For Your Lifeguard!
Chicken Scouts
Yes, We Have No Electricity
The One That Didn't Get Away
The Toothless Fairy
Slaphappy Birthday

KOOKY KLASSICS ‡
DIC Entertainment
(Direct-to-Video Animated Movie)

The Idiots and The Odyssey (story)

ZORRO †
Fred Wolf Films / Warner Brothers

The Beast Within
Two Zorros Are Better Than One
Tar Pit Terror
A King's Ransom
Pirates of San Pedro
The Anti-Zorro
Revenge of the Panther
The Iron Man
Poison Pen
Vision of Darkness
The Case of the Masked Marauder
Return of the Conquistadors
Raiding Party
The Hunter
The Four Horsemen
Nightmare Express
The Ice Monster Commeth
The Secret of El Zorro
Nordic Quest
Adios, Mi Capitan

DRAGON TALES †
*Columbia-TriStar / Children's Television
Workshop / PBS*

Co-Developed for Television by

One Small Step for Cassie (pilot)
Circle of Friends (pilot)

1996

FANTASTIC VOYAGES OF SINBAD
Fred Wolf Films

The Mystery of Elephant Island

SKYSURFER STRIKE FORCE
Ruby-Spears Productions

Water Hazard

TEENAGE MUTANT NINJA TURTLES †
Fred Wolf Films / CBS

The Return of Dregg
The Beginning of the End

The Power of Three (Part I of III)
A Turtle In Time (Part II of III)
Turtles to the 2nd Power (Part III of III)
Mobster From Dimension X
The Day the Earth Disappeared
Divide and Conquer

LOGGERHEADS
Neue Deutsche Filmgesellschaft

Hospitality & Insurance (story)

THE JOJOS ‡
DIC Entertainment

Series Bible
The Panama Root Canal (pilot)
Operation: Dessert Storm (pilot)

WACKY WORLD OF TEX AVERY †
DIC Entertainment

"EINSTONE" segments:

Saur Loser
A Bird In The Brain's Worth 2 In A Bush
Caveman And Wife
Cave Improvement
Out Of Shape, Out Of Mind
Once Upon A Time Traveler
Neanderthal Mom

"GHENGIS & KHANNIE" segments:

Humpty Dumpty Had A Great Wall
Aloha Oy!
You Take the High Road & I'll Take Cairo
A Pain In The Rain Forest
Who Kilt The Conqueror?
Up A Greek Without A Paddle

"MAURICE & MOOCH" segments:

Breakfast In Bedlam
Sitter Jitters
Black 'n' Blue Belt
Teacher's Pest
True Or False Alarm
Toy Store Story

1995

SKYSURFER STRIKE FORCE
Ruby-Spears Productions

The Crawling Horror (script only)
2-Minute Warning! (story only)

GOO GOO GADGET ‡
DIC Entertainment

Raiders of the Lost Mummies (Pilot)

1994

THE ADVENTURES OF SANTA CLAUS ‡
Will Vinton Productions

Multi-Media Animated Feature Film
Treatment by Jeffrey Scott

WEE STOOGES ‡
Jeffrey Scott Productions / ABC

Created by
Executive Producer

Drown And Out In Beverly Hills (pilot)
Last of the Moe Haircuts (pilot)

MEGA MAN †
Ruby-Spears Productions

Electric Nightmares
Mega-Pinocchio (story only)
Robosaur Park
Mega Man In The Moon
Ice Age

HAWAIIAN SLAMMERS
DIC Entertainment
(Half-Hour Animated Special)

1993

MOBY & DICK ‡
Will Vinton Productions
(Multi-Media Animated Feature Film)

Story & Screenplay by Jeffrey Scott

SONIC THE HEDGEHOG †
DIC Entertainment / SEGA

Robolympics
Magnificent Sonic
Black Bot the Pirate
Hedgehog of the Hound Table
Robotnik's Pyramid Scheme
Prehistoric Sonic
Baby-Sitter Jitters
Honey I Shrunk the Hedgehog
Robotnikland
The Mobius 5000
The Little Merhog
Road Hog

1992

WISH KID ‡
DIC / Fox Children's Network

A Dog's Breakfast (pilot)

THE SUPER TROLLS
DIC Entertainment
(Half-hour Animated Special)

GUARDIANS OF THE COSMOS ‡
Fred Wolf Films

Genesis (pilot)

1991

GOOF TROOP
Walt Disney TV Animation

Party Animal

JAMES BOND, JR. †
Murakami Wolf Swenson

A Worm in the Apple
A Race Against Disaster
The Chameleon
Leonardo Da Vinci's Vault
Nothing To Play With
The Inhuman Race
Hunt For Red Star One
Lamp of Darkness (story)
Pompeii & Circumstance

Fountain of Terror (story)
No Such Loch
Between A Rock & A Hard Place (story)
Cruise to Oblivion
Deadly Recall
Thor's Thunder (story)
Monument to SCUM (story)
The Art of Evil
A DeRanged Mind
SCUM on the Water
Quantum Diamonds (story)

WISH KID †
DIC Entertainment / NBC

Co-Developed for Television by

Top Gun - Will Travel (pilot)
A Matter of Principal
Haunted House For Sale
Captain Mayhem
Glove of Dreams
Love At First Wish
Lotto Trouble
Darryl's Dilemma
A Nick Off The Old Block
A Grand Ol' Time
Gross Encounters
Mom, Dad...You're Fired!
The Best of Enemies

1990

DUCK TALES
Walt Disney TV Animation

Attack of The Metalmites
Honey, I Shrunk The Gizmo Suit
The Golden Goose (Part I)
The Golden Goose (Part II)

TALE SPIN
Walt Disney TV Animation

My Fair Baloo
The Hunt

JIM HENSON'S MUPPET BABIES
Marvel / Henson / CBS

A Punch Line To The Tummy

WINNIE THE POOH
Walt Disney TV Animation

976-Trouble

1989

SWAMP THING ‡
Marvel Productions / Lightyear / CBS

Series Bible

HI & LOIS "TRIXIE & DAWG" ‡
Marvel Prods & King Features / CBS

Who's Minding The Baby (co-written)
Boo Hoo On Cue (co-written)
Think Fast! (co-written)

JIM HENSON'S MUPPET BABIES
Marvel / Henson / CBS

Romancing The Weirdo

CAPTAIN N: THE GAME MASTER †
DIC Entertainment / NBC

Kevin In Videoland (Pilot)
Mr. & Mrs. Mother Brain
How's Bayou?
Videolympics (Part I)
Mega Trouble For Megaland (Part II)
Nightmare On Mother Brain's Street
Three Men And A Dragon
Simon The Ape-Man
Wishful Thinking
The Most Dangerous Game Master
Metroid Sweet Metroid
In Search of The King
Happy Birthday, Mega Man

1988

STEVIE WONDER'S INNER VISIONS ‡
Stephen J. Cannell Productions

Series Bible

1987

THE GREATEST AMERICAN HERO ‡
Stephen J. Cannell Productions / ABC

Series Bible
Car Trouble (Pilot)

ULTRACROSS ‡
Stephen J. Cannell / Nelvana / LBS

Executive Producer
Developed for Television by

Like Father, Like Son (Part I)
Like Father, Like Son (Part II)
Like Father, Like Son (Part III)
The Wall
The Exterminator
Road Raiders
The Price of Freedom
A Crack In The Family
Operation: Killer Whale
The Prince And The Racer

1986

JIM HENSON'S MUPPET BABIES
Marvel / Henson / CBS

Pigerella
The Best Friend I Never Had
The Weirdo Zone
Muppets In Toyland
The Muppet Broadcasting Company
Kermit Goes To Washington
Fozzie's Family Tree
The Daily Muppet
Scooter's Uncommon Cold
Treasure Attic
Around The Nursery In 80 Days
Polly Wants A Muppet
Muppet Goose
Bad Luck Bear

CBS STORYBREAK ‡
Southern Star Productions / CBS

Sideways Stories From Wayside School
(Not the Broadcast Arts Version)

1985

JIM HENSON'S MUPPET BABIES
Marvel / Henson / CBS

Once Upon An Egg Timer
Piggy's Hyper-Activity Book
Fozzie's Last Laugh
The Great Cookie Robbery
Out-Of-This-World History
Snow White And The Seven Muppets
I Want My Muppet TV!
Musical Muppets
Who's Who At The Zoo?
The Great Muppet Cartoon Show
The Muppet Museum of Art

HULK HOGAN'S ROCK 'N' WRESTLING †
DIC Enterprises / CBS

The Junkyard 500 (Pilot)
The Four-Legged Pickpocket (Pilot)
Andre's Giant Problem (Pilot)
Cheaters Never Prosper
Ghostwrestlers
My Fair Wrestler
Battle of The Bands
Amazons Just Wanna Have Fun
The Art of Wrestling
A Lesson In Scouting
The Duke of Piperton
Ten Little Wrestlers
Ballet Buffoons
The Wrong Stuff
Junkenstein
Robin Hulk And His Merry Wrestlers
Gorilla My Dreams
Wrestling Roommates
Moolah's Ugly Salon
Ballot Box Boneheads
Big John's Car Lot
The Superfly Express
Rowdy Roddy Reforms
Captain Lou's Crash Diet
Junkyard Dog's Junkyard Dog
The Foster Wrestler
Driving Me Crazy
The Wrestler's New Clothes
Rock 'n' Zombies

1984

THE RIGHT STUFF ‡
Marvel Productions / CBS

Series Bible
Desert Encounters (Pilot)

THE SECRET WAR ‡
Marvel Productions

Series Bible

MENUDO ‡
Marvel Productions / ABC

Series Bible

TRANSFORMERS ‡
Marvel Productions / CBS

Series Bible
A Robot's Best Friend Is His Dog (Pilot)

THE LITTLES
DIC Enterprises & ABC Productions

Little Baby-Sitters
Looking For Grandma Little

DUNGEONS & DRAGONS
Marvel Productions / CBS

The Traitor
The Last Illusion

JIM HENSON'S MUPPET BABIES
Marvel / Henson / CBS

Developed for Television by

Noisy Neighbors (Pilot)
Who's Afraid of The Big, Bad Dark?
Dental Hijinks
Raiders of The Lost Muppet
Scooter's Hidden Talent
The Case of The Missing Chicken
8 Take Away 1 Equals Panic
What Do You Wanna Be When You Grow Up?
Close Encounters of The Frog Kind
Gonzo's Video Show

Fun Park Fantasies
From A Galaxy Far, Far Away
Good, Clean Fun

M.A.S.K.
DIC Enterprises & Kenner Toys

The Star Chariot
Video Venom

1983

SPORT-BILLY ‡
Sport-Billy Productions, Monte-Carlo

Now You See It, Now You Don't (Pilot)

X-MEN ‡
Marvel Productions

Series Bible

PAC-MAN †
Hanna-Barbera Productions / ABC

Here's Super-Pac!
Hey, Hey, Hey...It's P.J.
Pac-A-Lympics
Pac-Van-Winkle
Super-Pac Vs. Pac-Ape
The Old Pac-Man And The Sea
Journey Into The Pac-Past
The Greatest Show In Pacland
The Genii of Pacdad
Dr. Jekyll & Mr. Pac-Man
Computer Packy
Happy Pacs-Giving
Around The World In 80 Chomps
The Super-Pac Bowl
Public Pac-Enemy Number One
P.J. Goes Pac-Hollywood

THE LITTLES †
DIC Enterprises & ABC Productions

Beware of Hunter! (Pilot)
The Lost City of The Littles
The Big Scare
Lights...Camera...Littles!
Spirits of The Night
The Little Winner

A Big Cure For A Little Illness
The Rats Are Coming!
A Little Fairy Tale
Prescription For Disaster
The Little Scouts
A Little Gold...A Lot of Trouble
Dinky's Doomsday Pizza

DUNGEONS & DRAGONS
Marvel Productions, Ltd. / CBS

In Search of The Dungeon Master
Beauty And The Bogbeast
Servant of Evil (script only)
Garden of Zinn
The Box
Children of Darkness
P-R-E-S-T-O Spells Disaster

THE GREATEST STORIES OF ALL
DIC Enterprises & ABC Productions

David And Goliath (One-Hour Special)

MARSUPILAMI ‡
Marvel Productions / CBS

Series Bible

1982

STARCHASER: THE LEGEND OF ORIN
Mihahn, Inc. - Atlantic Releasing
(3-D Animated Feature Film)

Story & Screenplay by Jeffrey Scott

MORK & MINDY ‡
Hanna-Barbera Productions / ABC

Series Bible

ROXIE'S RAIDERS ‡
Ruby-Spears Productions / CBS

Terror By Telephone

CAPTAIN CARROT ‡
Ruby-Spears Productions / ABC

Frankenfrog (Pilot)

INTERNATIONAL FAST 111'S
General Mills Toy Group

T.E.R.R.O.R. At Roaring Pass (Special)

THE INCREDIBLE HULK ‡
Marvel Productions / NBC

Series Bible

SUPERFRIENDS †
Hanna-Barbera Productions / ABC

The Krypton Syndrome
Two Gleeks Are Deadlier Than One
Once Upon A Poltergeist
Playground of Doom
Space Racers
Terror On The Titanic
Mxyzptlk's Revenge
Roller Coaster
Day of The Dinosaurs
Revenge of Doom
A Pint of Life
Attack of The Cats
The Recruiter
Invasion of The Space Dolls
Bulgor The Behemoth
Warpland
An Unexpected Treasure
Video Victims
Prisoners of Sleep
One Small Step For Superman
The Malusian Blob
Return of The Phantoms
Bully For You
Superclones

PAC-MAN †
Hanna-Barbera Productions / ABC

Developed for Television by

Presidential Pac-Nappers (Pilot #1)
Hocus-Pocus Pac-Man (Pilot #2)
The Great Pac-Quake
Southpaw Packy
Pac-Baby Panic
Picnic In Pacland
Pac-Man In The Moon

Neander-Pac-Man
Super-Ghosts
Invasion of The Pac-Pups
Pacula
Trick Or Chomp
The Bionic Pac-Woman
Once Upon A Chomp
Journey To The Center of Pacland
Chomp-Out At The O.K. Corral
The Great Power-Pellet Robbery
Backpackin' Packy
The Abominable Pac-Man
The Pac-Boat
Sir Chomp-A-Lot
Goo-Goo At The Zoo
The Pac-Mummy
A Bad Case of The Chomps
The Day The Forest Disappeared
Nighty Nightmares

PAC-MAN †
Hanna-Barbera Productions / ABC

Christmas Comes To Pacland (Special)

PANDAMONIUM †
Intermedia / Marvel / CBS

Algernon's Story
Timothy's Story
The Itty-Bitty City
Ice Hastles
Methinks The Sphinx Jinx Stinks
Prehistoric Hysterics
Once Upon A Time Machine
20,000 Laughs Beneath The Sea
The Great Space Chase

1981

FONZ & THE HAPPY DAYS GANG
Ruby-Spears Productions / ABC

There's No Place Like Rome

THUNDARR THE BARBARIAN
Ruby-Spears Productions / ABC

City of Evil

GOLDIE GOLD
Ruby-Spears Productions / ABC

Night of The Walking Doom

SUPERFRIENDS
Hanna-Barbera Productions / ABC

Outlaws of Orion
Creature From The Dump
Three Wishes

TROLLKINS
Hanna-Barbera Productions / CBS

Escape From Alcatroll
The Troll Choppers Meet Frogzilla
Trollyapolis 500
Trollin The Magician
The Great Troll Train Wreck
Raiders of The Lost Troll-Mummy
Treasure of Troll Island
The Empire Strikes Trolltown
Pixlee And The Seven Trolls
Supertroll
Trolltown Trollympics
Dr. Frankentroll, I Presume
Flooky And The Troll Burglar
Agent Double-O-Troll
The Abominable Trollman

CAPT. AMERICA & THE BARBARIANS ‡
Marvel Productions

Series Bible

THE BOWSER BUDDIES ‡
Ruby-Spears Productions / ABC

Messed Up Mascots (Pilot)

1980

SUPERFRIENDS †
Hanna-Barbera Productions / ABC

One Small Step For Mars
Big Foot
Cycle Gang
Elevator To Nowhere

Journey Into Blackness
Haunted House
The Make-Up Monster
Dive To Disaster
The Ice Demon
Mxyzptlk Strikes Again
Yuna The Terrible
Rock 'n' Roll Space Bandits
The Incredible Crude Oil Monster
Voodoo Vampire
Invasion of The Gleeks
Around The World In 80 Riddles
The Man In The Moon
Circus of Horrors
Return of Atlantis
Termites From Venus
Eruption
Revenge of Bizarro
The Killer Machines
Garden of Doom

CAPTAIN ROB ‡
Polyscope B.V.

Rose Pearls of Tamoa (Pilot)
Mystery of Penguin Island (Pilot)

1979

SUPERFRIENDS †
Hanna-Barbera Productions / ABC

Rub Three Times For Disaster
Lex Luthor Strikes Back
Space Knights of Camelon
The Planet of Oz
The Lord of Middle Earth
Universe of Evil
Terror At 20,000 Fathoms
The Superfriends Meet Frankenstein

SPIDER-WOMAN †
DePatie-Freleng Productions / ABC

Pyramids of Terror
Realm of Darkness
The Ghost Vikings
The Kingpin Strikes Again
The Lost Continent
The Kongo Spider

Games of Doom
Shuttle To Disaster
Dracula's Revenge
The Spider-Woman And The Fly
Invasion From The Black Hole
The Great Magini
A Crime In Time
Return of The Spider Queen
A Deadly Dream

SPIDER-MAN
Marvel Comics & Depatie Freleng

Doctor Doom...Master of The World
Bubble, Bubble, Oil And Trouble
The Sandman Is Coming To Town
Lizards, Lizards, Everywhere
Curiosity Killed The Spider-Man

1978

CHALLENGE OF THE SUPERFRIENDS †
Hanna-Barbera Productions / ABC

Invasion of The Fearians
The World's Deadliest Game
Time Trap
Trial of The Superfriends
The Monolith of Evil
The Giants of Doom
Secret Origins of The Superfriends
Revenge On Gorilla City
The Swamp of The Living Dead
Conquerors of The Future
The Final Challenge
Fairy Tale of Doom
Doomsday
Superfriends: Rest In Peace
History of Doom
Rokan: Enemy From Space
The Demons of Exxor
Battle At The Earth's Core
Sinbad And The Space Pirates
The Pied Piper From Space
Attack of The Vampire
The Beasts Are Coming
Terror From The Phantom Zone
World Beneath The Ice
The Anti-Matter Monster
Invasion of The Brain Creatures

The Incredible Space Circus
Batman: Dead Or Alive
Battle of The Gods
Journey Through Inner Space
The Rise And Fall of The Superfriends

FOSSIL FACE ‡
Ruby-Spears Productions / ABC

Fossil Face (Pilot)

CAPTAIN CAVEMAN
Hanna-Barbera Productions / ABC

Old Cavey In New York
Cavey Goes To College
Kentucky Cavey
The Old Caveman And The Sea
Lights...Camera...Cavey!

PLASTIC MAN
Ruby-Spears Productions / ABC

The Minuscule Seven
The Clam

1977

SUPERFRIENDS †
Hanna-Barbera Productions / ABC

The Day of The Plant Creatures
Exploration: Earth
Planet of The Neanderthals
The Brain Machine
Joy Ride
Invasion of The Hydronoids
Hitchhike
Space Emergency
Drag Race
Fire
Game of Chicken
Volcano
Tiger On The Loose
The Antidote
The Collector
Alaska Peril
The Invisible Menace
The Monster of Dr. Droid
Vandals

Energy Mass
The Enforcer
Day of The Rats
Flood of Diamonds
The Fifty Foot Woman
Cheating
Attack of The Killer Bees
The Marsh Monster
The Runaways
Time Rescue
The Protector
Stowaways
Rampage
Frozen Peril
Dangerous Prank
Cable Car Rescue
The Man-Beasts of Xra
Tibetan Raiders

1976

DYNOMUTT: DOG WONDER
Hanna-Barbera Productions / ABC

Assistant Story Editor

The Glob (co-written)
Tin Kong (co-story)
Queen Hornet (co-story)
The Lighter Than Air Raid (co-story)
Blue Falcon vs. the Red Vulture (co-story)

CLUE CLUB
Hanna-Barbera Productions / CBS

One of Our Elephants Is Missing! (co-written)
2001

Live-Action Film, TV and Stage Credits

KISS OF DEATH
Trainingcape.Com

Quarter-hour dramatic Internet movie

1997

THE PUMPKIN THAT WASN'T PICKED ‡
Momentum Distribution

TV Special Treatment

1996

WISHAROO'S TREE HOUSE ‡
Just Your Pal, Inc.

Co-Executive Producer
Co-Created by

Series Bible
Cheap Skates (pilot)

1994

THREE STOOGES: NEXT GENERATION ‡
Columbia / Interscope / Jeffrey Scott
Productions

Producer

Story & Screenplay by Jeffrey Scott

1993

THE THREE STOOGES LIVE
AT THE MGM GRAND
Jeffrey Scott Prods. / Fred Moch & Assoc.
(Half-Hour Live Stage Show)

Executive Producer

Co-Written by Jeffrey Scott

1990

WAKE, RATTLE & ROLL
Hanna-Barbera / Sunn Classics

Co-Producer

Van Ready, Van Set, Van Gogh!
Pipe Dreams
Freedom Of Screech
Waste Makes Haste
Wake, Rattle & Wrestle
Rewind To The Future
Super Sam

Basement Of Thunder
How To Cure A Computer Virus
Sam Van Winkle
Harry Who?
Decks' Family Tree
Chariots Begin At Home
Surf's Down
Morning Of The Living Dead
Holmes Sweet Holmes
Fools Russia In
Read Any Good Minds Lately?
Basement Broadcasting Company
Wishful Thinking

1989

THREE STOOGES: 2ND GENERATION ‡
Columbia Pictures / Jeffrey Scott Productions

Shared Story Credit
Screenplay by Jeffrey Scott

1988

THE MARRIED COUPLE
Golden Era Productions

Story & Screenplay by Jeffrey Scott

1987

ADVENTURES OF SPADE & MARLOWE ‡
Paramount / Jaffe-Lansing Productions

Story & Screenplay by Jeffrey Scott

1985

DISNEY SUNDAY MOVIE ‡
Walt Disney Productions / ABC

Starbike

1983

BENJI, ZAX & THE ALIEN PRINCE
Hanna-Barbera / Mulberry Square / CBS

Thanks for the Memories (story)
Double Trouble (story)

1981

MISADVENTURES OF SHERIFF LOBO
Universal / NBC

Bang, Bang...You're Dead!
One Flew Into The Cuckoo's Nest
Keep On Buckin'

MR. MERLIN
Columbia Pictures / CBS

A Message From Wallshime

POWERS OF MATTHEW STARR
Paramount Television / NBC

Staff Writer

Daredevil

1979

MISADVENTURES OF SHERIFF LOBO
Universal / NBC

The Guns of Orly (Co-Written)

Glossary

2-D: Short for two-dimensional, used to refer to conventional cel animation.

3-D: Short for three-dimensional, refers to CG animation. Also refers to the illusion of depth created by wearing anaglyphic (red & blue) or Polaroid glasses to view 3-D comics or movies.

A-PAGES: When a script is edited, and scenes are lengthened, A-pages are used so that the entire script does not have to be renumbered. This is helpful so that what was previously discussed as having been on page 3, is not suddenly on page 4. Any writing that rolls over its original page onto a new page becomes an A-page. Thus, where in the first draft you might have page 3, in the next draft you might have page 3 followed by 3-A. If a scene is lengthened by several pages, you just continue with the alphabet, such as 3-B, 3-C, etc.

A-STORY: The main plot of the outline or script. It is often the action plot.

ACT: A division of a script or cartoon, usually falling between commercial breaks.

ACT BREAK: The end of an act generally a dramatic or suspenseful moment.

ACTION: The physical movement as described in a script. (See *Description*)

ANGLE: Used in shot lines when the writer wants to direct the viewer's or reader's attention to something, but isn't that concerned about exactly how near or far we are to it, such as ANGLE ON FRED & BARNEY.

ANIMATIC: A series of still drawings and pencil tests, edited together with the dialogue track to form a rough draft of the cartoon.

ANIMATIC REWRITE: In prime-time animation writing, the 1-2 day rewrite, during which the writers view the animatic and punch up gags, etc.

ANIMATION CAMERA STAND: An upright frame that holds an animation camera so that it can shoot the individual animation cels and backgrounds on a pegboard beneath the camera.

B.G.: Abbreviation for "background", as in "there's a forest fire in the b.g."

B-STORY: A B-story is a sub-story that is usually character driven and complicates or places a barrier in the way of the A-story.

BACKGROUND: In animation, a background is a piece of artwork or graphic depicting an interior or exterior scene, over which the animation is placed before being photographed, scanned, or output to media.

BACK TO or BACK TO SCENE: This simply means you're going back to the previous scene or character you just cut away from, such as BACK TO JOHN.

BACKSTORY: A description of the events that took place in the past that led to the present situation of the series and its characters.

BEAT: A single scene of an outline. Also sometimes refers to a pause or very short duration of time.

BEAT OUT: The process of working out the beats of an outline.

BIBLE: A complete description of a series containing four basic parts: the world, the characters, the stories, and the format.

BREAK: To break a story means to conceive the basic idea, and may also imply that the story is given initial approval to move forward. Stories are often broken by a group of writers.

BROADCAST STANDARDS & PRACTICES (aka BS&P): The person or office that reviews scripts to ensure that the material is suitable for the intended audience.

BROKEN: (see *Break*)

CAMERA ANGLES: The various positions of the camera, such as CLOSE SHOT (or CLOSE ANGLE), HIGH SHOT (or HIGH ANGLE), etc.

CAMERA MOVES: Any movement of the camera, or indication of such in the script, such as MOVE IN or PAN or ZOOM OUT, etc.

CAPPER: A final gag that caps a sequence of related gags, and is often a twist on the original intention.

CAST LIST: A list of the speaking characters sometimes found at the beginning of a script.

CASTING: The process of interviewing voice talent to choose who will perform the voices of the various animated characters.

CEL: A transparent piece of acetate on which 2-D animation is inked and painted. From celluloid, the original flammable material cels were made of.

CG: Short for Computer Graphics. *Toy Story* and *Antz* are examples of CGI animation.

CHARACTER ARC: The path of change a character takes in the course of a story.

CHARACTER NAME: The name of a character as it appears in a script, above that character's dialogue. Character names are always capitalized.

CLAYMATION: Stop-motion animation using clay for the characters, hardware, and environment, developed to a fine art by Academy-Award-winning producer Will Vinton.

CLOSE: Used in slug and shot lines, this indicates that we are seeing the character's head only. Close-ups can vary from chest up, to clipping the hair and chin.

CLOSER: Indicates the shot is closer in on the subject than the previous shot. If you were on a full shot of a marine squad you might call for CLOSER ON LIEUTENANT AND CORPORAL if you were going to have dialogue between them.

CONCEPT: The basic, undeveloped idea.

(CONT.) or (CONT'D): When there isn't enough room at the bottom of a script page to complete a character's dialogue it is often continued at the top of the following page, with the word (CONT.) or (CONT'D) immediately after the character's name.

CONTINUITY: An uninterrupted succession or flow; a coherent whole. In script writing it means that there are no discrepancies in the cutting from scene to scene, so that everything flows smoothly for the viewer, both visually and conceptually.

CONTINUOUS: Generally a new slug line means a new scene. However, there are times when there is a new setup (meaning another location) of the same scene. For example, if someone is inside a house and walks out the front door, the first scene might be INT. HOUSE

– DAY, but the second one would be EXT. HOUSE – CONTINUOUS. This means that the action is continuing, and not interrupted by a time cut.

CREDIT: A short piece of text at the beginning or end of a production which indicates what each person contributed to the production. Most writers receive a "Written By" credit on the cartoons they write.

CREDITS: 1) A list of a writer's works; 2) the list of creative and technical contributors shown at the end of a TV episode or movie.

CROSSOVER: An animated film or series that crosses over the adult and kid market and works well for both. *Beauty and the Beast* is an example of a crossover film.

CUT TO: The simplest and most common transition between scenes, and simply means that you are going from one scene to the next with no transition effect at all, just a straight change of scene.

DESCRIPTION: (sometimes called *action*) It is the describing of the physical part of the story. This includes all of the action that takes place, as well as the environment and what's in it, such as vehicles, characters, and anything else you might see on the screen. The description part of a script also includes any camera angles and moves, as well as notations of sounds or special effects which may be necessary to fully communicate to the storyboard man and animators.

DEVELOP: In TV*ese*, develop means to expand a concept into a fleshed out series, complete with format, characters, and story ideas. A writer who develops a series usually gets a "*developed for television by*" credit. To develop can also mean the fleshing out of any part of a series or story, such as the beats, characters, premises, etc.

DEVELOPMENT DEAL: The deal made with a studio or network, subsequent to which a series concept is developed into a bible and pilot.

May also include the development of character artwork.

DIALOGUE: The lines written in a script under the character names that will ultimately be read by the actors.

DIALOGUE TRACK: A recording of the cartoon's voices only. The dialogue track is made in a recording session during which the actors read their lines from the script.

DISSOLVE TO: When the current scene fades away as the new scene fades into view. It's a smooth transition, anywhere from one to three seconds or more, and is generally used to indicate that a substantial period of time has passed.

DRAFT: A version of a script.

EDITING: See *story editing*.

ELEMENT: One of the creative principals of an entertainment project, such as a writer, director, animator, producer, or actor.

ESTABLISHING, TO ESTABLISH: Either of these terms are used to indicate that the shot is designed to establish the location. The first time we cut to New York City in a story we might say EXT. NEW YORK CITY – TO ESTABLISH – DAY. This word might alternatively be used in the description immediately following the slug line.

EXECUTIVE PRODUCER: The top person who creatively runs a television show. In animation, there are many variations of the duties of an executive producer, from the creative person who oversees a series from high on to the owner or CEO of a studio, to the person who created the series, to a person hired to make the creative decisions. The usual duties of an executive producer are to oversee the creative content of the development, stories, designs, voices, music and post production.

EXT.: Short for exterior, meaning that the scene takes place outside.

EXTREME CLOSE: A variation of the close-up in which only a portion of the face is showing, such as EXTREME CLOSE – HARRY'S EYES.

F.G.: Used as shorthand to indicate something in the foreground.

FADE IN: Indicates that the scene is fading into view from black.

FADE OUT / FADE TO BLACK: The opposite of FADE IN, this means the picture fades away until it is black.

FAVORING: This tells the reader/director that one character or object is to be favored in the scene. For example, if you had a cat sniffing around for a mouse, you might call your next shot as FAVORING THE CAT'S FOOT if you wanted the mouse to stick a match between his toes and give him a hotfoot.

FINAL DRAFT: The last draft of a script, ready to go into production.

FLESH OUT: To expand a concept, beat or story by adding more detail.

FOAMATION: Stop-motion animation using foam characters.

FORMAT: The content and context of a television series. The content deals with what the series is about, how the characters interrelate, the theme, genre, etc. Context is the artistic and physical form that the production will be set in, such as episode length, type of animation, music, age of the intended audience, etc.

FRAME: Just as a cel is an individual drawing in an animated sequence, a frame is an individual image file in the computer. A frame can be created in the computer, or can be a drawing that is brought into the computer by scanning. A sequence of frames, shown in motion, creates an animated scene.

FREELANCE: A freelance writer is one who is not on staff or contracted to write multiple scripts, but is independent and finds script assignments on whatever shows are taking pitches. Freepencil would be a more appropriate term.

FULL: Used in the slug and shot lines to indicate that all of the subject matter is included in the shot. For example, if there were three cowboys in the street outside a saloon, FULL ON COWBOYS would mean that we see them all in this angle.

HIGH CONCEPT: A particularly clever or unique idea which, summed up in a sentence or two, creates an interesting image.

HOLE: Something illogical, incomplete, or missing within a story.

IN HOUSE: At the studio by the staff.

INKING: The process of tracing an animation drawing onto a clear acetate cel with (usually) black ink.

INT./EXT.: Used for the unusual circumstance when the scene is part inside and part outside, like in a car or perhaps in a doorway.

INT.: Short for interior, INT. means that the scene is taking place inside. It could be inside a house or office, or sometimes might refer to inside a cave or other natural structure.

INTERCUT: To cut back and forth between two or more locations, such as INTERCUT INDIANA AND THE BALL.

JOKE PASS: After a prime-time animated story is beat out, the staff all get together and do a joke pass, adding, deleting and improving the gags, and adding any new beats that may be needed.

LAYOUT: The process by which the lead animators lay out the basic background designs and character movements of the scenes. A layout can also be the physical background sketch or a sketch of the character(s) movement.

LEAD WRITER: In prime-time animation writing, the person who writes the first draft outline and script and whose name appears on the credits.

LONG: Used interchangeably with WIDE, such as LONG SHOT - AIRFIELD.

MASTER SCENE METHOD: In the master scene method you simply use a slug line to set up the scene and the rest of the action is handled with description, without the use of any camera angles.

MATCHED DISSOLVE: A dissolve in which some part of the new scene matches the old. For example, if you wanted to show a bushy headed character getting a haircut you might see him in the barber's chair, then after a MATCH DISSOLVE see him in the same chair with a crew cut.

MEDIUM: Used in slug and shot lines to indicate that we are seeing the characters from about their waists up.

MIX: Part of the sound production process whereby the music, sound effects, and dialogue tracks are mixed together, each at the optimum volume.

MODELS: Design artwork of characters, wardrobe, vehicles, props, etc. Model sheets show various angles of the characters or objects so that animators can draw them consistently from any angle.

(MORE): Used at the very bottom of a script page to indicate that the scene continues on the following page.

"MUST" SCENE: A scene that must be there. For example, in any superhero story, there "must" be a scene in which the superhero battles the villain. Finding the "must" scenes is an easy way to begin developing a story.

O.S.: Short for "off screen". This is used to indicate someone moving off camera, such as, the dog chased the cat o.s. It can also indicate action that is taking place off screen, such as, the man reacted to a LOUD O.S. CRASH. It is also used in parenthesis after a character name in script dialogue to indicate that the voice is coming from someone who is off camera, such as, JOE (O.S.), followed by his dialogue.

OPTION: To pay a fee for the exclusive right to develop an existing property for a period of time.

ORIGIN STORY: A story in which the characters and/or format come to be. An origin story is the backstory done as an episode.

OMIT or OMITTED: When this word is seen alone in a script it means that a scene, which appeared in a prior draft, has since been cut. It is actually a misnomer because the word means "to fail to include or mention," and thus implies that a scene was mistakenly left out. Deleted would be more correct, but why argue with tradition?

OTS: Short for "over the shoulder." When used in a shot line indicates that we are looking over someone's shoulder at another character or view. It is often used during conversations between two people.

OUTLINE: A complete story, in written prose form, laying out in detail every scene that will be in the final script.

PACING: The speed at which a scene or story plays out. You could also call it the "energy level" of a scene or script.

PACKAGE, PACKAGING: A package is two or more of the creative elements of a project already put together. Packaging means bringing together these creative people *before* a project is sold in an attempt to more easily sell it. Package also refers to a deal in which a writer is guaranteed a number of scripts, also known as a script package.

PAINTING: The process of hand-painting animation cels on the reverse side or, in the case of computers, automatically coloring in the frames.

PAN: A horizontal camera movement to the left or right, such as CAMERA PANS away from the farm to reveal a twister in the distance.

PANNING: Used the same as traveling.

PARENTHETICAL: An attitude, emotion, or in rare cases, action that appears directly beneath the character name in parentheses.

PASS: What you get when someone doesn't want to buy your series or script.

PEGBOARD: A flat, usually round plate, holding a piece of glass, below which are registration pegs that hold animation cels (which are punched to fit on the pegs). The pegboard is usually embedded into a drawing board with a light beneath it so that sequential drawings can be compared as they are animated, and so that the animation can be traced onto cels.

PENCIL TESTS: Animated sequences of pencil animation only, done before the animation is inked and painted to make sure it looks right in motion.

PILOT: The first episode written for a series.

PITCH: The act of verbally selling your series or script.

POLISH: A short, quick revision of a script. Most script deals include a first draft, a revision, and a polish.

POST PRODUCTION: That part of the animation process that comes after the animation has been produced. Post production includes editing, music, sound effects, mixing, etc.

POV: Used in shot lines to indicate that the scene we are seeing is the point of view of one of the characters. Usually we would have a shot of the character whose pov it is immediately before the POV shot. This allows the viewer to connect the pov with the person who's viewing it.

PREMISE: A simple telling of the story, generally from one-half to three pages.

PRESCHOOL: A genre of animation targeted at the audience of preschool children.

PRESENTATION: The written or verbal pitching of a series or story. An animated series presentation generally contains a description of the series and possibly some artwork.

PROP: An object. In cartoon writing, props are things used for gags.

PULL BACK: See *Zoom*.

PUSH IN: See *Zoom*.

READ REWRITE: The step in the prime-time animation writing process during which the staff does another rewrite, based on the table read notes, which usually takes another 1-1/2 days.

RECORD or RECORDING: The recording of dialogue as acted out by the actors in a sound studio.

RETAKE: A revised piece of animation correcting a poor or unusable scene, or to improve the overall cartoon.

REVERSE ANGLE: Indicates the opposite view. If you have a shot with the camera following a burglar as he breaks into an office, you might call for REVERSE ANGLE ON BURGLAR if you wanted to dramatically reveal a cop sneaking up on him from behind.

REVISION: A rewriting of a script.

REVISION MARKS: A symbol, usually in the right script margin, indicating that a change has been made in the draft. The most common revision mark is an asterisk (*). Some studios like writers to use revision marks on second and subsequent drafts so changes can be more easily identified.

RHYTHM: Rhythm in storytelling is similar to rhythm in music. It's a recurring wave.

RIPPLE DISSOLVE: Type of dissolve with a rippling visual effect, used for special purposes. For example, a ripple dissolve off a close-up would usually indicate that we are seeing something in the person's mind, such as a past event.

SAMPLE: A script or other piece of writing used as an example of one's work.

SCANNING: A process by which animation artwork (backgrounds or individual drawings) is digitally scanned in order to transfer the image into a computer.

SCENE NUMBERS: Numbers in the margins of outlines or scripts that help locate and identify scenes.

SCREENPLAY: The complete written blueprint of an animated or live-action film, consisting of scene description and character dialogue. Screenplay generally refers to film scripts whereas teleplay refers to television scripts.

SCRIPT: The complete written blueprint of an animated or live-action film or television episode, consisting of scene description and character dialogue.

SFX: Short for "sound effect(s)". It is quite common in animation scripts to note important sound effects. These are usually noted in the scene description, such as, SFX: LASER BLAST. This can be helpful for sound effects editors, though it is sometimes redundant and takes away from the smooth reading of a script.

SHOT-BY-SHOT METHOD: In the shot-by-shot method the writer calls out each shot in the script as he envisions them.

SHOT LINES or SHOTS: Capitalized lines in scripts that come after slug lines, describing subsequent angles in the same scene. They do not have INT., EXT., DAY or NIGHT notations, but describe more specific camera angles.

SIGHT GAG: A visual gag as opposed to funny

dialogue, such as a character stepping on a rake and having the handle thwak him in the kisser.

SLUG LINE: The capitalized line in a script that defines the basic setup of a particular scene. For example, INT. SALOON – DAY. Day or night are noted at the end of the slug line, or sometimes weather or more precise environment notations such as STORMY NIGHT or LATER THAT AFTERNOON. This gives the director an idea of the scene's general visual setting.

SOTTO, SOTTO VOCE: The word "sotto," used parenthetically below a character name, means the following dialogue is spoken softly, so as not to be overheard.

SPEC: Short for speculative, which means *engaged in risky business on the chance of quick or considerable profit.* Thus, a spec script is one that a person writes on his or her own time with the hopes of selling it to a studio or network.

SQUASH AND STRETCH: A style of animation in which the characters can literally be squashed and stretched, as in the classic Chuck Jones and Tex Avery cartoons.

STORYBOARD: A visual interpretation of the script made up of small, thumbnail drawings (generally three per page). Using rough drawings, the storyboard shows every scene in the script, and indicates action and camera moves by means of various symbols and sequences of pictures.

STORY ARC: The change that takes place over the beginning, middle, and end of a story.

STORY DYNAMICS: All of the separate patterns of change that are taking place in a story at any given time.

STORY EDITING: Reading scripts and giving notes to the writer. Also consists of rewriting the script to ensure it conforms to the series format.

STORY EDITOR: A member of the writing staff,

under the executive producer, who reads scripts and gives notes to the writer instructing him or her what to change. Once the writer has so rewritten a script, the story editor works with the executive producer and/or network making the final script changes.

TABLE PROCESS: In prime-time animation writing, a series of steps whereby the staff continues to develop the script after the lead writer has turned in his first draft. The "table" is simply the big conference table at which the staff can work en masse.

TABLE POLISH: The final stage of the prime-time animation table process, attended by the executive producer and writing staff.

TABLE READ: A step in the prime-time animation writing process in which the actors participate, coming to the table and reading their lines in real time (meaning the actual time it will take during the episode). The writers note which jokes work and which don't, and note any other problems as the story plays out.

TAKE: A continuous sequence of recording, either on film, video, or audio tape. When an actor flubs a line during recording they do another take.

TALKING HEADS: Too much time spent on dialogue. Called "talking heads" because sometimes that's all you see.

TEASER: A short scene at the beginning of an animated program that "teases" (piques the interest of) the audience with some kind of action or mystery related to the story.

TEXTURE MAP: The texture applied to the surface to a 3-D CG form, such as skin, metal, wood, water, etc. Buzz Lightyear was texture-mapped with a plastic surface. (See *wire frame*.)

THWAK: A made up onomatopoeic word that represents the sound something makes when it hits a toon character in the face or anywhere else. This is just an example of the many funny words that cartoon writers use to enhance a script.

TILT: An up or down movement of the camera. An example would be, the CAMERA TILTS UP to reveal the blistering sun above.

TOYETIC: A property that can be easily turned into toys and ancillary products.

TRANSITIONS: Special optical effects used to segue from one scene to the next.

TRAVELING: Used in a shot or slug line to indicate that the scene is moving, such as when the camera follows a car, or when there's a shot inside a car and the background is moving past the window.

TREATMENT: An outline of the story, including a description of most if not all of the scenes and the major characters. Whereas an outline lays out all the beats, a treatment can sometimes be more of a description of a movie, as if you're selling it rather than telling it.

TWO SHOT: A shot consisting of two people, usually from their waists up, generally used when there will be dialogue between them.

VISUALIZATION: To get a mental image of what you are writing.

V.O.: Short for voice over. This is also used parenthetically after a character name to indicate the voice is coming from someone not on camera. However, whereas O.S. indicates the person is off camera, V.O. indicates a "disembodied" voice, such as a narrator, a person's thoughts, a ghost, etc.

WALLA: Nonspecific dialogue such as that heard during a party. The word "walla" is sometimes placed parenthetically under a general character name, such as CROWD, to indicate we are hearing crowd murmuring.

WIDE: Used in the slug line or shot line to indicate that the camera view of the scene takes in the whole picture rather than just part of it. EXT. WIDE ON MOJAVE DESERT – DAY would indicate that we are seeing a panorama of the desert. The word LONG is sometimes used interchangeably with WIDE, such as LONG SHOT – AIRFIELD.

WIDEN / WIDER: Used to describe a shot that is a broader view than the previous shot. You might use one of these terms if you wanted to include more characters or more of the environment than the last shot. WIDER is used in shot lines, whereas WIDEN is usually used in description.

WIPE TO: Indicates that the new scene is "wiping" away the old one. There are hundreds of wipes. The most common is the horizontal wipe, in which the new scene replaces the old scene from left to right, like a sliding door closing. There are also diagonal wipes, circular wipes, checkerboard wipes, etc. A wipe indicates a passage of time.

WIRE FRAME: A 3-D model inside a computer which appears to be made of a wire frame (actually it's just lines). A wire frame can be of any object, animated or inanimate, such as people, cars, bugs, water, etc. After a wire frame is built by a computer artist it is mapped with a texture, such as metal, wood, skin, etc., then lighted

within the computer to give it shape and modeling. Finally, it is given motion, the result being a fully animated 3-D object.

WORD: A sound that has meaning. This, of course, is the spoken word. The only difference with a written word is that it has a symbol or symbols (letters) that represent the sound and meaning. So a written word is a symbol of meaning.

XEROXING: A method of copying pencil animation drawings onto acetate cels by means of a copying machine. The Xeroxing process turns the pencil line into a virtual ink line on the cel.

ZIP PAN: A rapid pan which, in animation, is usually accompanied by horizontal lines or blurring.

ZOOM: A forward or backward movement of the camera. For example, ZOOM IN on the mouse as he smiles devilishly, or ZOOM OUT to reveal the mouse is surrounded by a dozen cats! (Technically, a *ZOOM* is done with a lens whereas a PUSH IN or PULL BACK is a camera move. But in animation writing they are interchangeable.

Animation Links & References

Animation Industry Directory (www.animationmagazine.net)
Animation Magazine (www.animationmagazine.net)
Animation World Network (www.awn.com)
Animation Writers Caucus (of the Writers Guild of America, 323-951-4000)
Hollywood Agents & Managers Directory (www.hcdonline.com)
Hollywood Creative Directory (www.hcdonline.com)
KidScreen (www.kidscreen.com)
Jeffrey Scott's E-mail (go to Jeffrey's website)
Jeffrey Scott's Website (www.jeffreyscott.tv)
Online Dictionaries (www.onelook.com)
Women In Animation (www.women.in.animation.org)
Writers Guild of America (www.wga.org)
Writers Guild of America List of Agents (www.wga.org/agency.html)

Index